All-American

The Jacobin series features short interrogations of politics, economics, and culture from a socialist perspective, as an avenue to radical political practice. The books offer critical analysis and engagement with the history and ideas of the Left in an accessible format.

The series is a collaboration between Verso Books and *Jacobin* magazine, which is published quarterly in print and online at jacobinmag.com.

All-American Nativism

How the Bipartisan War on Immigrants
Explains Politics as We Know It

DANIEL DENVIR

VERSO
London • New York

First published by Verso 2020
© Daniel Denvir 2020

1 3 5 7 9 10 8 6 4 2

Verso
UK: 6 Meard Street, London W1F 0EG
US: 20 Jay Street, Suite 1010, Brooklyn, NY 11201
versobooks.com

Verso is the imprint of New Left Books

ISBN-13: 978-1-78663-713-0
ISBN-13: 978-1-78663-711-6 (UK EBK)
ISBN-13: 978-1-78663-712-3 (US EBK)

British Library Cataloguing in Publication Data
A catalogue record for this book is available from the British Library

Library of Congress Cataloging-in-Publication Data
A catalog record for this book is available from the Library of Congress

Typeset in Fournier MT by Hewer Text UK Ltd, Edinburgh
Printed in the US by Maple Press

CONTENTS

INTRODUCTION

We're going to build a wall ... We don't have a country anymore.

—Donald Trump, April 28, 2016[1]

On January 27, 2017, a week into his presidency, Donald Trump made partially good on his campaign pledge to effect a "total and complete shutdown of Muslims entering the United States until our country's representatives can figure out what the hell is going on," banning immigrants and visitors from seven majority-Muslim countries from entering the United States for 90 days. He also suspended the entry of refugees from everywhere for 120 days and prioritized the resettlement of persecuted religious minorities, by which Trump meant Christians.[2]

That Trump had promised a Muslim ban in his barnstorming mega-rallies didn't make its enactment any less shocking. Even lawful permanent residents were initially blocked from boarding planes to the United States or refused entry once they had arrived. Protesters flooded into airports, lawyers rushed to court to file emergency motions, and Trump was swiftly dealt the first in a series of defeats as judges around the country put the ban on hold. It demonstrated, liberals swooned, the importance and resilience of institutions and the rule of law. At least until June 2018, when the Supreme Court voted to uphold the third version of his executive order, which narrowed the ban but made it indefinite, concluding that Trump's unambiguous bigotry had been duly laundered by way of bureaucratic procedure.[3]

Despite Trump having proclaimed that he was motivated by anti-Muslim animus, the conservative majority ruled that the ban's final version passed muster because it had been administratively justified in the language of national security. Trump's language had seemingly broken with establishment precedent. But, as his lawyers persuasively argued, his policies had not. Racist policy in post-1960s America was perfectly legal if it was called something else. One of Trumpism's achievements was to resist the pretense of doing so.

Even today, that Trump is actually president is still hard for many to accept or, more basically, to comprehend. But for supporters, Trump was telling basic truths—truths that elites from both major parties had long denied and even covered up. He was doing bold things that his predecessors had been afraid to do because they were too weak, corrupt, compromised. The United States, he said, had been sold out by its leaders. They exported American jobs to foreign countries and imported foreign workers to steal jobs at home. They sacrificed American blood and treasure in futile wars for other people's freedom, spent hard-earned taxpayer dollars on a global welfare scheme called "foreign aid," and, too politically correct and squeamish, failed to protect "our people" from terrorism and immigrant criminality.[4]

Once in office, Trump rendered in administrative and legislative prose a nativist presidential campaign suffused with the toxic poetry of race, nation, and religion. Trump had won by portraying a country under siege from a globalist elite that prioritized themselves and the interests of a foreign-born underclass over those of forgotten white Americans. Trump, rambling through speeches that seemed incoherent to detractors, expertly struck a resonant chord with millions. And whenever the crowd grew restless, he snapped them back to attention with a phrase that summarized it all: "Build the wall." Nothing tied his multifarious warnings of criminal, economic and even existential threat together as tightly as immigration. His subsequent success in transforming anti-immigrant vitriol into a perfectly legal Muslim ban provides a clue to an unsettling truth. Far from an anomaly, Trump's rhetoric and policies alike draw on and expose a deep well of *all-American nativism*. He was, detractors charged, simply un-American. But that was far from the case. The revulsion Trump inspires among liberal elites is rooted not just in the fear of the unfamiliar; they're also shaken by the even more disturbing encounter with the uncanny.

Trump shattered political norms by launching vicious personal attacks and stating obvious lies frequently and without shame. 2016 was a year zero for American politics, establishment critics believed. An indecorous, authoritarian cartoon character, leading an army of extremist rednecks, threatened the rule of law as we knew it.

There is some truth to these caricatures. But the historical reality is less comfortable. Trumpism was the result of American politics at its most normal. It was also the logical conclusion of a decades-long trajectory. This is nowhere truer than with the long-standing bipartisan agreement that immigration is a "problem" in urgent need of solving. For decades, hard-core xenophobia had seeped into conservative politics, transmitted across an ascendant network of right-wing television, radio and, ultimately, internet outlets. Republicans and Democrats, facing a series of insurgencies on the right, provided ideological cover to a constellation of stridently anti-immigrant organizations and constructed an enormous machinery of repression. Escalating deportations, crackdowns that would explode the populations of jails, detention centers and prisons, restrictions on public benefits, the erection of hundreds of miles of fencing, and the deployment of thousands of agents to the border with Mexico were together intended to convince Americans that the immigrant threat was under control. Instead, these actions manufactured the threat and made it seem all the more real.

Until Trump's election, it had been almost a century since nativism had stood among the country's explicit and central governing ideologies. And Trump stands out as a president who has become the country's leading nativist. Yet nativist politics, if sometimes articulated in more sober tones, proved far from archaic, and its appeal was by no means limited to the followers of fringe far-right characters like David Duke, Richard Spencer or even Jeff Sessions.

As I tell it in this book, the proximate story of the Trump administration begins in the 1960s and '70s. But the *longue durée* of European settlement serves as historical backdrop and founding condition: since the colonial period and then the nation's founding, government has tried time and again to ensure that the United States is a white country for white people—and sometimes to ensure that it belongs to a specific subset of whites at that. That is not hyperbole. Whiteness was the documented, comprehensive, and official policy until 1965, when President Lyndon B. Johnson signed the Hart-Celler Act, ending a quota-based immigration system that had since the early 1920s brazenly sought to maintain a demographic majority descended from northern and western European nationalities.

After the passing of Hart-Celler, authorized immigration boomed. But rather than the largely English, Irish and German immigrants of prior decades, newcomers were mostly Asian and Latin American. At face value, the law was a major victory for civil rights. But the year before, the United States had also sharply restricted authorized migration from Mexico, terminating the massive mid-century Bracero guest worker program, which had brought millions to labor on US farms. That program's termination was followed, in the Hart-Celler Act and the Immigration and Nationality Act Amendments of 1976, by the government setting limits on Mexican immigration, initiating the transformation of a long-standing pattern of often temporary and circular migration from Mexico into a permanent and rapidly growing population of undocumented immigrants who were now declared "illegal."[5]

Political debates over immigration often involve competing ideas about how to solve a problem. But migration is not self-evidently a problem; for much of American history, European migration was in fact the solution. In a society that was expanding westward, dispossessing indigenous people, and seeking to grow its base of productive settler citizens, European immigrants were often desirable. As settlement consolidated and was normalized throughout the nineteenth century, Euro-American settlers simultaneously became natives *and* nativists. Then, in the "colorblind" post–civil rights era, they became members of a "nation of immigrants" confident that their families, unlike Mexicans, had "come the right way." Government action and nativist politics combined to make Mexican migration into a *problem* of illegality. That broad consensus created the conventional wisdom that enforcement was the solution.

As non-white immigration increased and Mexican migration became criminalized, it faced a white backlash. This backlash did not come from nowhere. Rather, it drew from a long history of white population politics, including another anti-migrant movement that is not often remembered as such: the resistance to the integration of African Americans migrating from the South into schools, neighborhoods, and workplaces in the cities of the North, Midwest, and West. Just as racial liberals joined the war on crime and helped propel mass incarceration in order to protect the post-1960s order, the ostensibly pro-immigration figures commanding the political establishment nurtured anti-immigrant reaction in an attempt to manage it.

Demographic change was accompanied by the rise of a new, neoliberal economic order. Though neoliberalism shaped only part of that immigration-driven demographic change, it decisively shaped the political response to it. Beginning in the 1970s, a coordinated political offensive on the part of big business dismantled the New Deal order and crushed labor militancy. It represented a corporate assault on the power of labor and the welfare state, seen as obstacles to profitability and restored growth in an increasingly cutthroat global economy. Working-class communities were eviscerated and union power was decimated as industry decamped. Undocumented immigrants joined black Americans on the lowest tiers of an increasingly unequal labor market; both were readily blamed for the violent social disorder and alienation that are neoliberalism's morbid symptoms. In the 1990s, President Bill Clinton and congressional Republicans responded to fears over the free movement of capital—particularly as those fears related to the North America Free Trade Agreement (NAFTA) implemented in 1994—by joining nativists in demonizing the free movement of people. After invasions of Afghanistan and Iraq violently destabilized the world, immigrants, particularly Muslim ones, were scapegoated for that, too.

Anti-immigrant politics became defined by attacks from both right-wing nativists and the bipartisan establishment on "illegal immigration." It was a form of security theater that functioned to safeguard not only neoliberalism but also (to nativist consternation) legal immigration. Legal immigration enabled by the 1965 reform is the largest driver of the demographic change that nativists oppose: more than three-quarters of foreign-born people in the United States are here with authorization.[6] But the larger and newly diverse large-scale legal immigration since the passing of the Hart-Celler Act has always been protected by ethnic advocacy organizations, labor unions, religious groups, business interests, and powerful figures within both major parties. Anti-"illegal" politics, then, have been at the center of a public immigration debate that has blamed undocumented people for most everything.

The historical record examined in this book demonstrates that the story is painfully simple: fences and cages for the lowest, racialized rungs of the working class gave political sustenance to an economic order punishing working people as a whole. American borders hardened and prison walls were erected for everyday people at the very moment that borders opened wider than ever for capital flows.

As social and economic welfare declined, public funds and political capital were earmarked for demonizing rhetoric and repressive policies. The system of mass incarceration locked up a disproportionately black surplus labor force and immigrant workers side by side. The immigration enforcement system, having grown to unprecedented scope and systematization, criminalized the very foreign-born workers demanded by business. The coincidence of a crisis in economic security and the massive expansion of the state's repressive institutions shifted political unrest onto the terrain of racial and cultural conflict, physical safety, and American sovereignty.

Nativism reemerged as a mass politics demonizing immigrants as a criminal and economic threat in the early 1990s, as the Republican Party openly courted an anti-Mexican revolt that took off in California. Many—though by no means all—Democrats followed suit as President Bill Clinton steered his party to the right. Through the Bush and Obama administrations, the deportation machine grew and became further enmeshed in the country's gargantuan criminal justice system. The unprecedented militarization of the country's Southwestern border and the systematic identification and removal of unauthorized non-citizens became routine in a bipartisan political theater to convince Americans that everything was under control. It wasn't.

The crackdowns were scripted for voter approval but rarely if ever achieved outcomes that substantively met stated objectives. It is unclear to what extent the militarization of the border reduced unauthorized migration. But it did clearly shift migration routes into the deadly heat of the Arizona desert. And, ironically, it made would-be circular migrants into permanent criminalized residents—ballooning the undocumented population. In the interior, deportations wreaked catastrophe on millions even as the undocumented population climbed above 10 million. A narcotic threat blamed on Colombian and Mexican cartels and on "inner-city" black criminals was met with an estimated trillion-dollar-plus drug war that resulted not in a drug-free America but rather in record-setting overdose deaths and the violent destabilization of Colombia, Central America, and Mexico.[7] Likewise, the war on terror led to more terrorism and war. All the while, the immiserating economic order that all this war and repression functioned to protect, however haphazardly, blew up in 2008, and long-standing inequality and deprivation reached crisis proportions.

Enforcement successes celebrated by Democrats and Republicans alike have always proved to be a mirage; demands for politicians to crack down on immigration have intensified over the past few decades. The contradictions remained unsolvable because anti-immigrant policy could not deliver the better country it promised. As symbolically satisfying as one might find them, you can't eat racism and war. The prevailing response, however, wasn't that the strategy was wrong, but that it simply wasn't being implemented with sufficient vigor. So the most appealing solutions increasingly became the maximalist ones: a border wall, mass deportations, and the "shutdown" of Muslim immigration.

This is the basic paradox at the heart of US immigration politics: the border has never been more militarized, our prisons never more full, and our military never more hopelessly entangled, yet a vocal minority of Americans have become apoplectically adamant that our nation is insecure, inside and out, and vulnerable to threats foreign and domestic. This is a story about Americans' deep sense of unease in a rapidly globalizing world, and their resentment toward elites who seem to conjure a world full of violence, uncertainty, and downward mobility. It's also about the racist anti-tax and pro-segregation politics that emerge among affluent people who believe that their wealth is solely the product of their own hard work and talent. Trump's wall was a simple answer to complex challenges that were created in significant part by the same established order that many politicians in the anti-Trump camp hope to revivify. Trump's predecessors built more walls and cages than he will ever manage to construct—an irony that contains an explanation for our present situation.

This is not a book about the social, political, and economic drivers of immigration, though it necessarily sheds some light on them. Also, though the struggles of immigrants make frequent appearances throughout, it is not about the immigrant rights movement. It is about their enemies. And while this book is primarily focused on the politics of *immigration* as it is conventionally understood—people's migration across national borders—it also unsettles the false presumptions of conventional thinking that is analytically constrained by those same borders. In particular, I argue that the logic animating white resistance to the black Great Migration and freedom struggle has been similar to that behind the anti-immigrant movement—and that the latter in many ways grew out of and alongside the former. The origin of the migrants who have been targeted should not obscure the shared resistance to racialized *migrants* foreign and domestic portrayed as posing an economic, criminal, and demographic threat. Nativism is a powerful subset of American racism and nationalism. Nativism is also, however, a concept that allows us to rethink racism itself as a bedrock nationalist population politics that functions to control the movement and status of racialized others—abroad, at the border, and in the interior. The commonalities are clarified when placed in deeper historical context: the continuation of a settler-colonial population politics, which from colonization through 1965 endeavored by law to maintain a white majority in a country that demanded racial others to do much of its least-valued labor.

Resistance to desegregation, a white identity politics of racial grievance, mass incarceration, the war on terror: all were dedicated to a quixotic mission to keep dangerous others from crossing US borders and to restrict the free movement of those already inside them. At a time when America's power to ensure economic and military dominance spun into crisis, government orchestrated repression to produce an illusion of order. In their fits and starts, these politics and policies were aimed at consolidating a neoliberal political-economic order that was threatened by dissent and contradiction from its inception.

And so how did the war on immigrants fare? It depends on how you measure success: Trump is in the White House, neoliberalism reigns, the privatized detention industry is booming. But this book argues that this moment of maximal nativist power is more like a supernova: a big, terrifying explosion marking the end, not the beginning, of a political cycle.

The future of the system that nativism stabilized is now in doubt. A global political and economic order that made the world smaller by intertwining economies and metastasizing foreign military intervention contained the seeds of its own crises: people followed the trails of weapons and money, but in reverse, to the center of the American empire. Immigrants traveled in large numbers to places where they were demanded as workers but rejected as neighbors, coworkers, and citizens. And with climate change, fossil-fueled capitalism is driving yet more people to move. But the politics of scapegoating have ultimately proven unable to compensate for neoliberalism's depredations, and Americans are increasingly more likely, not less, to see immigrants as allies rather than enemies.[8] The debate is polarizing, which is a good thing because it is destroying the bipartisan basis for the war on immigrants. The repression became so extreme under Bush, Obama, and Trump that it sparked a mass social movement to resist it, and polls show that Democratic voters have swiftly moved toward supporting immigrant rights. And, critically, nativists have been unable to leverage the bipartisan war on "illegal immigrants" and its Trumpian apotheosis toward their goal of permanently slashing legal immigration. Ironically, the bipartisan war on "illegal immigrants" has made Trump and his base obsessed with the Wall to stop immigrants from "coming the wrong way." Trump, for all his danger, has indeed heightened these contradictions: perhaps *never* have both socialism and immigrant rights alike received such high levels of public support in the United States.

In my account, the history of contemporary immigration politics is at the same time the history of mass incarceration's racist containment of the black Great Migration and freedom struggle; of the workers rendered expendable by economic restructuring; of the triumph of neoliberalism over the New Deal order; of the Democratic Party's rightward lurch; and of a national security state and military-industrial complex that was searching for a new direction after the Cold War and that, after the attacks of September 11, 2001, recklessly expanded.

The thesis of this book, in other words, is that nativism is a thread that connects much of the past half-century—and more—of American history. And its organization is therefore both chronological and thematic, telling a series of overlapping stories. Chapter 1 explains the rise of the contemporary nativist movement amid growing fears of ecological and economic scarcity that emerged in the 1970s. Chapter 2 details the rise of border militarization and the federal deportation pipeline, alongside the rise of mass incarceration and the post-9/11 national security state. Chapter 3 examines the explicitly racist population politics of a centuries-long history of American empire-building, from European settlement and Native genocide through the post-9/11 merger of the Mexican and Muslim threat. Chapter 4 lays out the history of immigration politics from presidents George W. Bush through Barack Obama, and shows how the establishment's campaign for "comprehensive reform" constantly escalated security politics, perversely elevating the very far-right nativists whom they hoped to placate. I conclude by appraising Trump's crimes to date.

Immigration politics have been at the center of much that has gone wrong in recent decades. Immigrant liberation will be indispensable to building a better world to replace it. Securing immigrant freedom will require a new politics that transforms this country root and branch for everyone. It's a challenge that we can only take on if it is understood clearly. The way mainstream politicians from the two major parties handled immigration after 1965—performing security while protecting free markets—ultimately made Trumpism an irresistible political force. In 2016, the curtain finally slipped away to reveal a gargantuan machinery of state that had violently repressed unauthorized immigrants for decades. Trump spoke of its purpose with chilling clarity. The movement to not only defeat Trump but to transform the rotten system that made him president will only succeed if a diverse and transnational working class unites to fight for a more lasting change.

This holds true elsewhere, too. Though this is a book about US history, a racist and Islamophobic xenophobia is also driving an ascendant far right in Australia, our Anglo settler-colonial sibling, and in Europe, which colonized the world and now, amid economic crisis, hysterically campaigns against a supposed colonization of its own territory by Third World and Muslim peoples. The current economic order has imposed misery in the center and periphery alike, provoking migration and a xenophobic reaction that is, in reality, a phantasmic projection of Europe's own violence against the world onto its victims. Migration politics are today conjuring ghosts of colonialism's past.

That is no doubt the case in the United States. This is the country where Chinese exclusion took root as Gilded Age inequality wrecked a myth that had portrayed the frontier as providing an endless bounty, itself forged amid indigenous genocide; where eugenics and the second Ku Klux Klan flourished during World War I's first Red Scare and the recession that followed in its wake. The wars on "illegals," crime, and welfare have been the politics that made and punished scapegoats. It's impossible to know whether Trump is a true believer in much of anything at all aside from his own greatness, white supremacy, and the prerogative of powerful men to do as they like. But he is a master showman, and speeches at campaign rallies that appeared to be a stream of semiconscious non-sequiturs to detractors were in reality reflections of his preternatural ability to read a crowd. The crowd wanted the Wall.

"You know," Trump told the *New York Times*, "if it gets a little boring, if I see people starting to sort of, maybe thinking about leaving, I can sort of tell the audience, I just say, 'We will build the wall!' and they go nuts."[9] Trump has said that "we don't have a country anymore," and this book seeks to explain why that resonates: how racism and nationalism are shaped by politics, economics, and history. My objective is an analysis far more systematic than commonplace accounts that blame in-born white resentment as though it's a static ahistorical force in American politics.

Works of social criticism often marshal forgotten histories to recast a normal-seeming reality as strange. This book does the opposite, analyzing what for decades was an all-too-normal anti-immigrant politics to explain how we ended up in such a seemingly bizarre present.

1

SCARCITY

Failing to reduce the current rate of immigration, legal and illegal, clearly means that our children and our grandchildren cannot possibly have the quality of life that we ourselves have been fortunate to have enjoyed.
—Representative Anthony C. Beilenson (D-CA), 1996[1]

In 1964, President Lyndon B. Johnson called on Americans to build a Great Society, where "an order of plenty for all of our people" would be directed to "elevate our national life, and to advance the quality of our American civilization."

The optimism soon curdled. Americans lost their sense of place in the world and found themselves in long lines at gasoline stations. The horn of plenty dried up as stagflation, a schema-shattering combination of high unemployment and inflation, took hold—setting the stage for a business reaction against organized labor and the New Deal order that had protected it. A slow, bloody, and expensive war on Vietnam not only defeated the US military but also, alongside Richard Nixon's hack crimi-nality, discredited government. Even prosperity's most taken-for-granted foundation appeared at risk: suddenly, our way of life appeared to push the earth beyond carrying capacity. In short, a future that had once seemed to offer limitless promise was abruptly and drastically circumscribed; the boundless Great Society devolved into a zero-sum game, with hostile camps competing over dwindling resources. A new era of immigration—mass, diverse and, in the case of Mexicans, criminalized—had the bad fortune of accompanying this proliferating uncertainty, conflict, and pessimism.

For decades, the debate over immigration has centered on empirical questions over whether immigrants put downward pressure on wages for native-born workers (by and large they do not) or are a strain on public spending (it depends on what level of government).* But the dynamics of American immigration politics can't be explained by seeking to answer these questions. What's revelatory is why and how these debates began to shape American politics in the first place.

The politics of immigration need to be understood in relation to the rise of mass incarceration, the crisis of empire, and white reaction against demographic change. But for the

---

* A National Academy of Sciences, Engineering, and Medicine study found that "the impact of immigration on the wages of natives overall is very small," and, "to the extent that negative wage effects are found, prior immigrants . . . are most likely to experience them, followed by native-born high school dropouts." It added: "There are still a number of studies that suggest small to zero effects." The authors found that "the fiscal impacts of immigrants are generally positive at the federal level and negative at the state and local levels." (Francine D. Blau and Christopher Mackie, eds., "The Economic and Fiscal Consequences of Immigration," Washington, DC: National Academies Press, 2017, 5, 11, 247–48.)

purposes of this chapter, I untangle the pervasive sense of economic scarcity that formed the core of contemporary immigration politics as it took shape in the 1970s. My concern here is not only economics narrowly construed but also the fundamental resources provided by non-human nature—the fragility of which had come into view and become the object of widespread anxiety. But making sense of this recent history first requires explaining how Americans became primed to blame racialized others for economic problems in the first place.

Workers of the world divided

The Naturalization Act of 1790 opened citizenship to most "any alien" who was a "free white person" and barred all those who were not—forging a deep and permanent link between citizenship, race, and the status of labor. "Free white" workers would consistently scapegoat immigrants and others for an unequal system; it was that system, in turn, that made those others other, as the invention of racial difference came to explain the status of the labor they performed. W.E.B. Du Bois described this dynamic in *Black Reconstruction in America*, writing that slavery caused poor whites to hate enslaved black workers and their work. Instead of identifying as workers, they dreamed of emulating planters and owning an enslaved workforce of their own. "To these Negroes [the poor white] transferred all the dislike and hatred which he had for the whole slave system," wrote Du Bois. "The result was that the system was held stable and intact by the poor white."[2] White-supremacist naturalization law and slavery alike established who counted as a true American.

The white man's republic celebrated a "free labor" ideal that depended upon but also rejected menial labor, performed first by black people and then later by racialized immigrants. Assignment to menial labor became an inherited, racial trait, appearing in the false guise of a feature of biology. This also meant that sex and gender were central to white supremacy and capitalism, because it was through reproduction that race—and thus the division of labor—became a social reality.

Racism on the basis of the free labor ideology became a ground for racist nativism. In 1850, California imposed a special tax on foreign miners and then, briefly, five years later, imposed it specifically on those ineligible for citizenship: Asians. Approximately 250,000 Chinese workers arrived between 1850 and 1882, many to mine gold in California or to labor on the transcontinental railroad, the economic backbone of an American empire stretching to the Pacific.[3] After the Civil War and amid the counterrevolution against Radical Reconstruction, a recession took hold in the 1870s as the United States expanded its genocidal frontier. Anti-Chinese sentiment grew across the West, particularly in California.

Industrial capitalism squeezed farmers and labor alike, a dilemma to which free and cheap land on an expanding frontier no longer provided an exit. So many genocidal wars against Native people had been won and yet the new system made the economic independence promised by the frontier myth plainly untenable. Westward migration no longer offered an escape valve for the masses of people lacking wealth or land.[4] Xenophobia offered a temporary fix. Many businesses no doubt wanted immigrant labor.[5] But anti-immigrant politics was a compromise that facilitated industrial capitalism's ascent in the face of the increasingly militant movements of the 1870s and 1880s. One such movement, the Populist alliance of workers and farmers, posed a truly radical threat. The movement drew strength from its rejection of the racist divisions at home and abroad that fundamentally shape American capitalism. It was undermined in part by its failure to fully move beyond those divisions: the Knights of Labor voted to back Chinese exclusion, and members of the white Farmer's Alliance failed to support Colored Farmers' Alliance boycotts and strikes, which were met with lethal violence in the South.[6] Populism's defeat, in turn, only helped consolidate racism's hold.[7] Although elite strategies of racial division and stratification can prove to be explosive and unpredictable, it has for American capitalism been an indispensable feature.

Cultural theorist Stuart Hall wrote that "race is the modality in which class is lived." Whites blaming Chinese workers' racial "servility" for the economic system that subjugated them all was a case in point. The first restrictive federal immigration law, the Page Law of 1875, targeted Chinese people precisely as a racialized labor threat, increasing criminal sanctions for transporting and contracting "coolie" workers and barring the entry of Asians suspected of being prostitutes.[8]

In 1882, a ten-year ban on Chinese workers became law.[9] The Chinese Exclusion Act was repeatedly renewed, and finally made permanent in 1904.[10] Nativists were adamant that no other Asian laborers fill the void. In 1907, the US government succeeded in obtaining the Japanese government's agreement not to issue passports to laborers, which prevented the immigration of Japanese workers to the United States. In 1917, an entry ban was enacted to cover people from across an expansive "Asiatic Barred Zone," which did not include Japan or the Philippines, a colonial possession. The exclusion was cemented and expanded to Japan by the 1920s national origins quota laws, which also sharply restricted immigration from southern and eastern Europe. Racial bars to naturalization were not fully abolished until 1952 and Asian immigration was severely limited until 1965, when President Johnson signed the Hart-Celler Act, repealing the quota system.

The labor movement of the late nineteenth and early twentieth century was divided over mass immigration. The Knights of Labor's model of industrial unionism extended to many immigrants but not to European contract laborers or, after internal debate, to Chinese workers. The American Federation of Labor (AFL) embraced a craft-based model, an exclusionary approach that also manifested in its support for excluding newcomers. The radical Industrial Workers of the World organized not only people from every nation but even across the US-Mexico border alongside the radical Partido Liberal Mexicano, with whom they mounted an insurrection in Baja California.[11] The Socialist Party, radical labor's most important electoral force, was riven by debates over immigration. But the SPUSA ultimately embraced restriction to the consternation of its tribune, Eugene Debs.[12]

The labor movement won spectacular victories when it organized the entire working class. But business retained the upper hand as workers from the world over remained divided.

Less desirable as a citizen than as a laborer

With Asian workers banned and European workers heavily restricted, industries in the Southwest, especially agriculture, and others as far away as Chicago demanded Mexican labor. In the early twentieth century, recruiters traveled into Mexico's west-central states, enticing workers into a system of indentured servitude known as *el enganche*, or "the hook." Those recruited to work in the United States fled the privatization and consolidation of rural land, falling wages in the cities and, eventually, a country battered by the chaos of the Mexican Revolution.[13]

Mexicans—those who migrated and those who simply found themselves on the wrong side of the border after the Mexican-American War—were tolerated as workers but disdained as neighbors. They were subjected not only to exploitation on the job but to segregation and discrimination in housing and public accommodations, and to rampant state and vigilante violence.[14] As the congressional Dillingham Commission, which laid the groundwork for the massive restriction of the 1920s, put it: Mexican workers were "providing a fairly adequate supply of labor . . . While not easily assimilated, this is of no great importance as long as most of them return to their native land. In the case of the Mexican, he is less desirable as a citizen than as a laborer."[15]

A Los Angeles Chamber of Commerce official declared that agricultural work was best done by "the oriental and Mexican due to their crouching and bending habits [to which they] are fully adapted, while the white is physically unable to adapt himself to them."[16] Race was defined by the sort of work someone did, and then work was organized by those racial categories. This created the problem of what to do with racialized others. Mexicans, portrayed as deportable and impermanent laborers, were not excluded alongside Asians or restricted together with Europeans. Instead, a compromise between nativists and agricultural interests was struck in 1929 that made crossing the border without authorization a misdemeanor—the law that would one day make Trump's family separations possible.[17] It also made illegally reentering after having been deported a felony.[18]

During the Great Depression, federal, state, and local government drove hundreds of thousands of Mexicans from their jobs, the relief rolls, and ultimately the country as part of a massive "repatriation" campaign that combined coerced deportations and voluntary departures, including of US citizens.[19] But World War II soon increased demand for low-wage labor. In response, the United States and Mexico established the Bracero program, through which guest workers could work temporarily north of the border. Much of the wages were deposited in a Mexican bank to induce them to return (though some funds never were returned to workers).[20] The program issued 4.6 million temporary visas between 1942 and 1964.[21] Many others entered without authorization.[22] The program laid the groundwork for large-scale Mexican migration—what scholars have called "the largest sustained flow of migrant workers in the contemporary world"—that would last until the Great Recession of 2008.[23]

Business demanded immigrant workers; indeed, growers in the Southwest adamantly resisted enforcement targeting their employment of undocumented Mexican workers. But politicians would feel compelled to expel, repress, or exclude those same workers in order to placate public sentiment. In these early years, much opposition to both unauthorized Mexican immigration and the Bracero program came from labor: the restrictionist AFL; the Congress of Industrial Organizations (CIO), formed in the 1930s to organize the ethnically diverse masses of mass production workers neglected by the AFL, and which did staunchly oppose racist national origins quotas; and Mexican-American organized labor. In 1949, the National Agricultural Workers Union (NAWU) mobilized six thousand people at the border in California's Imperial Valley to protest imported Mexican labor. "Braceros and 'wets' are the two sides of the same phony coin," said NAWU organizer Ernesto Galarza. Their purpose was to "cut down the wages of farm labor, to break strikes and to prevent [union] organization; to run American citizens off farm jobs, especially on the corporation ranches."[24]

Mexican labor migration was for decades protected from union and nativist critics by an "iron triangle" comprising Southwestern agricultural interests, Southern and Western conservatives in Congress, and the Federal Immigration Bureau.[25] The 1952 Immigration and Nationality Act made "harboring" undocumented immigrants a felony, but included a measure known as the Texas Proviso that exempted employers. Enforcement often targeted braceros who attempted to organize.[26]

In 1954, President Eisenhower appointed Lieutenant General Joseph M. Swing to run the Immigration and Naturalization Service (INS). Swing launched Operation Wetback in June and soon thereafter boasted that it had removed more than a million from the country, mostly Mexicans. It was a program that Trump would approvingly cite in a 2015 Republican primary debate—"moved 'em way south, they never came back"—making a racist past usable to legitimate his present-day nativist agenda. Yet those deportation numbers were an enormous distortion. In reality, as Kelly Lytle Hernández writes, it wasn't a one-off roundup but rather the culmination of a decade-long Border Patrol crackdown that had prompted massive farmer resistance (and support from many Mexican Americans).[27] It aimed to discipline rebellious farmers and their labor force—"drying out the wetbacks" (rather than removing them) by driving them into an expanded Bracero program.[28]

In 1964, the United States terminated the Bracero program amid the exposure of widespread abuses and strong opposition from organized labor. The next year, Johnson signed the Hart-Celler Act, which put an end to the overtly racist national origins quota system that had since the 1920s restricted immigration by nationality. The new immigration system simultaneously eliminated official racism and introduced a novel colorblind form, imposing the first-ever numerical caps on immigration from Western Hemispheric nations like Mexico. It also for the first time required that prospective immigrants seeking employment visas file a "labor certification" proving that they would not displace US workers.[29] The situation was exacerbated in 1976, when universal country caps were imposed, allotting Mexicans the same number of slots as Argentines or Nicaraguans. The firmly established pattern of Mexican migration would continue but the new system, as historian Mae Ngai writes, "recast" it as "illegal," "naturalized the construction of 'illegal aliens' and, increasingly, of illegal aliens as 'Mexican.'"[30]

Organized farmworkers fought employers' use of undocumented workers to break strikes, and their leader, Cesar Chavez, called on Senator Robert Kennedy to "remove Wetbacks" from the fields.[31] From the perspective of many in the farmworker movement, undocumented migrants were doing just what guest workers had done: driving down wages and thwarting unionization.

During a 1967 strike in California's Central Valley, the union protested outside the Bakersfield INS office demanding action against "illegal aliens" and also "green carders."[32] In 1974, the United Farm Workers deployed people to the border wearing "UFW Border Patrol" armbands to form a "wet line" against migrants crossing the Arizona border. Multiple Mexicans were beaten, allegedly by "wet line" members. Chavez said that he had found no evidence of union wrongdoing.[33]

In 1965, when national origin quotas were abolished, the United States admitted 296,697 immigrants. By 1973, it admitted 400,063. They came alongside a large but unknown number of unauthorized migrants from Mexico. Authorized immigration from Asia grew by 500 percent, while immigration from northern and western Europe declined by two-thirds.[34] Just as a social and economic order that had delivered considerable gains for a generation of white American workers began to collapse, a historic influx of non-white immigrants arrived—all amid the violent racist reaction that greeted the black Great Migration, which government facilitated by imposing an intensive system of residential segregation. Segregation was and remains a system of domestic bordering. And as with the border with Mexico, those on the "wrong" side of the line are portrayed as a criminal threat that must be contained. Both migrations, transnational and domestic, challenged the racist demographic norms that tenuously held the New Deal order together; in response to both, white reaction helped destroy that order.

The economic crises of the 1970s no doubt made for what historian Judith Stein called a "pivotal decade": high inflation driven by soaring oil prices, high unemployment, and intensified global competition battered the economy.[35] Many people, however, benefited from inflation, as wages rose to meet price increases, and the value of their debts eroded.[36] But white middle-class homeowners nonetheless shifted their allegiance to the right and to the rich, and business launched a coordinated assault on labor after a decade of militant organizing drives.[37] Middle-class members of the so-called Silent Majority aggressively resisted school and housing integration while former New Deal Democrats and Republicans alike foregrounded the demonization and punishment of "welfare mothers as a nonproductive rentier class."[38] In constructing racially and economically exclusive suburbs, postwar liberalism created the social basis for its undoing.

This was the emerging economic dynamic that facilitated the turn of the public mood against foreign workers. Perhaps surprisingly, though, neither suburban homeowners nor unions founded the contemporary nativist movement— environmentalists fixated on overpopulation did. The scarcity of natural resources would soon be demoted to a decidedly minor theme as anti-immigrant politics emphasized anxieties over the English language, the white numerical majority, crime, welfare expenditures, job competition, and, ultimately, terrorism. But it was the belief that America's air, water, and land were threatened by foreign invasion that first began to weave the complex tapestry of fear and hatred that would shape immigration politics for the next half-century.

Lifeboat ethics

Paul R. Ehrlich's 1968 bestselling book, *The Population Bomb*, placed these American anxieties into a terrifying global context, warning that rapid human population growth would lead to mass famine and ecological catastrophe. Fear of overpopulation complemented an ominous vision of the future foretold by a landscape of blighted and violent cities, poisoned water and closed factories.

Though Ehrlich's book wasn't about immigration, some of his fans seized on it obsessively. Ecologist Garrett Hardin, who in 1968 published his landmark *Science* article "The Tragedy of the Commons," helped connect the dots. Hardin popularized the now-famous thought experiment as a problem of collective action: if every herdsman maximally grazed their cattle in a common pasture they would be acting in their rational self-interest but also to the collective ruin.[39] The pasture is destroyed this way. Though there are, of course, countless examples of people efficaciously managing commonly held resources,[40] Hardin's paranoid myth quickly became a staple of neoliberal thought—an argument for the indispensability of private property. What many who are familiar with the concept today might not know is that Hardin was a racist, and that his article, which advanced this seminal concept, was a polemic against overpopulation, arguing, "Freedom to breed will bring ruin to all."

That same year, astronaut Bill Anders took his famous photograph of the whole earth at the horizon. National borders were invisible, bolstering a vision opposite to Hardin's: humanity's shared fate within the common home of Spaceship Earth. Adlai Stevenson, then the US ambassador to the United Nations, described the concept in 1965: "We travel together, passengers on a little spaceship, dependent on its vulnerable reserves of air and soil; all committed, for our safety, to its security and peace; preserved from annihilation only by the care, the work and, I will say, the love that we give to our fragile craft."[41]

Neo-Malthusians took the dimmer view that, since the spaceship was running low on supplies, it would have to do with fewer passengers. Instead of universalist environmentalism, they demanded First World resource hoarding. In 1974, Hardin made the nativist implications of his philosophy clear when he published two versions of an article called "Lifeboat Ethics." "Environmentalists use the metaphor of the earth as a 'spaceship' in trying to persuade countries, industries and people to stop wasting and polluting our natural resources," Hardin wrote. "The spaceship metaphor can be dangerous when used by misguided idealists to justify suicidal policies for sharing our resources through uncontrolled immigration and foreign aid."[42]

"Metaphorically, each rich nation amounts to a lifeboat full of comparatively rich people," he continued. "The poor of the world are in other, much more crowded lifeboats. Continuously, so to speak, the poor fall out of their lifeboats and swim for a while in the water outside, hoping to be admitted to a rich lifeboat, or in some other way to benefit from the 'goodies' on board. What should the passengers on a rich lifeboat do?"[43] Hardin's sober-minded implication was to let them drown. Given today's massive crisis in the Mediterranean—thousands of migrants dying each year trying to reach Fortress Europe— it was morbidly prescient.[44]

Resources, whether they be jobs or food or clean water, seemed to be in short supply. Difficult questions required forthright answers. Or, this was at least one way to justify opposing non-white immigration to a country that had been founded by genocidal white settlers. "The press of numbers, of masses of humanity, have made migration obsolete as a solution to human problems," said Democratic Colorado governor Richard Lamm.[45] What this perspective rendered invisible was that severe exploitation of Third World people had rendered the First World so much richer than the Third. Lamm's imperative was to uphold the global color line.

A similar argument was made in a 1973 *New York Times Magazine* cover story, which warned that Americans would either have to choose dramatically smaller families or restrict large-scale immigration if the population were to be stabilized. "There are rumblings," the author wrote, "of a desire for new changes in immigration law, a desire motivated not by prejudice but by concerns for the environment, dwindling resources and the quality of our lives." Limiting immigration, the author wrote, would allow us to "catch up on better housing; eliminate unemployment; help the poor, the blacks, realize their aspirations; provide better quality education, health care, welfare and more imaginative care for our senior citizens; conserve our natural resources; improve mass transportation." Shutting down the border could cure "the whole laundry list of ailments we suffer."[46]

The next year, Zero Population Growth (ZPG), the leading US organization founded in response to *The Population Bomb*, declared that "legal immigration should be reduced to a level approximating emigration"—in other words, all but eliminated.[47] Meanwhile, Hardin became involved in the Environmental Fund (later renamed Population-Environment Balance), a new organization funded by Mellon heir Cordelia Scaife May.[48] It successfully lobbied for legislation that made it harder for the immigrant parents of US citizens to gain legal status. The group's president, Justin Blackwelder, said that the law sought to dissuade migrant women from crossing the border "to have their babies on the levee." The comment anticipated the later nativist vilification of so-called "anchor babies," a slur against immigrant women who allegedly arranged to birth in the United States so that their children would gain birthright citizenship—thus "anchoring" dangerously fecund Mexicans to a country where they by no right belonged, claiming resources they had no right to.[49]

In 1975, John Tanton, a Michigan ophthalmologist, abortion rights advocate and former chair of the Sierra Club's National Population Committee, took over as ZPG president. But the organization's leaders rejected Tanton's proposal to forcefully take on immigration, according to one former staffer, because "they were uneasy about getting into ethnicity—they didn't want to be called racist." Tanton and company, they said, "talk in very legitimate terms, about protecting our borders and saving the nation's resources and so on . . . but the trouble is, after you've heard them, you want to go home and take a shower."[50] In 1979, Tanton founded the Federation for American Immigration Reform (FAIR) and became the godfather of the modern nativist movement.[51] Tanton, whose correspondence with May included an alarmed discussion over women in wealthy countries having fewer babies than poor ones, described her as FAIR's single largest supporter as early as 1983.[52] Hardin, in turn, claimed that FAIR and the Environmental Fund had "interlocking directorates . . . We exchange ideas, we exchange personnel."[53] He joined FAIR's board and published frequently in Tanton's journal *The Social Contract*, founded in 1990. Ehrlich and his wife would join FAIR's leadership, too.

FAIR remains among the most consequential anti-immigrant organizations today. Remarkably, Tanton created and nurtured a network that ultimately included every major nativist group in the country: U.S. English founded in 1983; the Center for Immigration Studies in 1985; FAIR's legal arm, the Immigration Reform Law Institute, in 1986; and NumbersUSA in 1996.[54] Tanton's network benefited enormously from May's wealth, receiving more than $150 million since 2005 (the year that she died) from her Colcom Foundation.[55] Gradually, the environmental movement drifted away from anti-immigrant politics, though nativists would throughout the late '90s and 2000s try, and fail, to bring the Sierra Club in line. The flagship organization of the environmental movement from which the new nativists emerged wanted nothing to do with what its leadership called "extremists acting from racial prejudice."[56]

Initially, however, FAIR had proclaimed a desire to seek "a middle-of-the-road stance, eschewing the far right," and avoid "an image of racism, jingoism, xenophobia, chauvinism or isolationism."[57] Its first executive director, Roger Conner, was a liberal who said that he wanted to pursue restriction "without bringing the crazies out of the woodwork," or drawing on "the racist, anti-immigrant feelings we all know exist in the country."[58]

But the only mass base for red-hot nativist politics was on the right. Initially, FAIR sent its appeals to mailing lists full of liberals who had contributed to populationist and environmental causes. But they also sent appeals to other lists and experimented with other messages. "Over and over again," writes Charles Kamasaki, longtime immigrant rights advocate and author of a history of immigration politics, "the lists that produced the highest returns were of conservative activists, and the most effective anti-immigration messages emphasized cultural if not necessarily explicitly racial concerns about immigration."[59]

Conner moved on in 1988. But before doing so, he recommended that Dan Stein, the head of the Immigration Reform Law Institute, take his place. Stein embraced Tanton's more forthright racism. He suggested that immigrants were "getting into competitive breeding" and described immigration as posing a political and partisan threat, warning: "Immigrants don't come all church-loving, freedom-loving, God-fearing . . . Some of them firmly believe in socialist or redistributionist ideas. Many of them hate America, hate everything the United States stands for. Talk to some of these Central Americans."[60] He warned that "we're going to have a bloody battle . . . [that's] either going to be settled by effective political leadership or it's going to be settled in the streets."[61]

It was the "dynamics of direct mail," said Conner, that made FAIR "more culturally conservative."[62] According to historian Carly Goodman, FAIR initially welcomed President Bill Clinton's hard-line approach—but then seemingly realized that more could be gained by attacking him.[63] The emphasis on overpopulation was replaced by arguments that immigration posed dangerous threats. "FAIR's evolution toward the right both reflected and drove the movement of grassroots conservatives toward immigration restriction," as Kamasaki writes.[64]

The environment faded as a core nativist issue. It would reemerge three decades later, however, as climate change spurred not only new migrations but also a still-nascent right-wing response, a politics of eco-apartheid that envisioned walls and military force to safeguard hoarded resources in a warming world.

Inventing "illegal immigration"

Not only did immigration increase, but Mexicans began to travel further afield in search of work as the mechanization of agriculture decreased demand for farm labor, and neoliberal economic restructuring increased demand for low-wage labor everywhere. At first, it was more a curious phenomenon than a crisis. A 1969 Associated Press article reported that "the prosperity Dallas and Fort Worth have experienced" had brought with it the "new problem" of large numbers of "wetbacks" to the area. But it also noted that the INS was assisting the undocumented migrant "in obtaining a visa so he can stay with his family."[65]

The "problem" of illegal immigration had not yet been fully developed as such. That changed after economic crisis took hold in the 1970s. The anti-immigrant movement that emerged in response was distinct from those of prior eras. Immigration had long elicited opposition. But in the past opposition had nakedly targeted racial others. After 1965, immigration law was formally race-neutral but de facto discriminatory—against Mexicans, who became the face of the "colorblind" era's problem of "illegal immigration."

Civil rights and labor figures, including representatives of the NAACP, the League of United Latin American Citizens (LULAC), and the AFL-CIO unified behind a solution: sanctions on employers who hired unauthorized workers. Yet liberal anti-immigrant sentiment tended to avoid overt racism. Many blamed bosses for hiring immigrants, and government for failing to stop them from doing so, rather than immigrants themselves.[66] Organized labor, often simplistically caricatured as forever stalwart restrictionists, played a complicated role. The AFL-CIO had helped to bring an end to both the abusive Bracero program and then, thanks in part to the progressive influence of the CIO over the restrictionist AFL and allegiance to Cold War liberal foreign policy aims, the racist national origins quotas. They believed that "illegal immigration," like the Bracero program, abused imported labor to the detriment of domestic workers.[67]

In 1971, California governor Ronald Reagan signed the nation's first law penalizing employers for hiring undocumented immigrants (ultimately blocked in court) amid recession and in response to a powerful farmworker boycott of grapes.[68] Soon after, the House of Representatives, led by Representative Peter Rodino, a New Jersey Democrat and labor ally, passed legislation to impose employer sanctions only to be blocked by agriculture-aligned interests in the Senate.

Unlike today, the major opposition was not to the legalization of undocumented immigrants but rather to cracking down on the bosses who employed them. Specifically, advocates of employer sanctions struggled to find their way past Senator James Eastland, a Dixiecrat from Mississippi, where he owned a 5,800-acre cotton plantation.

Eastland opposed employer sanctions, though not because he supported civil or immigrant rights. Indeed, he had helped lead the fight against repealing the racist national origins quotas in the 1960s.[69] Eastland was an arch-segregationist senator who had defended Jim Crow on the grounds that it forestalled the "mongrelization" of the black and white races.[70] But he was a tenacious champion of agricultural interests. In 1972, a call from his office shut down an INS raid of Mississippi cotton gins in its tracks.[71]

Rodino's continued push for employer sanctions, however, prompted growing resistance from the left as well. Established Hispanic organizations had shifted from their longtime opposition to undocumented immigrants. In part, that's because Chicano radicalism had re-envisioned Mexican immigrants as compatriots exploited by a racist and capitalist order rather than as competitors who threatened Mexican American wages and white ethnic assimilation.[72]

The Chicano movement was substantially nationalist in orientation. But the leading left-wing Mexican American organization, the Centro de Acción Social Autónomo-Hermandad General de Trabajadores—led by legendary radical Bert Corona—emphasized solidarity with immigrants as a matter of class struggle under the motto *Somos un pueblo sin fronteras* (We are one people without borders). This transnational inclusivity began to win out. By the mid-1970s, the UFW and mainline organizations like LULAC reversed their historic position and demanded rights for the immigrants they had long opposed.[73]

Meanwhile, many whites shifted right. In 1970s New York City, the population of Latin American immigrants—people not from Mexico but from Caribbean countries like the Dominican Republic and South American ones like Colombia—was growing in white neighborhoods where longtime residents had begun to relocate to the suburbs amid a fiscal crisis that elites used to impose deep austerity.[74] Black people were moving in, too. Both groups were met with intense resistance. A New York Board of Education spokesperson announced that some schools were turning away students who could not provide a green card. The NYPD reported that it dutifully notified the INS when an immigrant was arrested. In 1950, the Queens where Donald Trump grew up had been 96.5 percent white; it became known everywhere as the home of Archie Bunker, TV's reactionary white working-class icon. By 1970, roughly 13 percent of the borough was black and 8 percent Hispanic, with a growing Asian population. The president of the civic association in the neighborhood of Jackson Heights called "illegal aliens" "an unbearable burden" and "an American tragedy."[75]

In Elmhurst, a crowd of three hundred jammed a community board meeting. "Get these illegals out of this country," one man demanded. "It's time to protect the Americans," stated another, overwhelming one woman's plea not to make "illegal aliens," as the reporter referred to them, a "scapegoat, like in Nazi Germany." South Americans were blamed for overcrowded schools and job competition.[76] Advocates responded that they were being made "scapegoats" for poor city services and the bad economy. Residents attending the meeting called by the Community Board for Corona and Elmhurst wailed about "illegal aliens," though most of the Latin American immigrants were in fact documented.[77] In the same neighborhood, whites quickly moved out of the massive, 4,600-unit Lefrak City apartment complex after a federal housing-discrimination lawsuit fully opened the complex to black renters smeared as "welfare" tenants.[78]

"The crisis saw a group of almost universally white elites remake life in a city that was becoming increasingly black and brown," writes historian Kim Phillips-Fein. "The collapse of the postwar social compact in New York happened at the very moment when it was losing its white middle-class population, when more and more of those using city services were low-income minorities. Many of the elites at the time blamed those impoverished African Americans and Latinos (and the public sector workers who served them) for New York's financial problems."[79]

But it wasn't just elites who scapegoated black and brown people. Across the city, the Great Migration and new international migration led to conflict. In Brooklyn, Crown Heights had undergone a massive and conflictive transition with the arrival of West Indians and Hasidic Jews and the exodus of former residents. Its Taxpayers and Civic Association encouraged members to report migrants to the authorities. "Thousands of illegal aliens here are sending their children to public schools," a lengthy 1974 *New York Times* story warned, "using municipal hospitals and receiving welfare benefits while often paying minimal taxes and sending large amounts of money abroad."[80] The *Times* warned that "illegal aliens have mounted what immigration authorities call a 'silent invasion' of New York and northern New Jersey."[81]

Immigrants might have valid reasons for migrating, but, the argument went, the United States was too hard pressed to make room for them. For many, the problem was clear. Or at least it was clear that there *was* a problem. The INS and the Border Patrol responded with workplace and community raids and deportations.[82] But potential policy solutions and the political coalitions that might either pursue or oppose them were still in the earliest stage of formation.

Nixon's hyperbolic and hard-line INS commissioner Leonard Chapman said that the situation had become "hopelessly out of control."[83] His successor under Jimmy Carter, Leonel Castillo, the agency's first Hispanic leader, praised unauthorized immigrants' "drive and ambition."[84] A *Los Angeles Times* story summed up the prevalent ambivalence: "Many are exploited and become, at once, pathetic victims and victimizers of the social system."[85]

In 1977, President Carter proposed that Congress increase the size of the Border Patrol, legalize unauthorized immigrants, and (following in the footsteps of President Gerald Ford's "illegal immigration" committee) sanction wayward employers.[86] Carter also affirmed the culture of scarcity and the loss of liberal faith in the power of government that was nurturing budding nativist sentiment. Beginning in 1979, Federal Reserve chairman Paul Volcker resolved the economy's troubles in favor of the wealthy with a spectacular interest rate hike that precipitated widespread deindustrialization, crushed worker power, and pushed ordinary people into unemployment.[87]

No wonder that Ronald Reagan's vision of "Morning in America"—from the man who had insisted that "the American people, the most generous on earth, who created the highest standard of living, are not going to accept the notion that we can only make a better world for others by moving backwards ourselves"—would resonate so powerfully.[88] And no wonder that a country where citizens no longer believed that they had the power to rule would come to so aggressively defend the boundaries of citizenship against outsiders. Narrowly defining the contours of "the American people," for many, would protect its value: an *exception*, for liberals and conservatives alike, drawn in contrast to a world of lesser peoples and nations.

Yet even as anti-immigrant sentiment intensified, it had yet to take powerful institutional form: right-wing conservatism of the era was so untouched by the nascent nativist movement that Reagan launched his campaign by calling for a North America "in which the peoples and commerce of its three strong countries flow more freely across their present borders than they do today."[89] Free markets, militant anti-communism, and a commitment to the transformative power of unbridled presidential optimism carried the day.

Reagan's right-wing breakthrough in 1980 changed the conservative movement forever—but the basic approach to immigration reform remained the same. In 1978, legislation backed by Senator Ted Kennedy had created the Select Commission on Immigration and Refugee Policy (SCIRP), chaired by Reverend Theodore Hesburgh, the president of the University of Notre Dame and an acclaimed Catholic liberal. In 1981, the Hesburgh Commission proposed employer sanctions and a national identification card, measures to deal with the root causes of migration, increased Border Patrol funding, a modest increase in legal immigration, and amnesty for unauthorized immigrants. And importantly, it separated the issue of "illegal" from legal immigration, contending that Washington had to "shut the back door" to the former and "open the front door" to the latter. This basic policy framework would guide the next three decades of mainstream immigration reform efforts.[90]

While celebrating immigrants' general contribution to the economy, SCRIP asserted that undocumented workers harmed "some U.S. citizens and resident aliens who can least afford it . . . hurt by competition for jobs and housing and a reduction of wages and standards at the workplace." Since labor demand drove migration, "some form of employer sanctions is necessary if illegal migration is to be curtailed." Legalization was also necessary, however, because "legalized aliens would no longer contribute to the depression of U.S. labor standards and wages."[91]

Economic anxiety didn't by itself make the immigration "problem" a reality. But it powerfully shaped its contours.

In 1982, the INS launched a series of nationwide raids dubbed Operation Jobs, which rounded up thousands of unauthorized immigrants at workplaces nationwide, including at a Denver meatpacker, Trinity Valley Steelworks in Fort Worth, and an auto parts business near Chicago.[92] That same year, two white men in Detroit, including a Chrysler plant supervisor, beat Chinese American Vincent Chin to death with a baseball bat during his bachelor party. They did so under the apparent and false belief that he was Japanese and so, by racist logic, culpable for the auto industry's decline.[93]

Most economic-based antipathy wasn't expressed directly through vigilante street violence. But Walter Mondale's warning that Americans would one day be relegated to "sweep[ing] up around the Japanese computers" seemed all too plausible.[94]

Opening the front door

Democratic representative Romano Mazzoli and Republican senator Alan Simpson of Wyoming led a bipartisan effort to legislate Hesburgh's "solution" to "illegal immigration" into law.

The Reagan administration was divided between law-and-order forces hostile to undocumented immigration and business opposition to employer sanctions, including from growers in the president's home state.[95] And though Reagan terrorized Central American refugees as part of his dirty war against communism, he certainly was no nativist: "You don't build a nine-foot fence along the border between two friendly nations," he said.[96] Meanwhile, the liberal left was split on the question. The AFL-CIO backed sanctions.[97] But Hispanic leaders of a movement that was taking institutional form in Washington, alongside the American Civil Liberties Union, contended that sanctions would incentivize discrimination against people who looked or sounded like they might be from somewhere else. As is often the case in immigration politics, there were motley coalitions on all sides of the debate.

In 1986, after years of conflict and negotiation, Reagan signed the landmark Immigration Reform and Control Act (IRCA). It ultimately legalized an estimated 2.7 million immigrants, authorized a 50 percent increase in funding for the Border Patrol and included what was billed as tough fines against employers who hired unauthorized immigrants.[98] It made the targeting of immigrants convicted of criminal offenses a deportation priority. It also created the first iteration of what became the Diversity Visa program, which was intended to benefit Irish immigrants but ultimately provided a plurality of visas to Africans—and was thus maligned a few decades later by President Trump for bringing migrants from "shithole" (or maybe, according to some meeting attendees, "shithouse") countries.[99] IRCA also created the little-remembered Commission for the Study of International Migration and Cooperative Economic Development to research economic policies that would reduce migration. They endorsed free trade with Mexico as a solution.[100]

IRCA is today generally considered to be an immigrant rights victory because it legalized a massive number of undocumented people. At the time, however, FAIR supported IRCA over considerable internal dissent, opposing its legalization provisions but hopeful that employer sanctions might work to choke off undocumented immigration. Even before IRCA became law, however, they were rightfully nervous it would not turn out that way. "In order to get the employer sanctions to turn off the job magnet that draws illegal aliens here, we had to drag along the baggage of a general amnesty," FAIR's Gerry Mackie lamented as the legislation headed to Reagan for his signature. "No one knows if there will be a new surge of illegal immigrants, but if the INS doesn't have the money it needs to defend the borders, there could be some real problems."[101]

Just as today, establishment politicians believed that enforcement paired with legalization would solve the immigration "problem." Ultimately, however, the law didn't work as advertised. It successfully legalized a large swath of undocumented residents, thanks in part to aggressive litigation challenging a restrictive INS process. The employer sanctions, however, had been watered down during negotiations, were easily evaded with fraudulent documents, and only lightly enforced.[102] Four years in, the number of unauthorized crossings, having once dropped to as low as 50 percent of 1986 levels, were creeping back up to those record highs, and the number of Mexicans sponsored for visas by their newly legalized relatives grew.[103] According to Otis Graham, a historian and a key figure in FAIR founder Tanton's network, restrictionists and pro-immigrant forces alike overestimated sanctions' impact.[104] Either way, IRCA was a provisional solution that could never have resolved the underlying contradictions. The United States and Mexico together formed an integrated binational economy, albeit an unequal one. Mexicans would continue to migrate regardless of whether there was a legal avenue for them to do so.

And they did. Migration was pulled by US labor demand and pushed by Mexico's economic crisis: the flood of petrodollars recycled by Wall Street into loans to Latin America was squeezed off by the Federal Reserve's interest rate hike. In 1982, Mexico defaulted, deepening the power of international banks and financial institutions, and precipitating market-liberalizing structural adjustments. Then, declining oil prices hit Mexico's fiscal base hard, further growing its public debt.[105]

Two decades later, reform politics would be flipped on its head. A bipartisan establishment alliance emerged again to push reform legislation under presidents George W. Bush and Barack Obama. These later efforts, however, won support from business and many civil rights organizations— the same coalition that had initially resisted IRCA—alongside organized labor, which had backed employer sanctions. Nativists who had supported IRCA came to reject any new proposals to legalize unauthorized immigrants no matter how much border and interior enforcement was included.

In the 1980s, hard-core anti-Mexican nativism, let alone civilizational Islamophobia, had not yet become a decisive force in national immigration politics—far from it. If it had, IRCA would never have passed with such broad legalization provisions. The business wing maintained the upper hand, and Reagan's successor, President George H.W. Bush, signed legislation passed by a Democratic Congress that dramatically *expanded* authorized immigration through the Immigration Act of 1990, which raised the global ceiling for annual admissions to 700,000 until 1994 and 675,000 after that, a cap from which immediate relatives of American citizens remained exempt.

Senator Simpson opposed an early form of the bill and had initially persuaded President Bush to as well. But opposition was steamrolled by business and ethnic advocacy groups. One internal administration memo, in a powerful reflection of a bygone conservatism, fretted that Bush would become publicly identified with "restrictionists" if he didn't support the law.[106] The legislation also, however, authorized the hiring of one thousand Border Patrol agents, replicating in miniature what had become the conventional wisdom of protecting the political space for authorized immigration by cracking down on "illegals."

In 1982, Simpson had warned that if immigration reform didn't pass Congress there would be growing calls "for more enforcement, more border patrol personnel, more immigration investigators." He continued:

We shall see a change in public attitudes toward immigrants and refugees. We shall see public support for our fine immigration and refugee programs eroding as American citizens perceive that their short-term interests are being threatened by the continued uncontrolled numbers of legal and illegal immigrants competing for jobs and scarce resources.

We might well then see all of the latent nativism, xenophobia, racism and scapegoating come fully to the surface and begin to tragically and profoundly influence public policy. We can expect increased public pressure for stricter enforcement of the existing immigration laws; increased raids upon the workplaces; the prospect of continued long-term detention, and the possibility of mass deportations.[107]

Simpson's predictions of growing nativism proved prescient, though not for the reasons he supposed. Enforcement escalations indeed became commonplace. But they would only lead to calls for yet more dramatic enforcement and the very extreme xenophobia he had warned against.

The next major attempt to fix these impossible contradictions was the North American Free Trade Agreement (NAFTA), with its promise that integrated markets would improve Mexicans' living standards to the point where they would no longer feel compelled to migrate north. NAFTA's globalizing framework, of course, neither stopped migration nor mollified its nativist critics. It inflamed them, creating the specter of a New World Order that moved both labor and capital across borders at corporate whim while undermining American wages, neighborhoods, security, and sovereignty. As IRCA failed to deter unauthorized immigration and the NAFTA debate ripped through both major parties, radicalized nativists moved toward the center of American politics.

Hardworking, hardly working

In the early 1990s, an anti-immigrant insurgency took root in California, the center of the movement to bar Chinese immigration more than a century earlier. A major economic slump had taken hold, thanks in part to declining defense industry jobs after the Cold War drew to a close. Chinese people had moved into the San Gabriel Valley, and Latinos into the San Fernando Valley, as area aerospace manufacturers spun into sharp decline.[108] Immigrants joined black Americans in the racist white imaginary as lazy and unworthy welfare dependents.

As jobs became scarcer, the number of immigrants, authorized and not, was growing. In 1990, an estimated 3.5 million undocumented immigrants lived in the United States, more than 40 percent of them in California.[109] "Illegal immigration is the hottest issue in the state," said Republican assemblyman Bill Morrow, who represented a wealthy district encompassing portions of Orange and San Diego Counties, in 1993. "We've got to say to the Federal Government, 'If you don't close the border, we will.'"[110]

In a familiar contradiction, immigrants were seen as both competing for scarce jobs and refusing to work at all, mooching off the state. Citizens identified as "taxpayers" were forced by a hostile government to fund the dangerous fecundity of non-white layabouts. One Republican legislator from an LA suburb circulated a ditty composed by a constituent to that effect:

Everything is mucho good.

Soon we own the neighborhood.

We have a hobby—it's called breeding.

Welfare pay for baby feeding.[111]

Latina childbearing was a dominant theme, deeply enmeshed with the era's demonization of poor black mothers. It tied the government's fiscal irresponsibility to the encouragement of irrepressible and irresponsible reproduction. To many in Southern California, Mexicans illegally invaded by crossing the border, and then illegitimately expanded their numbers by having children who would consume benefits funded by, and thus rightly belonging to, hardworking taxpayers.[112]

California was sold to turn of the twentieth century Anglos as an "Eden for the Saxon Homeseeker" and organized on profoundly racist principles from the inception of colonization. Spanish rule brutally reduced the indigenous population, which fell from 310,000 in 1769, to 150,000 in 1850, when California became a US state; Americans continued this trend, overseeing a fall to fewer than 20,000 by 1900.[113] In 1950s Los Angeles, media and police stoked a panic that "wolf packs" and "rat packs" of Mexican American youth were "invading white communities to peddle drugs and commit violence," using the same cars that had enabled California's low-density utopia to trespass the racial boundaries that defined its social order. Criminal others, as historian Matthew Lassiter writes, made "pretty white females into heroin addict-victims who invariably descended into the living death of prostitution across the urban color line." Racist criminalization recapitulated the events of a decade prior, when Mexican American youth dressed in Zoot Suits were portrayed as delinquents and assaulted by masses of rioting servicemen.[114] The state of California officially endorsed residential segregation as the best way to prevent delinquency.[115] Border enforcement, whether within American cities or along international boundaries, functioned and continues to function to protect the spatial organization of race and class hierarchy.

But by no means was a nativist revolt in California inevitable. In 1979, a poll had found that residents of the Southwest were much *less* likely than those in the Northeast to believe that undocumented workers took jobs from Americans, something that one expert credited to the concentration of immigrants in areas with the lowest unemployment rates.[116] Anti-immigrant sentiment was by no means dominant.

California lieutenant governor Mike Curb, a Republican, told members of the Republican National Committee in 1979 that "undocumented workers are not committing crime, they are coming here to work. Very few of them are on welfare, very few of them are violating our laws, most of them are extremely good citizens. We should begin to treat them with respect. We should treat any worker who is putting in an honest day's work with respect."[117] Imagine a Republican politician saying that in 2020.

Early 1990s California is the first chapter of a story about how such sentiments became politically impossible in the Republican Party. California proved for nativists that mass non-white immigration led to crime, the growth of a racialized underclass unassimilable to American culture, and, critically, excessive expenditures by hardworking taxpayers on behalf of an indolent minority shamelessly reproducing without the means to pay the costs of their offspring.

The nativist revolt culminated in voters' 1994 passage of Proposition 187, an act of spectacular cruelty that among other things denied public services to suspected undocumented immigrants—even schools—and required public officials to report those immigrants to the INS. The stated goal was to deter new undocumented immigrants from arriving by driving those already present out of bedrock services.[118]

The measure began by asserting that the people of California "are suffering economic hardship caused by the presence of illegal aliens in this state" and from "personal injury and damage caused by [their] criminal conduct."[119] The measure, originating in the right-wing suburban stronghold of Orange County, simultaneously conjured up a law-abiding and taxpaying victimized citizenry (the suffering people) and those who were to blame: criminal and moocher aliens. White injury was premised on white innocence, which in turn relied on ignorance: absent was the history of Mexican migration and its criminalization; also missing was a good explanation for why all these Anglos even lived in a state and cities with Spanish-language names, places that had in fact previously belonged to multiple indigenous peoples before European genocide.[120]

Two of the key Prop 187 organizers, former border agent Bill King and soon-to-be leading nativist Barbara Coe, summed up the kaleidoscopic dynamic of immigrant threat and white victimhood in a 1992 ad they had placed in the *National Review*. The ad sought out people who had "been victims of crimes either financial (welfare, unemployment, food stamps, etc.), educational (overcrowding, forced bilingual classes, etc.) or physical (rape, robbery, assault, infectious disease, etc.) committed by illegal aliens."[121]

Proposition 184, affirming a draconian new "Three Strikes" sentencing law, was on the same ballot, and likewise passed in a landslide. As scholar Daniel Martinez HoSang writes, both measures "depicted an angry and vulnerable populace drawing the line against an incorrigible criminal class that lay beyond the pale of society."[122] So many threats had been rolled into one alien menace. Unsurprisingly, FAIR was involved. One of its lobbyists, former INS commissioner Alan C. Nelson, helped write 187 alongside the agency's former western regional chief, Harold W. Ezell. FAIR then spent thousands on pro-187 ads after the propositions' opponents attacked 187's ties to FAIR, highlighting its receipt of hundreds of thousands of dollars from the eugenicist Pioneer Fund.[123]

This was the moment that the movement's most right-wing demands entered mainstream conservative politics— and thus mainstream politics as a whole—in full force. And though the law's full implementation was quickly blocked in court, it nonetheless terrorized immigrants. Prop 187 supporters pointed to the fear the law had unleashed in immigrant communities—to celebrate its success. "A number of people have pulled children out of school for no apparent reason. All these things add up to illegal aliens leaving the state of California," crowed Ron Prince, an Orange County accountant who served as co-chairman of Save Our State, which was the name of the organization backing the measure and also a shorthand for the measure itself.[124]

Republican governor Pete Wilson made 187 and the defense of "Californians who work hard, pay taxes, and obey the laws" a centerpiece of his reelection campaign, and rode anti-"illegal" politics to victory.[125] Wilson made it clear that "illegal immigration" could be a partisan issue that Republicans would seek to own. As Clinton moved his party right, that also meant it was a wedge issue that centrist Democrats would try to co-opt in a bid to outflank them.

Indeed, it was Senator Dianne Feinstein, the California Democrat and former San Francisco mayor, who led the way in connecting immigration to the economic slump and making "illegal immigrants" a top political issue.[126] It was Feinstein who inspired Governor Wilson "to become more aggressive," according to a *Los Angeles Times* analysis at the time. "She has provided 'cover' for politicians of both parties, lending respectability to a sensitive area where it is easy to be branded a demagogue and a bigot." Feinstein suggested that political correctness had made others too afraid to "speak out."[127]

Feinstein, who had narrowly lost the 1990 gubernatorial election to Wilson, claimed that her "moderate approach" was necessary "to avoid a serious backlash against all immigrants," articulating establishment politics that would define the coming decades: crackdowns on bad "illegal immigrants" to protect good "legal immigrants" and to defuse extreme right-wing measures.[128]

One Wilson election ad similarly invoked the specter of bad immigrants tarnishing the good. Against images of the Statue of Liberty and a naturalization ceremony, he declared: "There's a right way, and there's a wrong way. To reward the wrong way is not the American way."[129] The Hart-Celler Act of 1965 had purportedly replaced a racist system with a fair and liberal one. In the "colorblind" era that followed, "illegal immigrants" could be portrayed as violating the citizenship compact and meriting just punishment.[130] Prop 187 was simultaneously right-wing and liberal, racist and capacious: it passed by eighteen percentage points with 63 percent of the white vote, but also nearly half of black and Asian votes and nearly a quarter of Latinos.[131] A racist law could be presented as racially neutral opposition to illegality.

Feinstein and the rest of the liberal establishment did oppose 187—but on terms that entirely conceded its premise. The establishment campaign, Taxpayers Against 187, targeted white suburbanites with the case that the war on "illegal immigration" was necessary but that right-wingers were waging it ineffectively. "Something must be done to stop the flow of illegal immigrants coming across the border," their official statement read. "Illegal Immigration is a REAL problem, but Proposition 187 is NOT A REAL SOLUTION." The campaign warned that 187 wouldn't actually deport anyone and that undocumented students expelled from school could become criminals.[132]

Grassroots activists who mounted their own immigrant-centered campaign as part of a mass movement of protests and student walkouts were appalled. Prop 187 was unbeatable. So, instead of attempting to co-op nativist language, they built the immigrant power that would over the following decades help transform California politics and relegate the state's Republicans to the margins.[133]

Meanwhile, Feinstein released an ad attacking her opponent in the Senate race on border security, boasting that she "led the fight to stop illegal immigration."[134] In September, less than two months before the vote, Attorney General Janet Reno announced Operation Gatekeeper, a massive federal crackdown on the San Diego border area, declaring: "The days when the border served as a revolving door for illegal immigrants are over."[135] Feinstein and Reno's approach encapsulates a central argument of this book: the liberal and mainstream establishment attempted to outflank their right-wing opponents by co-opting their message, but in doing so they simply amplified the nativists' politics and advanced their policies. Democrats worked with the right to convince voters that immigration was a problem. They voted "yes" on 187 because it was a tough solution.

Balanced-budget nativism

In the late nineteenth century, "the alleged racial inferiority of immigrants became the *explanation* for depressed wages, labor strife, and the emerging 'sweatshop system,'" just as their un-Americanness explained left-wing radicalism, writes sociologist Kitty Calavita.[136] In the 1990s, a fiscal frame was front and center, and "this scapegoating of immigrants as the cause of the crisis found a ready audience among the white middle-class who disproportionately make up the electorate."[137] Assessing the history of anti-immigrant politics then requires not only accounting for why nativism waxes and wanes in intensity at particular moments—the *quantity* of nativism—but also its *quality*. "If immigrants serve as scapegoats for social crises, it stands to reason that the specific content of anti-immigrant nativism will shift to encompass the prevailing malaise."[138]

And so it did. The movement that took off in California was the product of intertwined fiscal and social conservative accounts of long economic and social crises. The nativist resurgence of the 1990s was heavily focused on "immigrants as a tax burden, a focus that is unusual, if not unique in the history of U.S. nativism," Calavita writes. It was a larger piece of the "balanced-budget conservatism" that accompanied "workers' stagnant wages and increasing insecurity, and the dismantling of the welfare state."[139]

The argument that immigrants were exploiting social services to which they had no right offered conservatives a less offensive way to make the familiar argument that hardworking taxpayers were funding programs for a poor and often non-white underclass that did not deserve them. Indeed, the foundation for fiscal nativism had been set years prior. Historian Mike Davis writes that, in 1964, suburban opposition to black people in their neighborhoods spurred the success of Proposition 14, which aimed to thwart integrated housing; then, in the late 1970s, suburban parents mobilized against busing to integrate schools; and in 1978,

California kicked off a nationwide tax revolt after middle-class white suburbanites led the successful campaign for Proposition 13, which restricted property taxes in the name of defending the home and the families who occupied it from a redistributive state that was transferring their wealth to the undeserving poor.[140]

Felicitously, victories won by California's suburbanite right, a movement that went national with Nixon and Reagan, created new crises for that movement to exploit. HoSang explains: "The large-scale cutbacks in public services that fueled so much of the animosity driving Proposition 187, nearly all of which could be traced to the wave of property tax–slashing measures in the late 1970s and early 1980s as well as to the increase in state prison spending, became almost singularly understood as a result of the impact of undocumented immigration."[141] The upshot was that the crisis would be met by white reaction more than working-class resistance.

To say that xenophobia is shaped by the politics of economic life does not mean that economically precarious whites are its exclusive source, as the muddled debate over the causes of Trump's election suggest. Quite to the contrary: the New Deal order had quietly subsidized white middle-class suburbia by financing homes in segregated neighbor-hoods where children attended segregated schools and also built the highways that led to them. But these subsidies were often invisible to their recipients, and so the New Deal perversely laid the material foundation for the reaction against it: middle-class white suburbanites living in racially exclusive suburbs who believed that their status was solely the product of their own hard work, and who fought to protect the world they had built from undeserving others. Nowhere was this more true than in the Sun Belt, where defense spending dramatically remade the economy and spurred a population boom.[142]

The New Deal state created not only racially exclusive suburbs but also a new identity for the people who inhabited them: "homeowner, taxpayer, and schoolparent status," as Lassiter writes.[143] The result, writes Davis, was that "affluent homeowners, organized by notional community designations or tract names, engaged in defense of home values and neighborhood exclusivity," became "the most powerful 'social movement' in contemporary Southern California."[144]

American capitalism had created an iconic and proudly self-made white bourgeois family that simultaneously depended upon and disparaged low-paid immigrant workers who performed their cooking, cleaning, landscaping, and childrearing. The New Deal order's "Fordist family wage," as scholar Melinda Cooper writes, "not only functioned as a mechanism for the normalization of gender and sexual relationships, but it also stood at the heart of the mid-century organization of labor, race, and class."[145] That system broke down, and women entered the paid workforce in massive numbers, exciting a panic over sexual abuse of children who had been placed in daycares, and over Satanic cults.[146] In the 1990s, middle-class Californians confronted the uncanny reality that a way of life for which they gave only themselves credit was premised upon the labor of people whose presence they found uncomfortable and with whom sharing citizenship seemed impossible.

Nativism and the sex panic grew from the same soil; indeed, nativism was itself a form of sex panic. The defense of "family values," of course, had become central to conservative politics. And while some religious right leaders have no doubt supported immigrants on Biblical grounds, many ordinary adherents have not; protecting their families, it seemed, required banning and expelling all sorts of other families whose difference constituted a threat to their future.

New world order

Even as 187 was almost entirely blocked in court, Arizona, California, Florida, New Jersey, New York, and Texas sued the federal government to recuperate immigration-related costs, including for incarceration.[147] Governor Wilson fought on by attempting to deny prenatal care to undocumented women—a telling priority.[148]

Californians, on the same ballots upon which they voted to pass 187, helped Newt Gingrich's Republicans win unified control of Congress for the first time since 1952. Simpson, who had led the fight for IRCA, took the chair of the Senate Immigration Subcommittee and restrictionist representative Lamar Smith took over its House counterpart. Both were dedicated to restricting legal immigration, cracking down on "illegal immigration," and denying welfare to immigrants.[149] Ron Prince, co-chair of the pro-Prop 187 organization Save

Our State, called the California measure a bid "to get the attention of our government."[150] They got the message.

"Never before has this level of action been taken toward reforming immigration and never this early in a Congressional session," Dan Stein, FAIR's leader, gloated. "Immigration, thanks to the success of Proposition 187 and growing popular opinion as reflected in all major opinion polls, has Congress's attention."[151]

Among the decade's anti-immigrant laws was a retrenchment in public benefits targeting poor people in general and permanent residents in particular: Clinton and congressional Republicans' so-called welfare "reform" law of 1996, an extension of the same balanced-budget racism that fueled Prop 187. It is seldom remembered that the Personal Responsibility and Work Opportunity Reconciliation Act included major restrictions on authorized immigrants' access to public benefits (though Clinton did criticize these provisions as tarnishing an otherwise "extraordinarily important bill").[152] The bill cut cash assistance to poor families who had for years been racialized and portrayed as black, Latino, and pathologically dependent on government. Ironically, a judge struck down provisions of Prop 187 that denied state benefits not because they violated immigrant rights but because the federal welfare reform law preempted them.[153]

Republicans at a national level learned a lesson from California: the war on "illegal immigrants" could mobilize more white voters to the right. It offered a new way for a party remade in reaction to black civil rights to highlight fears over what *Time* had in 1990 called the "browning of America"—to run a new version of the same play that had brought the GOP such success through the 1970s and 1980s. The nativist movement's long-term goal, however, was the much larger task of reducing overall immigration—which meant sharply restricting legal arrivals as well.[154] But attacking legal immigration would mostly prove to be impossible: it was protected by powerful bipartisan forces and, since 1965, had become deeply embedded in American institutions and politics.

The 187 campaign's simultaneous demonization of undocumented immigrants and public benefits was well suited to a conservative politics that mobilized a cross-class coalition of whites behind social and fiscal conservatism. But another central debate of that era, over NAFTA, evinced a coalitional fracture: the business-aligned factions of both parties advocated corporate globalization amid populist revolts on both the right and left.

In fact, Prop 187 attracted a huge number of volunteers from one of the largest anti-NAFTA forces of the era: United We Stand America, founded by independent presidential candidate Ross Perot.[155] Immigration was a major issue for many of Perot's supporters.[156] But not explicitly for Perot. He trained most of his fire on NAFTA, which he warned would create "a giant sucking sound" of American jobs disappearing into Mexico. Opposition to globalization was often an inchoate mix of feelings about the movement of capital and people, over national sovereignty, and identity. Perotism marked the midway point of a political transition, allowing a heterogeneous mass of disaffected people to express their grievances.[157]

Perot's 1992 independent campaign for president won an astonishing 19 percent of the vote—including tallying 24 percent in Orange County. Perot's politics included an idiosyncratic assortment of positions reflecting a homespun philosophy that he used his vast personal wealth to promote in lengthy and popular infomercials. He called for campaign finance reform, direct democracy, and balancing the budget through tax hikes and spending cuts. He also criticized excessive CEO pay, the First Gulf War, and America losing the game of nation-based global competition.

In retrospect, Perot's success was the product of a moment when anti-globalization sentiment was still early in the process of ideological consolidation, which unfolded within a two-party system led by avowedly pro-globalization politicians. Perot, whose share of the vote was cut by more than half in 1996 when he ran on his Reform Party ticket, failed to define a systematic ideology that would outlive his extraordinarily bright moment in the national spotlight. By contrast, Pat Buchanan, an alumnus of the Nixon and Reagan administrations, became the prophet for a politics that would ultimately transform the Republican Party by way of Donald Trump. "His message is not mine," Perot said. "We don't want to build a wall around America."[158] It turned out that Perot didn't speak for many of his voters. Buchanan did.

In 1992, Buchanan ran an insurgent and racist primary campaign against President George H. W. Bush opposing the globalization of both labor and capital, and homosexuality. He did well enough to secure the keynote address at the Republican National Convention. Buchanan delivered an infamously homophobic and sexist speech that terrified many swing voters, warning of a "cultural war, as critical to the kind of nation we will one day be as was the Cold War itself."[159]

In 1995, Buchanan received an ecstatic reception at Perot's United We Stand America conference, where he demanded to know, "What are we doing to our own people? What are we doing to our own country?"[160] In the 1996 primary, Buchanan pledged to "bring back the Perot voters and the lost Reagan Democrats back to the GOP."[161] Meanwhile, Perot that same year fought off a serious challenge for his own Reform Party's presidential nomination from hard-core nativist Richard Lamm, the former Democratic governor of Colorado, who insisted that "we must place as a first priority our own huddled masses."[162]

During the 1990s, Buchanan crafted a nascent coalition around social conservatism, libertarian opposition to the slice of government spending directed specifically at a racialized minority portrayed as the nonworking poor, and an economic nationalism that placed white, blue-collar workers at its center. He simultaneously appealed to whites' European heritage and their status as workers threatened by globalist business, warning of the "anti-NAFTA rage of the populist right." It "is about more than trade," he wrote. "NAFTA is the chosen field upon which the defiant forces of a new patriotism have elected to fight America's foreign policy elite for control of the national destiny." For Buchanan, NAFTA was just one skirmish in a battle against a New World Order, foreign aid, foreign military entanglements, feminism, the United Nations and illegal immigration. NAFTA was, he wrote, "part of a skeletal structure for world government."[163] As Frank Guan notes, however, "it was his defense of workers in American manufacturing and his opposition to foreign wars, not his racial bigotry and moral puritanism that estranged the aspiring demagogue from the party he had served."[164]

Establishment Republicans attempted to stitch racism and neoliberalism into a majority coalition. Buchanan exploited the fact that white working-class voters, motivated to defect from the New Deal coalition over economically entangled racial animus, had never signed on to the nakedly anti-labor policies advanced by the business side of the Republican coalition. It was one thing to oppose school busing and neighborhood integration, or cut benefits to poor people, characterizing them as non-white and nonproductive. It was another to attack white workers, and it drove support toward the right-wing insurgent.

Buchanan combined opposition to free trade and illegal immigration into a right-wing nationalist agenda, the potency of which would only be realized by many with the election of Trump. At the time, the New Democrats and their Republican opponents sought to disentangle three closely entwined issues—"illegal immigration," legal immigration, and economic globalization—playing nativism to their advantage by focusing it on "illegals" and thereby protecting both neoliberalism and legal immigration.

"We can't afford to lose control of our own borders at a time when we are not adequately providing for the jobs, health care, and the education of our own people," said Bill Clinton, directing voters to place their blame on criminalized migrant workers instead of on the capital whose mobility he was protecting through a sophisticated global legal framework.[165]

Instead of addressing the economic stresses that underlay Americans' sense of insecurity in the world, politicians projected them onto the border. Without a strong left, and with union resistance curbed by Clintonism, opposition to corporate globalization was increasingly (though by no means entirely) captured by the right-wing anti-globalist position that saw mobile labor and capital as twin evils. The Soviet Union's collapse supposedly heralded the triumph of American capitalism and the end of history as we knew it. But for many Americans, what was supposed to be an epochal victory marked a great sense of doubt, a story of which they were no longer certain to be the author and protagonist.

Clinton deftly framed Republicans as extremists even as he co-opted less extreme variants of their positions. As far as short-term electoral matters were concerned, it at least didn't appear to hurt given that Clinton won reelection in 1996. Republican demagoguery also drove a boom in naturalizations as eligible immigrants who had previously declined to do so became citizens in huge numbers to defend themselves against the nativist onslaught.[166] And Clinton won an even greater share of Latino and Asian voters than he had in 1992 (though overall voter turnout reached near-historic lows).[167]

In any case, the New Democrats' short-term political victory reinforced the perception that immigrants posed a danger, that public benefits incentivized sloth and overbreeding among a racialized underclass, and that muscular

repression on the borders and in the interior would be necessary to contain the threats. Unsurprisingly, then, the long-
term advantage would accrue to the right, which was better
positioned to link the immigrant threat to crime, welfare,
globalization, and terrorism—and to package it all into a
potent white and nationalist force.

2

SECURITY

*Our nation was built by immigrants . . . But we won't tolerate
immigration by people whose first act is to break the law as
they enter our country.*

— President Bill Clinton, weekly radio address, May
1995[1]

In 1981, the Hesburgh Commission declared that "undocumented migration flouts U.S. immigration law [and that] its most devastating impact may be the disregard it breeds for other U.S. laws."[2] In the 1990s, politicians increasingly portrayed "illegal immigration" as an intrinsic source of criminality, as President Bill Clinton and his Republican antagonists sought to out-tough each other. It was a war on crime that demonized an immigrant threat, spurring border militarization and mass incarceration alike — all while deepening the connections between the criminal justice system and immigration enforcement, which traditionally was a largely civil matter.

"Every day, illegal aliens show up in court who are charged," said Clinton in a 1995 radio address. "Some are guilty and surely some are innocent. Some go to jail and some don't. But they're all illegal aliens, and whether they're innocent or guilty of the crimes they were charged with in court, they're still here illegally, and they should be sent out of the country."[3]

Amid high murder rates and long-term economic restructuring, Clinton not only fueled anti-crime sentiment but also helped ensure that crime had a black and Latino face. He described ungoverned streets and an insecure border as the sources of a violent and narcotic threat, and proposed policing, imprisonment, and deportation as solutions. Critically, Clinton cracked down both on "criminal aliens" who committed crimes and on "illegal immigrants" as a whole by insisting that all were by definition criminals: "people whose first act is to break the law as they enter our country," as he put it.

The histories of building walls along the border to keep foreigners out and erecting cages to contain those who live here already are inextricably entangled. As historian Kelly Lytle Hernández shows, they long have been so. Dominant politics, portraying a combined domestic and foreign criminal threat, built and legitimated a massive machinery of repression that operated through the Border Patrol, immigration agents from INS (later ICE), civil detention centers, local police, federal law enforcement, and a system of local, state, and federal jails and prisons. By the end of Obama's first term, immigration enforcement and criminal justice institutions would be almost seamlessly linked. The result was a deportation machine unprecedented in both efficiency and size.

The government response to September 11 under George W. Bush affixed these systems of domestic and border repression to the national security state and the military's war on terror—a war in and against Muslim-majority nations abroad that ultimately boomeranged into a politics of mass Islamophobia at home (which I discuss at length in the next chapter). This chapter's story begins at the border with Mexico, where the criminalization of human migration and the war on drugs became pretexts for a spectacular increase in the size of the Border Patrol and the construction of hundreds of miles of fencing. It ends by explaining how the wars on drugs and "illegal immigrants" failed to prevent the entry of either, leading to demands for yet more escalation rather than a reexamination of whether the wars should be waged at all.

In recent decades, the border has become more an idea than a place. Since the 1970s, it has served as a lens through which Americans see their myriad, growing fears. At the same time, politicians have weaponized the border to serve political ends. Nativism is a recurrent feature of American history. But it was only in recent decades that the sort of border that Donald Trump would make use of came into existence. It was the politics and policies of those who came before him—including Clinton, Bush, and Obama—that paved the way for criminal violence and terrorism to displace economic insecurity as nativism's central focus.

Creating the crisis

The continental United States has two land borders. But when people talk about "the border," they typically refer to the one shared with Mexico. That border has existed as a geographic place cutting across a certain set of longitudes and latitudes, with slight adjustment, since the 1848 Treaty of Guadalupe Hidalgo and the 1853–54 Gadsden Purchase rendered the US conquest of roughly half of Mexico's territory a legal reality.

Through the nineteenth century, the nation's land borders marked the limits of an expanding settler empire's contiguous territory. They were not a source of anxiety about immigration. In a sense, they were the opposite: they were a frontier, marking the territorial boundary of an empire-in-waiting that only white settlement could make a reality. Even in the early twentieth century, when the federal government first instituted light patrols, it was to catch barred Chinese who might slip in—not Mexicans.[4] Congress first created the Border Patrol in 1924 just two days after it passed the Immigration Act of 1924, a law that imposed racist national origins quotas targeting eastern and southern Europeans and extended the bar on Asian immigration to formally exclude nearly the entire region.[5]

Mexicans were not barred, but many crossed without authorization anyway, preferring to avoid securing a passport and paying an expensive visa fee and head tax that were first instituted in 1917.[6] The Border Patrol targeted barred Chinese and restricted Europeans and also liquor smugglers.[7] Yet it became more than anything a force for social control over Mexican "illegals," regulating and disciplining the Mexican labor supply, not attempting to end it. For white working-class agents, it was also about "community, manhood, whiteness, class, respect, belonging, brotherhood, and violence," writes Hernández. "Border Patrol officers in the Texas-Mexico borderlands thus broadly policed Mexicano mobility instead of enforcing the political boundary between the United States and Mexico."[8] It was only the "fears of invasion and subterfuge" surrounding World War II that "transformed the U.S. Border Patrol from a series of small and locally oriented outposts into a national police force with the resources to pursue immigration control on a much larger scale."[9] And it was only with the wartime creation of the Bracero program that, at the Mexican government's prodding, more agents were assigned to the border with Mexico than the one with Canada, leading the number of Mexicans returned south to skyrocket.[10]

Yet before violent battles between drug cartels, military, and police erupted in Mexico, and before militarization took root north of the line, the border had for many Americans been simply a gateway to a short vacation. During Prohibition, the streets of Ciudad Juárez and Tijuana were lined with high-end clubs. For decades, party seekers made their way from San Diego through the busy San Ysidro port of entry to Avenida Revolución's expansive street party. Just east in Tecate, women on the Mexican side hung their wash on a fence that stood less than five feet tall and was intended to block cattle rather than people. Nearby, the fence was simply a steel cable that children employed as a swing.[11]

For many, the international boundary was long a bridge to a sister city, perhaps where an actual sister lived. It was easily traversed for family visits, or for lunch.[12] Through the 1960s, the Border Patrol was a minor agency barely known to many who lived outside the borderlands.[13] After mass Mexican migration became criminalized in the 1960s, however, immigration became a growing concern most everywhere. At the border itself, the situation slipped into what looked like a spontaneous invasion as massive numbers of undocumented Mexicans surged past an overwhelmed Border Patrol. In reality, the scene was the direct outcome of the US government criminalizing long-standing Mexican migration by squeezing off legal immigration pathways.

In the late 1950s, roughly 450,000 Bracero migrants and 50,000 permanent residents entered from Mexico each year. In 1964, the Bracero program was terminated.[14] In 1965, the first-ever caps were placed on Western Hemisphere immigration as part of the Hart-Celler Act, which repealed the racist national origins quotas. In 1976, Congress criminalized a larger swath of Mexican migration by establishing a global ceiling of twenty thousand visa slots per country. President Gerald Ford signed the bill, but he also complained that the cookie-cutter low cap imposed on Mexicans failed to take into account the "very special historic relationship" between the two countries.[15]

The effect, as Douglas Massey and Karen Pren write, "was predictable": undocumented migration exploded.[16] In 1960, total apprehensions in the Southwest stood at 21,022, rising to 40,020 by 1965. By 1970, they had risen to 201,780, and to

690,554 by 1980. In 1983, they topped one million and would remain in the seven figures, save for a few dips, until the era of mass unauthorized Mexican migration ended with the Great Recession's onset.[17]

Meanwhile, Mexico created the Border Industrialization Program to create jobs that would compensate for the shuttered Bracero program. The result was the rise of what would become a massive maquiladora industry, through which US corporations export components to Mexican border factories duty-free and then re-import the manufactured product into the country, paying a tariff only on the value added in Mexico. This created a population boom in border cities like Juárez and Tijuana and allowed US corporations to take advantage of cheap Mexican labor without hiring Mexican migrants inside the country: a "disembodied export of the Mexican workforce."[18]

As the United States began to sharply restrict Mexican migration in the mid-1960s, a new service economy took hold, hollowing out the middle of the labor market and expanding the ranks of low-wage workers to occupy its bottom rungs, which in turn spread demand for Mexican workers far beyond Southwestern agriculture.[19] Mexico's export of migrants facilitated economic restructuring on both sides of the border, functioning as an "escape valve" for a Mexican economy with insufficient good jobs and providing "a reserve army of workers, at the disposal of the U.S. economy, the training costs of which are mostly borne by Mexican society."[20] Mexican workers, like Chinese in the late nineteenth century, were emblems of a distrusted new system.

The border, an ordinary place for people who lived there, became a symbol of trouble for millions who didn't. Still, until the 1990s, it could be crossed with little difficulty. Perhaps not on the first try but then, if caught, on the second.[21]

"All we ever do is delay them a little," said a Border Patrol supervisor in San Ysidro, the largest site of illegal crossings, in 1983. "I'll never forget this one guy we caught four times. The last time we got him, he just threw his hands up in the air and shook his head. I felt sorry for him . . . But that's rare. He just had bad luck. Usually they make it through on their second try."[22]

Many understood that the new system was plainly nonfunctional—including, quite remarkably in retrospect, INS officers' union head Michael Harpold, who complained that "relatives of legal U.S. residents who had been waiting years to immigrate legally were forced to come in illegally in order to join their families."[23] Thanks to the "colorblind" equality that followed 1965 reform, Mexican applicants for visas—to which they had rights by virtue of their US citizen relatives—were confronted with backlogs that by 2017 stretched as long as twenty-one years.[24]

The result was a chaotic nightly scene. As darkness fell one night in 1984, hundreds of migrants—mostly Mexicans but also Central Americans fleeing poverty, war and repression—gathered by Tijuana's Colonia Libertad neighborhood where beer, tacos and used coats were for sale.[25] Heading to Los Angeles's Pico Boulevard and other points north, they met up with the *polleros*—like *coyote*, a Spanish word for what English-speakers disparagingly call a smuggler—who would guide them across borderland canyons as agents waited across the line in San Diego. Some would be caught and would promptly try again.[26]

The futile dynamic seemed almost choreographed, with *polleros* reportedly timing their attempts to coincide with agents' shift changes. The San Ysidro cat-and-mouse game, however, was taking a violent turn, as bandits targeted migrants for theft, assault, rape and murder, and engaged in shootouts with San Diego police. Neither the possibility of apprehension nor the violence deterred the migrants. "Fear is not having beans on the table," said one Mexican from the state of Guerrero.[27]

Meanwhile, the militarization of the border increased alongside the criminalization of Mexican migration. It was a war zone, Americans remarked, something like a not-so-distant Vietnam. Or, perhaps, like the long hot summer of black urban uprisings in 1967. The fight was waged with buried electronic sensors, helicopters, four-wheel drive vehicles, and infrared scopes that might identify migrant groups as large as thirty, ghostly figures against a green backdrop.[28]

Much of the Border Patrol's equipment was initially developed for military use—sensors to surveil the Ho Chi Minh Trail, scopes for Marine Corps snipers at Khe Sanh.[29] It was, said INS commissioner Alan C. Nelson, an effort to stop "the greatest surge of people in history across our southern border."[30]

"It's part of the Rambo mentality . . . that every problem that confronts this country can be solved through law enforcement or military action," said Herman Baca, chairman of the Committee on Chicano Rights in San Diego. "It parallels Vietnam. Our government policy makers are fighting a war that they don't understand . . . And you know who won in Vietnam."[31]

Border Patrol violence was rampant. One agent said that it was commonplace for agents to carry unregistered "throwaway" guns: "They explained to me that if you shoot an alien 'by accident,' all you have to do is throw away that gun next to him and say he was shooting at you." An immigration inspector confirmed the account, saying that he had been taught how to do so in the academy. "I've seen many such shootings," said one former agent, "and these are unarmed people, people who come across just to get jobs."[32] Rape accusations were commonplace, as was the trading of access to the United States for sex. Migrants were called "wetbacks," "wets," and "tonks," referring to the sound agents' flashlights make when they smash against detainees' heads.[33]

Those who spoke out reported being ignored and fired. A supervisor alleged that one "tends to overempathize with people trying to get into this country legally or illegally" and so "does not have the proper attitude to become a successful immigration inspector."[34]

Complaints of abuse were so rampant that in 1980 two Hispanic agents were sent undercover, dressed as Mexican workers, to investigate the San Clemente, California, checkpoint on the I-5 highway.[35] The result was that the agents on duty allegedly beat them with a chair and a flashlight, resulting in criminal charges for that assault and for others allegedly committed against civilians, including a fifteen-year old US citizen.[36]

A Border Patrol agent charged in a separate case of physical abuse allegedly told a trainee that beatings were necessary "because the criminal justice system doesn't do anything about these people."[37] "These people," however, would soon become one of that system's priority targets.

Taking down the surrender flag

The southern border was viewed not only as the entryway for "illegal" humans but for illicit drugs as well. The quixotic goal of stopping both created contemporary border politics. The Border Patrol had enforced Prohibition, and in 1956 had created the Criminal, Immoral, and Narcotics program.[38] But the war on drugs was something of a different magnitude, launched as a supply-side war that blamed *others*, whether black drug dealers at home or Latin American traffickers abroad, for the drug consumption that seemed to be sapping American's virtue and vitality. Many worried that the youth had, like society as a whole, lost their way. President Nixon privately fumed that the problem with marijuana was that "once people cross that line from . . . straight society to the drug society, it's a very great possibility they are going to go further . . . You see, homosexuality, dope, immorality in general. These are the enemies of a strong society. That's why the communists and left-wingers are pushing the stuff, they are trying to destroy us."[39]

Nixon had a border strategy for his 1968 campaign,

promising California parents that he would protect their children from Mexican marijuana.[40] The war on drugs, Matthew
Lassiter writes, was fought in the name of defending innocent white youth from the perceived threat from lower class
black and Mexican peddlers invading across social boundaries[41]—including, in Southern California, from across the
border.[42]

In 1969, Nixon launched Operation Intercept,* a massive
crackdown that subjected all cross-border traffic to dragnet
inspection and drove it to a near-halt.[43] It didn't stop the
flow of marijuana. In fact, drug interdiction repeatedly
backfired. For example, the shutdown of the famed French
Connection, which smuggled heroin from Turkey through
France to the United States, shifted sourcing of heroin to
Mexico, which was then trafficked across the US southern
border.[44]

Crackdowns created new crises to exploit. But crises
were already plentiful: changes in the economy, the
geographic organization of housing, work and education,
and gender roles; the rise of crime rates, the counterculture,
the anti-war movement, and second-wave feminism; militant black struggle and uprisings; a national identity

---

* Operation Intercept was run by Treasury Department senior advisor
G. Gordon Liddy, who would go on to be convicted over the Watergate
break-in. Remarkably, future Maricopa County sheriff Joe Arpaio—an offi-
cial once stationed in Mexico with the Bureau of Narcotics and Dangerous
Drugs, the DEA's precursor—claims to have played a leading role too. (Joe
Arpaio and Len Sherman, *Joe's Law: America's Toughest Sheriff Takes on
Illegal Immigration, Drugs and Everything Else That Threatens America*, New
York: Amacom, 2008, 45–47.)

shattered by Communist victory in Vietnam. The capacity of American families and the American people to perpetuate themselves into the future was in doubt.

President Reagan then campaigned on banishing doubt from the American mind, branding the Carter presidency a paragon of abdication and decline. Any restraint on drugs was capitulation. "We're taking down the surrender flag that has flown over so many drug efforts; we're running up a battle flag," Reagan announced in June of 1982. "We can fight the drug problem, and we can win. And that is exactly what we intend to do."[45]

The drug war was global, from Colombia to New York and beyond. The border was stigmatized as the open door through which drugs came; in fact, the border was an unlucky, consummately in-between place in a global drug market governed by American demand. Unsurprisingly, the campaign quickly faltered. Reagan escalated, proclaiming drugs to be a national security threat emanating from Sandinista Nicaragua, Communist Cuba, and Colombian revolutionaries.[46] As government was deemed unfit to do most anything aside from repression, and as the Soviet menace evaporated, an unwinnable war on drugs became urgently necessary even in the face—and maybe because—of its constant failure. Drugs, and the people who sold, transited, and consumed them, became an enemy perfectly suited to late twentieth-century American politics, stitching back together a once-unitary threat that defeat in Vietnam had cast into doubt and the Cold War's end would shatter into fragments.

Illegal activity was no doubt widespread at the border. Yet ironically, drug trafficking was and is such an attractive business not in spite but because of border enforcement and interdiction. Borders generate a stratified hierarchy of nationally bounded markets because enforcement raises transaction costs: every border and law enforcement obstacle, then, is an opportunity for criminals to reap a profit. In 2013, a kilo of cocaine that sold for $2,200 in the Colombian interior might sell for between $5,500 and $7,000 at the ports, $10,000 in Central America, $12,000 in southern Mexico, $16,000 in a Mexican town on the US border and then $24,000–$27,000 once it has been smuggled into the United States.[47] Drug traffickers use the border to make a profit in the same way that maquiladoras do.

The drug war took on a life of its own as it intensified. The bureaucracy and frontline officers dedicated to stopping drugs swelled, with funding for drug interdiction doubling between 1982 and 1987 alone. Officials boasted of major drug seizures, though larger seizures also reflected more drugs being trafficked.[48] Law enforcement has a stake in making the case that the drug scourge was huge and required a sizable force to confront it.[49] Even so, the enterprise was and would always be beset by a sense of futility. "I'd like to think that we're making a difference," said one customs agent in 1985. "Are we seizing a significant amount? Probably not."[50]

Interdiction efforts expanded from the border to US-backed, militarized interventions abroad, while domestic police forces fed drug dealers large and small, foreign and domestic, into the country's ballooning prison system. The seminal Anti-Drug Abuse Act of 1986, which infamously created draconian mandatory minimum sentences for crack cocaine, also required that the US government condition economic and military aid and related matters on nations' "full cooperation" with drug war aims.[51] The entirety of Mexico, the United States, and beyond became a borderland: fantastical lines were drawn everywhere between areas where drugs were produced and where they were consumed. The delusion made the border into the epicenter of a diffuse war zone that invited repression in every direction.

As a matter of politics and law, the modern war on drugs was from its early years a war on immigrants. Prosecutor and police power expanded, and immigration enforcement was commandeered by the war on crime. IRCA, Reagan's landmark immigration law, had made deporting immigrants who had been convicted of crimes a priority. The Anti-Drug Abuse Act of 1986 empowered federal immigration authorities to issue "detainers," or requests for local law enforcement to hold suspected undocumented immigrants.[52] Later, those detainers would be transformed into a key tool under Obama's Secure Communities program, facilitating the transfer of immigrants from local to federal custody.

The Anti-Drug Abuse Act of 1988 tied immigrants to the narcotic threat, subjecting non-citizens convicted of the newly coined category of "aggravated felonies"— murder, drug trafficking, and firearms trafficking—to mandatory detention. That same year, INS created the Institutional Removal Program and the Alien Criminal Apprehension Program, which targeted the class of "aggravated felons" created by the Act.[53] Congress also created harsh additional penalties for immigrants who illegally reentered the country after having been convicted of a felony or aggravated felony.[54]

By tying the burgeoning narcotic menace to immigrants, politicians waging the war on drugs during the 1980s and 1990s helped build our present-day system of what legal scholar Juliet Stumpf first called "crimmigration." This new system encompassed a growing number of criminal convictions that can lead to deportation; the increasing treatment of ordinary actions by unauthorized immigrants, like crossing the border between ports of entry or using someone else's Social Security number to secure work, as criminal offenses; the Border Patrol's growing role in domestic law enforcement, and domestic law enforcement's increased role in identifying and detaining undocumented immigrants.[55]

As was made all too clear in 2016, the right builds its most compelling political narratives by linking distinct sources of perceived external threat to one another. Drugs were a Swiss Army knife of statecraft, providing a conduit for the simultaneous criminalization of the domestic poor, the repurposing of the post–Cold War US national security state toward foreign interdiction, and the militarization of the border in both rhetoric and reality.

After IRCA

The Border Patrol was, by 1986, "undeniably the largest and most well-equipped staff in Border Patrol history," with its size increasing to more than three thousand agents.[56] It was quite modest compared to the roughly twenty thousand agents that would fill its ranks three decades later. But the Border Patrol had been radically transformed into an increasingly militarized force charged with the improbable task of stopping illegalized drugs and humans.[57]

As agents gave chase through the canyons, other migrants slipped through authorized ports of entry with fraudulent documents—as did large amounts of smuggled drugs.[58] Yet it remained common sense in policymaking circles and even among agents that enforcement could not fix the problem without attending to the factors pushing people to migrate. "If we had twice the manpower, we'd cover more area and make more apprehensions, but they'd still be coming," said one agent. "The answer is not in enforcement, the answer is to keep these people in Mexico."[59]

IRCA had briefly cut unauthorized migration but apprehensions soon ticked back up. IRCA had to "fail": a one-off legalization could never have regularized long-term migration flows. The border once again appeared to Americans as a porous made-for-television fiasco as fortified green-and-white INS buses were loaded up with detained immigrants.[60]

"Of course, I don't qualify for amnesty," said a nineteen-year-old Tijuana native detained on one bus. "None of us do. But there is still work in Los Angeles and there are still people who will hire us. Besides, having grown up as close to the border as I did, I knew life was better on this side."[61] One man had been picked up on the way to grab food with a friend. Others were nabbed at work, including several captured while picking onions in a Valencia field. "All of this is crap," said one. "They catch you. They send you back. You come back. And then La Migra catches you again. And the boss still wants you to come back." "We're not a very viable deterrent," one Border Patrol official lamented. "We see a lot more than we have officers to catch them."[62]

It wasn't just the land border. The specter of asylum seekers, particularly Haitian "boat people" fleeing widespread violence and repression after the 1991 military coup against President Jean-Bertrand Aristide, consumed politics. President George H. W. Bush detained thousands at the US colonial military outpost in Guantanamo Bay, Cuba, and turned thousands more back to the island. During his presidential campaign, Clinton had condemned Bush's inhumanity but reversed course before he even took office, pledging to continue the policy.[63] In office, Clinton fought and lost a fight to indefinitely detain HIV-positive Haitians who had legitimate asylum claims at Guantanamo—in horrible conditions within what the presiding judge described as an "H.I.V. prison camp"—because US law barred HIV-positive people from entry.[64]

In New York, Representative Charles Schumer warned that the influx into JFK airport of thousands claiming persecution "jeopardizes our security, and it jeopardizes the people who come here legally."[65] The New York Times claimed that many were actually economic migrants gaming the system, and that "the overwhelmed asylum system cannot tell the terrorist from the terrified."[66] This was in the wake of the 1993 World Trade Center bombing, and it was revealed that a key suspect had entered after requesting asylum. Federation

for American Immigration Reform (FAIR) executive director Dan Stein fanned the flames on *60 Minutes*: a terrorist
could gain entry, he said, with "two magic words: political
asylum."[67] Terrorism inspired fear. So did the entire Global
South. "The issue is," said New York INS district director
William S. Slattery, "Who's going to control the borders of
the United States? . . . The aliens have taken control. The
third world has packed its bags and it's moving."[68] Meanwhile,
the *Golden Venture*, a ship carrying nearly three hundred
unauthorized Chinese migrants, ran aground off Long
Island—provoking an enormous media spectacle.[69]

IRCA's failure and high-profile conflicts over asylum
made enforcement seem like the only solution. Near San
Diego, the INS considered a stronger fence to replace the
hole-filled one that stretched eastward from the Pacific
Ocean. "It's ludicrous," said Herman Baca, a frequent and
prescient critic of border enforcement. "We don't need a
Berlin Wall . . . You can't expect to stop illegal immigration
without getting at the root causes."[70]

But that argument lost its hold. In 1989, gatherings of
hundreds of anti-immigrant motorists staged "Light Up the
Border" protests in San Diego, shining their headlights
toward Mexico to ward off migrants and demand government action.[71] In 1990, the Border Patrol installed stadium
lights along a mile of the Tijuana River and it began to erect
the first fourteen miles of modern fencing—made of ten-
foot-tall welded steel landing mats from the Vietnam War—
along the border at San Diego with assistance from the Army
Corps of Engineers and the California National Guard. It

would become the first installment of an actually existing border wall that twenty-five years later made Trump's call to "build the wall" possible—a campaign that was premised on pretending that the wall didn't already exist.[72]

Under control

In September 1993, just two months before Congress voted to approve NAFTA, the spotlight shifted 620 miles to the east of San Ysidro to West Texas. There, large numbers crossed illegally from Ciudad Juárez into El Paso, not as immigrants but as part of their daily commute. Cross-border migration, with and without authorization, was sewn into the twin cities' fabric.[73]

Silvestre Reyes, chief of the Border Patrol's El Paso sector, launched Operation Hold the Line—originally given the indecorous name Operation Blockade—deploying hundreds of agents directly across the Rio Grande from Juárez and effectively shutting down urban crossings. In doing so, he created a framework for border militarization that emphasized deterring entry over apprehending immigrants after they cross. It's a framework that has shaped American border politics through today.[74]

A *New York Times* story gushed that Reyes had "accomplished something no other officer of the Immigration and Naturalization Service ever had. He got the border in his sector under control. Not just for a brief, flashy demonstration, but permanently."[75] It was true: he had transformed border enforcement by making the seemingly inconceivable—effective border security—suddenly seem possible.

It appeared to be the beginning of the end of border history. Reyes was celebrated as an iconoclast rebelling against Washington norms. Washington was paying close attention. All that was needed to secure the border, many quickly agreed, was the political will. The Clinton administration rushed to replicate his model, extending the El Paso crackdown along the border.[76] Politicians from both major parties would thereafter quixotically strive to make permanent security a reality.

The first Hold the Line replica appeared in October 1994, when Operation Gatekeeper was implemented in the San Diego sector. Immigration dominated California politics just ahead of the vote on Prop 187, whose advocates blamed the federal government for inaction. "California cannot raise its own border patrol, but California can say we will refuse to pay for bills," said Ira Mehlman, a California spokesperson for FAIR. Governor Pete Wilson had, as a grower-friendly US senator, denounced employer sanctions and called for a guest worker program. But like Clinton, he embraced the border war, correctly discerning that nativism was a potent campaign issue.[77]

One campaign ad for Wilson showed immigrants running through the San Ysidro port of entry in what was called a "Banzai run," darting through southbound traffic. "They keep coming," said the narrator. "Two million illegal immigrants in California. The federal government won't stop them at the border, yet requires you to pay billions to take care of them." In fact, the spectacle was the result of an escalation of Border Patrol enforcement making it more difficult to cross at unauthorized crossing points.[78] Tanton-network groups would take advantage of the spectacle as well, organizing "border tours" to dramatize their cause. (Years later, in 2015, they even had the help of active duty agents and their union.[79])

By the early 1990s, anti-immigrant activists were making the case that, as FAIR's Dan Stein put it, "Immigrants are not all honest and hardworking. Some are here to commit crimes, while others are part of a growing number of international organized crime rings that specialize in everything from alien smuggling to computer and credit card fraud."[80]

After the 1992 Los Angeles riots, far-right Republican presidential contender Pat Buchanan charged that "foreigners are coming into this country illegally and helping to burn down one of the greatest cities in America." "I can't understand why this Administration fails to enforce the laws and close that border," Buchanan told a crowd of senior citizens. "If I were President, I would have the Corps of Engineers build a double-barrier fence that would keep out 95 percent of the illegal traffic. I think it can be done."[81]

The uprising was centered in heavily black South Central Los Angeles. But Hispanics, who had moved into the neighborhood in large numbers, made up a significant portion of those killed and arrested.[82] The police who swept through the city arrested immigrants and turned many over to the INS for deportation.[83] INS and Border Patrol agents were also deployed to police the streets and make arrests, including of undocumented immigrants.[84] For leading nativist Garrett Hardin, the riot exemplified the threat posed by black and

Latino criminality alike. In a letter to Mellon heir and Tanton network funder Cordelia Scaife May, Hardin rejoiced that the riots had demonstrated that "maybe the blacks are less than saintly" while complaining that "newspapers in coastal California have neglected to point out the predominant Latinity of apprehended criminals."[85]

In 1992, Buchanan lost the primary, after a surprisingly strong challenge to the incumbent George H. W. Bush. But the Republican Platform incorporated his agenda in an effort to energize its right-wing base.[86] The new platform pledged to "increase the size of the Border Patrol in order to meet the increasing need to stop illegal immigration and . . . equip the Border Patrol with the tools, technologies, and structures necessary to secure the border." But it also departed from Buchanan's agenda by hitching anti-"illegal" politics to a free trade agenda, promising that "in creating new economic opportunity in Mexico, NAFTA removes the incentive to cross the border illegally in search of work."[87]

Buchanan's campaign also shaped the victorious Clinton's border and migration agenda. In 1994, the Border Patrol created its first national strategy. Developed with help from the Defense Department's Center for Low Intensity Conflict, it explicitly cited El Paso's Hold the Line as the future of border enforcement.[88]

"Those attempting to illegally enter the United States in large numbers do so in part because of the weak controls we have exercised over the southwest land border in the recent past," the strategy document declared. "Although a 100 percent apprehension rate is an unrealistic goal, we believe we can achieve a rate of apprehensions sufficiently high to raise the risk of apprehension to the point that many will consider it futile to continue to attempt illegal entry." Border Patrol called this strategy "prevention through deterrence," and emphasized that its "success . . . depends on continued Congressional support throughout its duration."

Congress was more than happy to oblige. In 1992, the Border Patrol deployed 4,139 agents. That number rose to 5,942 in 1996 and to 9,212 in 2000. Between October 1994 and June 1998, the San Diego sector received a 150 percent staffing increase along with new seismic sensors, vehicles, infrared night-vision goggles, and helicopters. Permanent lighting was extended from one mile in length to six.[89] San Diego and El Paso were locked down.[90] The border that mattered was the Mexican one. By 1999, there were nearly seven times more agents in the San Diego sector than along the entire northern border. Before the September 11 attacks, half the country's ports of entry with Canada were left unguarded overnight. As the United States demonized Mexico for being a conduit for drugs, the cocaine and guns entering Canada from the United States were ignored.[91]

In 1996, Reyes, the Border Patrol's first Hispanic sector chief, was elected to Congress by voters in his heavily Hispanic El Paso district, becoming its first Hispanic congressman. "It is rare that any immigration issue unifies El Pasoans, but Reyes did so with his strategy," the *El Paso Times* noted in its endorsement.[92] What once seemed impossible now seemed achieved. "People laughed at us," said Operation Gatekeeper architect and former San Diego

Border Patrol chief Johnny Williams in 1998. "They said, 'You're crazy to try this.' They just didn't think it was possible to control the border."[93] The new faith was embraced with a convert's zeal.

Goods and not people

NAFTA had exacerbated a pervasive fear that the United States, after winning the Cold War, had swiftly passed from world history's protagonist to the object of globalization's inchoate powers. Amid widespread but diffuse anti-globalization sentiment, "border security" would protect capital mobility. As senior advisor Rahm Emanuel put it in a 1996 memo to President Clinton: "We should be honest, that if we want continued public support for trade and friendly relations with Mexico, we must be vigilant in our effort to curb illegal trade (e.g., narcotics and immigrants)."[94]

Even as the demonization of "illegal immigrants" quietly offered political protection for NAFTA, however, proponents publicly spun the accord as a measure that would so improve the Mexican economy that people wouldn't feel so compelled to escape it. "In a sense, the whole point of NAFTA for Mexico is to be able to export goods and not people," said Mexican president Carlos Salinas de Gortari in 1993. "That means creating jobs in Mexico."[95]

The Border Patrol concurred. According to its 1994 National Strategic Plan, NAFTA "should reduce illegal immigration as the Mexican economy improves."[96] Attorney General Janet Reno campaigned hard for NAFTA—an unusual assignment for the nation's top cop—calling it "our best hope for reducing illegal immigration, in the long haul."[97]

In the more than two decades since, however, Mexico's growth rates have been sluggish, and poverty rates have remained high.[98] Meanwhile, researchers have found evidence that "employment generated by manufacturing production, and maquilas in particular, may indeed reduce the level of undocumented migration to the US."[99] But maquiladoras are part of a broader economic structuring that fuels migration, Raúl Delgado Wise and Humberto Márquez Covarrubias argue. Neoliberalism deepens an asymmetric form of binational economic integration, creating a vast surplus labor force in Mexico for export, and increasing dependence on those migrants' remittances.[100] Meanwhile, foreign investment that had flooded into Mexico suddenly flushed back out after the 1994 assassination of Luis Donaldo Colosio, the presidential candidate for the ruling Institutional Revolutionary Party (PRI).[101] The result was the 1994–95 peso crisis, which radically devalued Mexican wealth, contributing another major push factor for migration.[102]

And the border crackdown—intended to quell the border anxieties unleashed in part by NAFTA, which in turn was sold as a migration deterrent—in reality served to deter many Mexicans, who would otherwise have migrated back and forth across the border, from going back to Mexico.[103] Instead, they experienced a "caging effect," and stayed in the United States.[104]

Meanwhile, drug traffickers found respite in free trade, "hiding their drug shipments within the rising volume of commercial trucks, railcars and passenger vehicles crossing the border." Under NAFTA, illicit drugs became tiny needles in a growing haystack of unshackled global commerce. A single truckload was enough cocaine to satisfy the entire US market for over a month.[105] And increasingly, those drugs were coming across the southern border because US policy assisted Mexican cartels in diversifying and growing their business. By the mid-1990s, the United States had squeezed the cocaine-smuggling route that had run from Colombia through the Caribbean to Florida. The result was that Colombian traffickers began to route cocaine through Mexico. The power and economic clout of Mexican cartels grew, and they leveraged their critical intermediary role to demand payment not in cash but with a cut of the cocaine. Mexican traffickers, the Congressional Research Service found, evolved from being "mere couriers for the Colombians to . . . wholesalers."[106]

The result was that the Gulf, Tijuana, Sinaloa, Juárez cartels and others bloomed into massive criminal enterprises that helped plunge Mexico into a murderous bloodbath.[107] Meanwhile, the destruction of the Medellín and then Cali cartels did nothing to stop cocaine: Colombia was recently estimated to supply roughly 90 percent of the US market.[108] The result was a gruesome drug war death toll for Mexicans, with murders nearly tripling over the five years that followed President Felipe Calderón's 2006 US-backed deployment of military forces into the streets, according to one measure.[109]

The outcome was entirely foreseeable. The political response, however, was not to rethink interdiction as a strategy. Using legalization and regulation to seize the market from criminal actors was and remains taboo, with the exception of marijuana. Rather, policymakers doubled down. Government turned to more enforcement in the hope that a surge in officers and technology could accomplish the impossible—or at least convince Americans that they were trying.[110] Perversely, more drugs flowing across the border made it easier to accomplish and celebrate large seizures, redounding to the benefit of Clinton and Salinas, the two NAFTA-boosting presidents.[111]

In response to deepening integration, as political scientist Peter Andreas notes, politicians, officials and journalists turned the border into a stage upon which security was performed. "Border policing" became "not simply a policy instrument for deterring illegal crossings but a symbolic representation of state authority; it communicates the state's commitment to making and maintaining the borderline."[112] It was, like prison expansion, a way for a government that failed to ensure social and economic welfare to use repression as a means to present itself as an energetic protector of the public good. The ostensible purpose of border enforcement is to send a message to Mexicans that they are unwelcome. But the performance's greater purpose is to assure Americans that the government is sending that message to Mexicans. And that, despite appearances to the contrary, everything was going to be all right.

Neoliberalism "promised freedom and self-determination," sociologist Dylan Riley writes.[113] It created radical insecurity and uncertainty instead, a sense that people no longer had control over their lives. Opposition to "illegal aliens" and growing interest in aliens from other planets surged side by side during the 1990s as Americans searched out stories that explained who ran the world—because *they* plainly didn't. Xenophobia was at the core of a flourishing but still inchoate conspiracist culture that would, a couple decades later, merge into a total and paranoiac right-wing worldview anchored by the likes of Alex Jones and President Trump.

Crimmigration

The war on illegal immigration did more than transform the border. It also drastically changed, and merged with, a metastasizing carceral state. During his 1996 reelection campaign, President Clinton signed the Illegal Immigration Reform and Immigrant Responsibility Act, or IIRIRA, which called for a thousand new Border Patrol agents to be hired annually for five years; barred deportees from lawfully entering for three or ten years; empowered the attorney general to construct border barriers and authorized construction of a layer of secondary fencing in San Diego; and, critically, operationalized the criminal justice system to facilitate deportations.[114]

In a November 1996 memo to Clinton, written a few months after IIRIRA was signed into law and a week after the president had won reelection, Emanuel advised the president that "illegal immigration legislation provides that same opportunity" to perform a tough-guy co-optation of Republican politics as the 1994 crime bill had. It was important, he said, that Clinton could "claim and achieve record deportations of criminal aliens." Like welfare and crime, immigration was an opportunity for vintage Clinton triangulation: "By incorporating the opposition's rhetoric, you remove their policy claims."[115]

Yet that strategy also, of course, advances their policy aims. So-called welfare "reform" was a case in point. It not only targeted poor mothers generally but also immigrant women specifically, denying many permanent residents access to the program.[116] As the government cut back on welfare, it both grew the penal system and subjected poor people to government surveillance and control as a condition of receiving public benefits. Poor women's child birthing and rearing were framed as triply perverse: excessive in quantity; requiring taxpayer aid as a substitute for a man's wage; and producing dangerous men from whom the citizenry required the repressive "daddy state's" protection.

As historian Julilly Kohler-Hausmann argues, these were "policies [that] actively degraded the social, economic, and political status of already stigmatized categories of Americans."[117] The state didn't shrink but rather changed, deploying its repressive powers to safeguard the law-abiding, taxpaying citizen from those who broke the citizenship contract through criminality or through receiving stigmatized forms of state aid. The very category of "American" excluded undocumented immigrants, so they were seen as fundamentally unworthy. These politics created characters like "drug pushers, welfare queens, and criminals"—and they helped create the figure of the "illegal immigrant" too.

IIRIRA incorporated the war on immigrants into the core of the war on crime, which made it easier to deport immigrants (undocumented and permanent residents alike) for a growing number of criminal offenses, made those individuals' detentions mandatory, and foreclosed most opportunities for administrative relief. It also included a statute called 287(g), which would under the Bush administration allow the federal government to deputize local law enforcement and jails to enforce immigration law.

"There certainly were things that the administration did not like in the bill," Doris Meissner, INS commissioner under Bill Clinton and currently a senior fellow at the Migration Policy Institute, told me. "But [Clinton] was not about to be vetoing an immigration enforcement bill in '96 given the law enforcement agenda that he was pursuing, of which immigration enforcement was a part."[118]

But what's perhaps least understood about IIRIRA was that its demonization of "illegal immigrants" served to protect legal immigration, a template for mainstream immigration politics ever since. At the time, restricting legal immigration still had powerful supporters not only on the right but also among black liberals, including former representative Barbara Jordan, who warned against competition for poor US workers whom "reform" had pushed off welfare and into the low-wage labor market.[119] Not long before signing IIRIRA, Clinton had endorsed the deep cuts to authorized immigration recommended by Jordan's Commission on

Immigration Reform, including the elimination of visa pref-
erences for siblings of citizens.[120]

But the original vision—to achieve a crackdown on "illegal immigration" and deep cuts to legal immigration—was
dropped. Immigration moderates, in a bid to defend legal
immigration, successfully fought to split the bill: though the
law made it easier to deport legal permanent residents
convicted of crimes, relatively high levels of legal immigration were protected. It was "illegal immigrants"—who now
found it extremely difficult to gain legal status and were
subjected to three or ten years of banishment from the country—alongside "criminal aliens" that bore the brunt of the
crackdown.[121] The move was led by Frank Sharry, a leading
establishment advocate and executive director of the National
Immigration Forum, and denounced by advocates for undocumented people.[122] Repression of "illegal immigrants"
received support from across much of the political spectrum.
By contrast, legal immigration was fiercely protected by a
strange-bedfellows coalition encompassing advocacy groups,
business interests, and religious organizations that held sway
in both parties. As Clinton had put it in 1993: "We must say
no to illegal immigration so we can continue to say yes to
legal immigration."[123]

On the right, lining up to support legal immigration were
Americans for Tax Reform's Grover Norquist, the *Wall
Street Journal*'s editorial board, and Godfather's Pizza chain
and National Restaurant Association head Herman Cain—
later a right-wing presidential candidate. Legal immigration
was, House Speaker Newt Gingrich proclaimed, what "has

given America many of its most dynamic and creative citizens."[124] Republican House majority leader Dick Armey, a Texas free marketer, called Jordan's proposals "a misguided attempt to make legal immigrants the scapegoats for America's problems." Republicans and New Democrats agreed to make "illegal immigrants" the scapegoats instead.

In 1996, Clinton signed a second piece of legislation that deepened the emphasis on "illegal immigration" by further embedding it in the country's expanding criminal justice system. The Antiterrorism and Effective Death Penalty Act, like IIRIRA, required mandatory detention for many immigration offenders and expanded the number of crimes defined as "aggravated felonies," crimes for which a conviction made it virtually impossible for a non-citizen to fight deportation.[125] It also further tied immigration to the politics of terrorism—a linkage that would become inextricable after the September 11 attacks.

Clinton did criticize the bill's immigration provisions. But he signed the legislation anyway, and did so on the one-year anniversary of the bombing of the federal building in Oklahoma City, which killed 168 people.[126] It was an attack that was carried out by native-born US citizens, including Timothy McVeigh, a far-right member of the white power movement that raged against the New World Order—a movement, incidentally, that also embraced the racist conspiracy that Jews plotted to destroy the white race through mass immigration.[127] But immigrants and criminal defendants would suffer the consequences. After the two 1996 laws, deportations skyrocketed.[128]

That same year, Clinton signed a budget that increased INS funding from $2.1 to $2.6 billion, most of which was slated for border enforcement and deportations.[129] Altogether, the INS budget nearly tripled between 1993 and 1999, reaching $4.2 billion.[130] In 1995, ICE had a detention capacity of fewer than 7,500 beds.[131] That nearly doubled to 14,000 in 1998.[132]

Meanwhile, federal prosecutors dusted off an old, little used statute that made it a felony for someone to cross the border illegally if they had already been deported. Janet Reno's Justice Department implemented a "fast track" program that pressed migrants to quickly plead guilty in exchange for a shorter sentence. As a result, the number of illegal reentry prosecutions doubled between 1993 and 1996.[133]

Simultaneously, the INS Violent Gang Task Force was working with local police to target immigrant gang members for deportation—including members of the Salvadoran-American gang Mara Salvatrucha, or MS-13, which had formed in Los Angeles among refugees who had fled Reagan's dirty war.[134] Ultimately, Clinton and his successors' policies of deporting "criminal aliens" would export American-made gangs into a region with governments and societies ill-equipped to respond. These policies ultimately stoked another wave of refugees that President Trump would expertly weaponize toward nativist ends.

Who's tougher

The Clinton administration declared victory ahead of his 1996 reelection campaign. "After years of neglect, we are finally restoring the rule of law, locking down the Southwest border," said Emanuel.[135] Republicans nonetheless continued to try to use nativism against a Democratic president who had all but outflanked them. California governor Wilson announced his anti-immigrant presidential candidacy before the Statue of Liberty, declaring that "illegal immigration is not the American way."[136]

Wilson dropped out before any actual voting amid fund-raising shortfalls and damaging reports that he had once hired an undocumented maid.[137] But immigration didn't disappear from the campaign. Pat Buchanan made a second run for office, decrying illegal immigration and hoping to woo would-be Wilson voters into his camp.[138] "I will stop this massive illegal immigration cold. Period. Paragraph," said Buchanan at one campaign event. In another, he made it clear how he would do this: "I'll build that security fence, and we'll close it, and we'll say, 'Listen Jose, you're not coming in!'"[139] Buchanan sounded extreme. He was. But his right-wing agenda successfully prodded his conservative and liberal opponents to embrace lite versions of it.

Senator Bob Dole, the establishment standard-bearer who won the Republican primary, made strident nativism a center-piece of his campaign, going so far as to support a proposal that would allow states to deny undocumented children access to public schools.[140] He accused Clinton of making it so that "illegal aliens afflicted with AIDS cannot be denied taxpayer-funded medical treatment, no matter how high the cost."[141]

One fearmongering Dole attack ad slammed Clinton for opposing California's Prop 187 and accused him of giving "citizenship to aliens with criminal records" against a stark backdrop of prisoners and young, apparently Chicano men walking down the street. "Twenty thousand in our prisons; four hundred thousand crowd our schools. Every year they cost us $3 billion tax dollars," the narrator intoned. "We pay the taxes. We are the victims. Our children get shortchanged. If Clinton wins, we lose."[142]

Clinton responded to the attacks with an ad that boasted his signing of "a tough anti-illegal immigration law protecting US workers."[143] Another ad, from the Democratic National Committee, turned heads by explicitly linking immigrants to crime and suggesting that Clinton would fight both by putting more cops on the street.[144] "The most striking feature of the ads is that they reveal no ideological or policy differences between Dole and Clinton on the issue," a report in the *San Francisco Chronicle* noted. "The only point of contention is which one has been tougher on illegal immigrants."[145]

That year, a victorious Clinton won California, including Orange County, where Prop 187 had been launched. As Andreas notes, "The images of a chaotic border that were so masterfully exploited by Governor Wilson in 1994 were unavailable for Bob Dole in 1996."[146] The Democratic Party's 1996 platform heaped praise upon Clinton, asserting that before he took office "our borders might as well not have existed . . . President Clinton is making our border a place where the law is respected and drugs and illegal immigration are turned away."[147] Top Clinton strategist Mark Penn reportedly explained the campaign strategy in a presentation to the cabinet: "We did this by co-opting the Republicans on all their issues—getting tough on welfare, tough on crime, balancing the budget, and cracking down on illegal immigration."[148]

The more powerful the bipartisan coalition defending neoliberal economics and authorized immigration grew, the more border militarization and measures targeting criminal "illegal immigrants" became a point of broad consensus. What's more, draconian Republican proposals made Clinton's crackdowns seem reasonable by comparison.

Raul Yzaguirre, president of the National Council of La Raza, then and now Washington's most powerful Latino organization (since renamed UnidosUS), called Clinton's border militarization "sound policy . . . because the most effective, most humane method of reducing undocumented immigration is enforcement at the point of entry, including the Southwestern U.S. border. It is good politics because I.N.S. efforts in this area stand in sharp contrast to some of the high-profile, irresponsible and draconian proposals currently being debated in Congress."[149]

But Clinton's program was plenty draconian: it laid the groundwork for a deportation pipeline that operationalized a rapidly growing criminal justice system for deportation, militarized the border, and nurtured a paranoiac far-right narrative about a criminal alien invasion. This was all an attempt to outflank Republicans. "Law enforcement," Meissner told me, was "as an issue that [Clinton] wanted Democrats to take back from Republicans."[150] And the war on "illegal immigration" was core to that. But to what end?

Clinton capitulated to nativist demands that would only escalate in response. The parameters of the 1990s debate over "illegal immigration" and a broader security politics agenda were set by conservatives and amplified by New Democrats.

Clinton didn't concede that illicit drugs would make their way to the United States as long as Americans wanted to buy them. Instead, he promised that "new border patrol agents and . . . the most sophisticated available new technologies" would "help close the door on drugs at our borders."[151] Rather than countering the nativist argument that immigrants posed a criminal threat, Clinton promised to crack down on immigrants whose criminality was rooted in their very existence. Ultimately, all sides of the mainstream debate accepted the premise that border insecurity, "illegal immigration," and drug trafficking were problems that a repressive government response would solve.

By the new millennium, the border and "illegal immigration" receded from the spotlight. The economy was booming. Illegal crossings in San Diego had been effectively obstructed, pushing migrant routes east, toward Arizona. Although border-wide apprehensions remained in the seven figures, the border no longer resembled the one that Clinton had inherited. The xenophobic fever had broken. "The daily chaos which reigned along the San Diego border has, at long last, been replaced by scenes of control and order," the Border Patrol declared in 1999.[152]

As Andreas noted at the time, "Although the escalation of policing has largely failed as a deterrent and has generated perverse and counterproductive consequences that reinforce calls for further escalation, it has been strikingly successful in projecting the appearance of a more secure and orderly border."[153] The problem had seemingly been solved.

"A couple of years ago people were advocating to build a wall around the country," Senator Spencer Abraham, a Michigan Republican and immigration moderate, said in 1998. "That's no longer the case. Before, we had heard only one side of the immigration issue. Now, we get to talk about some of the positive contributions immigrants have made."[154]

A push to legalize unauthorized immigrants, who numbered an estimated 8.6 million in 2000, took shape.[155] That year, the AFL-CIO, with more progressive leadership in power, announced a historic shift to embrace legalizing the undocumented workers whom the labor movement had often viewed as a threat.[156] The move was spearheaded by labor leaders in California, a microcosm of an increasingly diverse working class whose major victories at a time of union decline were often immigrant-led.[157] Labor activists were also increasingly outraged at employers using immigration law against workers, including in 1999 when undocumented workers organizing at a Minneapolis Holiday Inn Express were detained after their manager called INS.[158]

But in national politics, the subject faded into the background. A *New York Times* story on presidential candidates Al Gore and George W. Bush's aggressive courtship of the Hispanic vote only mentioned immigrants once in passing and the subject of immigration not at all.[159] Unemployment was down and, remarkably, immigration was not discussed in a single presidential debate. On the fringes, Buchanan had broken from the Republican Party and mounted a successful takeover of what had been Ross Perot's Reform Party. New York real estate icon Donald Trump flirted with a run for the nomination, calling Buchanan a seeming "racist" with a "prehistoric" agenda who appealed only to the "really staunch right wacko vote."[160] Buchanan bombed, and establishment conservatives secured the presidency.

The scene, however, was just scenery. The solution was inevitably provisional because the underlying political, social, and economic dynamics fueling immigration were ignored. As the Congressional Research Service noted in a 2009 report, the Border Patrol "made 1.2 million apprehensions in 1992 and again in 2004, suggesting that the increased enforcement in the San Diego sector has had little impact on overall apprehensions."[161]

As apprehensions plummeted in targeted urban zones, huge numbers began to cross through remote areas, particularly the lethal Arizona desert.[162] Ultimately, this would precipitate more immigrant deaths and calls for yet more enforcement. In 2005, according to one count, the number of migrants who died crossing the border hit 472, up from 241 in 1999.[163] The long-running border crackdown has also systematically exposed migrant women and children to sexual assault by criminal actors and state agents alike.[164] Meanwhile, those who made it across were more likely to stay put once they arrived and few resources were committed to detecting the large number of immigrants who become undocumented after entering legally and overstaying a visa. The supply-side approach also left business unscathed, with INS investigations of employers plummeting from 15,000 in 1989 to roughly 6,000 in 1995.[165] Fines against employers fell throughout the 1990s.[166]

The nativist right didn't win the White House in the 1990s. But it did decisively make the decade's politics, shaping a bipartisan consensus of commonsense xenophobia while incubating the ideological germ of an ascendant far right. Over the next two decades, this dynamic would push the mainstream consensus so far to the right that it encapsulated the furthest fringes. As one headline later put it, "Trump is Pat Buchanan with better timing."[167]

Line of defense

Briefly, there was a Bush administration before September 11 that few today recall. An immigration deal seemed to be politically smart for the White House. Bush had just won a third of the Latino vote, and his pollsters believed he would have to do better to win reelection in 2004. Nativism was at a nadir, and wooing Latinos was a priority. A major legalization initiative connected to a guest worker program was a tantalizing possibility.[168]

"[Karl] Rove appears willing to do anything to try to expand alleged outreach to Hispanic voters," complained FAIR executive director Dan Stein, referring to Bush's political advisor.[169]

After Bush took office in 2001, his aides were busy discussing a legalization initiative. The president was negotiating with his Mexican counterpart, Vicente Fox, who made the reform a top priority. Fox's foreign minister, Jorge Castañeda, wanted a major legalization program, "the whole enchilada."[170] The entire political climate seems in hindsight almost unrecognizable. States like Utah, North Carolina, and Tennessee were issuing driver's licenses to undocumented immigrants.[171] Bush was no Pete Wilson. He liked to break into Spanish at campaign events and touted a "compassionate conservative" agenda.[172] "Where do they turn to? There's no room for them to move," said National Immigration Forum head Frank Sharry, referring to the nativist movement. "They're reduced to praying for a severe recession, and hoping that will put wind in their sails."[173]

Even then, however, the White House remained sensitive to the nativist right. Secretary of State Colin Powell insisted that the deal would not amount to "blanket amnesty." The administration's preferred term was "regularization." But they weren't fooling nativists who, despite a few years on the margins, immediately made it clear that they held veto power over Republican votes. "There's a lot of euphemisms out there," said Texas Republican representative Lamar Smith. "Whether it's an immediate amnesty or an amnesty after five years, it's still an amnesty."[174]

The September 11 attacks and the response to it, however, cut the whole debate short, closing the briefly open window for bipartisan, establishment-led reform. Even some on the right clamored to protect immigration reform from the backlash. Republican senator Sam Brownback, a right-wing evangelical from Kansas and a key reform advocate, echoed New York mayor Rudy

Giuliani's warning against post-9/11 xenophobia.[175] But as the US military rendered an expansive "Muslim world" into a battlefield, the country became a home base, the borders of which required maximal fortification. Most immediately, border traffic slowed to a crawl as customs agents undertook intensive car-by-car inspections.[176] That the 9/11 attackers had lawfully entered the country carrying visas on airplanes predictably didn't matter. The land border would only become an even more potent symbol of the country's vulnerability to just about anything bad in the world. Under Bush, government directed a rush of funds toward protecting a country that had almost overnight been renamed "The Homeland" (a term strange to Americans, and with Nazi antecedents).[177]

In 2003, immigration and border enforcement were reorganized under the newly created Department of Homeland Security (DHS). Bush, undergoing a rapid-fire makeover from judicially imposed election cheat to wartime president, presided over the addition of thousands of new agents and signed a law that led to the construction of hundreds of miles of fencing. Immigration had officially become first and foremost a security matter; meanwhile, the entirety of security had been subordinated to the overriding goal of preventing the rarest of events: terrorist attacks. Border Patrol appropriations rose from $263 million in fiscal year 1990 to $1.4 billion in 2002, $3 billion in 2010, and $3.8 billion in 2015.[178]

Those figures are not adjusted for inflation. But if they were, the increase in expenditure would still be tremendous:

a sevenfold increase in funding between 1990 and 2015.* And
that does not include the billions more allotted in other border
security spending. The militarism of the early war on terror
briefly pushed immigration from the center of public debate.
But it also revolutionized the government's approach. The
wars on drugs and immigrants had strengthened federal
police forces; the war on terror consolidated that development, and linked it to an unprecedented machinery for
permanent global conflict. The border became a virtual one
that expanded outward: customs agents were deployed to
foreign airports and foreign visitors required to submit to
being fingerprinted and photographed.[179] As the 9/11
Commission Report declared: "The American homeland is
the planet."[180]

A few years into the terror war, the Institutional Removal
Program and Alien Criminal Apprehension Program, established in 1988 to target "criminal aliens," were combined into
the Criminal Alien Program, which, according to the
Congressional Research Service, by April 2016 had "approximately 1,300 CAP officers . . . monitoring 100% of federal
and state prisons, a total of over 4,300 facilities."
Appropriations for targeting "criminal aliens" rose from
$23.4 million in fiscal year 2004 to $504.6 million in 2017.[181]

Within DHS, immigration and border security agencies
were relocated to Customs and Border Protection (CBP), and
massive funding was directed their way. A new reality demanded

---

* Using the Bureau of Labor Statistics calculator, $263 million in 1990
was equivalent to $506 million in 2015.

a new approach, regardless of that new reality being more the product of the government's response than of the attacks. The Border Patrol was directed to develop a new National Border Patrol Strategy.[182] The resulting document, released in 2004, reformulated the agency as a frontline defender against potential terrorists—including, critically, everyday migrants.[183]

"The priority mission of CBP, specifically including all Border Patrol agents, is homeland security—nothing less than preventing terrorists and terrorist weapons—including potential weapons of mass destruction—from entering the United States," wrote CBP commissioner Robert C. Bonner in his introductory letter. "The Border Patrol's traditional missions of interdicting illegal aliens and drugs and those who attempt to smuggle them across our borders remain important. Indeed, these missions are complementary. We cannot reduce or eliminate illegal entry by potential terrorists without also dramatically reducing illegal migration across our borders."

Worry ensued that the government had no clue who was in the country "illegally," and which among them might be what Attorney General John Ashcroft called "terrorist aliens."[184] This anxiety was exacerbated in 2002 when it was discovered that INS had mailed visa extensions to two 9/11 hijackers, by then long deceased along with their victims.[185] The government, targeting people of Middle Eastern and South Asian descent, moved to petition for detained immigrants to be held without bond.[186]

After the attacks, hundreds of Muslim, South Asian, and Arab non-citizens were quickly jailed and held on immigration charges—often in what the Justice Department inspector general found to be physically and verbally abusive conditions—and then deported.[187] Tens of thousands of visitors from a list of exclusively Muslim-majority nations—plus the token non-Muslim North Korea—were forced to register with authorities.[188] The program was directed by Kris Kobach, a young White House aide who would later become a lawyer with the Immigration Reform Law Institute, FAIR's legal arm, then Kansas's secretary of state, and ultimately a leading legal architect of both the anti-immigrant and "voter fraud" movements that nakedly linked nativism, anti-black civil rights reaction, and the effort to secure white Republican political power.

The self-reinforcing dynamic of border security and immigration enforcement escalation during the Bush administration became conjoined to a paranoid national security state that scoured the earth for potential threats. The connections could be rather explicit. Deputy Assistant Attorney General John Yoo, the infamous "torture memos" author, cited the Haitian migrants' case against the Clinton administration to argue that suspects indefinitely detained at Guantanamo had no legal recourse to US courts. Clinton had settled with the HIV-positive asylees in exchange for vacating the ruling so that the government could in the future maintain "maximum flexibility" at the base.[189]

Bush also followed Clinton in linking immigration enforcement to the criminal justice system. In 2002, the Florida Department of Law Enforcement signed the first-ever 287(g) agreement to deputize state and local law enforcement to enforce immigration law under IIRIRA, signed into law by Clinton in 1996.[190] It was, according to the *Miami Herald*, "an unprecedented terrorism-fighting tactic" that Florida presumably required since "at least 15 of the 19 hijackers had Florida connections."[191] In 2005, the government launched Operation Streamline as part of its "enforcement with consequences" approach to target a much broader swath of migrants for illegal entry and reentry than in the past.[192] Federal law enforcement used magistrate judges to oversee "cattle calls": mass guilty pleas from as many as dozens of defendants at once, at times prosecuted not by assistant US attorneys but by immigration officials who were not even necessarily licensed to practice law.

Bush would return to immigration reform. But whatever had existed of its bipartisan support had been displaced by a growing anti-immigrant consensus on the right. Tanton-network powerhouse NumbersUSA and rabidly nativist representative Tom Tancredo mobilized enormous grassroots pressure against even a relatively modest proposed 2002 reform that would have allowed some undocumented immigrants to apply for legal status without leaving the country. Tancredo correctly predicted that large-scale Republican support for the nativist position would make reformers "think twice about the next play that they're gonna call in this game."[193] "I had people come up to me on the floor of the House saying, 'O.K., O.K., call off the dogs'—meaning Numbers USA."[194]

Initially, Bush had hoped that border enforcement would be part of comprehensive legislation that included legalization. Indeed, the comprehensive bill that passed the Senate in May 2006 featured hundreds of miles of border fencing thanks to an amendment offered by Senator Jeff Sessions.[195] Bush aggressively courted House nativists to support it, visiting a Border Patrol training center and pledging to "get this border enforced." But the Senate bill failed in the House after nativist Republicans, true to form, revolted. So Bush gave Congress a tough-looking, stand-alone border wall law to campaign on instead: the Secure Fence Act of 2006, which accelerated the construction of the southern border fencing complex that had first taken root in 1990.[196]

Passed just ahead of the mid-term elections, the Act directed DHS to build fencing along at least 700 miles of the Southwest border.[197] It won eighty votes in the Senate. Many liberals voted "no" but centrist Democrats like Barack Obama, Hillary Clinton, Joe Biden, and Dianne Feinstein joined all Republicans save for Rhode Island's Lincoln Chafee to support it. Instead of being a component of comprehensive reform, intensified border enforcement became a down payment for a law that would never materialize. Instead of border enforcement succeeding at stopping migration, its failure to do so simply signaled the need for yet more border enforcement.[*]

DHS secretary Michael Chertoff cheered the Secure Fence Act, saying it would "enable the department to make substantial progress toward preventing terrorists and others from exploiting our borders and provides flexibility for smart deployment

---

[*]   And ironically, given the nativist movement's environmental pretexts, the construction of border barriers has caused immense ecological damage in part by blocking wildlife migration. (Stephanie Innes, "Beyond the Wall: Costly Answer in California Altering the Landscape," *Arizona Daily Star*, July 11, 2006.)

of physical infrastructure that needs to be built along the south-west border." No foreigners plotting a terror attack, however, have ever been found to have entered the United States by illegally crossing the border with Mexico. Indeed, the State Department has asserted that "terrorist groups likely seek other means of trying to enter the United States."[198]

In November 2005, DHS began to treat unauthorized immigrants even more like presumed criminals, moving to detain all non-Mexicans apprehended at the border as part of the Secure Border Initiative. Previously, most would have been released pending the outcome of deportation proceedings. To deal with the influx of inmates, DHS added two thousand new beds to the detention system.[199]

DHS entertained wild techno-fantasies, developing the SBInet surveillance program to integrate remote video surveillance, sensors, and other intelligence into a computer network and thus "ensure seamless coverage of the border," a "virtual fence." (The program was managed by Boeing, beset by criticism from the Government Accountability Office, deemed a technical failure, and ultimately shut down in January 2011 after $1 billion had already been spent on fifty-three miles.)[200]

South of the border, the professional smuggling business boomed as a crossing that could have previously been accomplished on one's own or with a small-time *coyote* now necessitated skilled, more expensive expertise.[201] In the 1980s, reported prices for a *pollero* were as low as $50 to $300. In 2008, they reached as high as nearly $3,000, rising alongside increased Border Patrol expenditures.[202] In March 2017, DHS secretary John Kelly boasted that fees had skyrocketed to as high as $8,000.[203] Recently, according to some US officials' estimate, Central Americans pay fees as high as $15,000.[204]

Meanwhile, the intensification of border policing was accompanied by a radicalization of policy goals. The Secure Fence Act called for "operational control" of the border, defined as "the prevention of *all* unlawful entries into the United States, including entries by terrorists, other unlawful aliens, instruments of terrorism, narcotics, and other contraband" (emphasis mine). There had been prior aspirations for "effective control" of the border. And the Clinton administration had in its first term sought "satisfactory management of the border," which entailed a strategy of "prevention through deterrence" to make crossing so tough that it would dissuade most migrants from even trying.[205]

The Secure Fence Act's aspirations for total control were extreme, reflecting the fact that border policy, for government and many of its constituents alike, became cruelly utopian. Although that utopia was by definition impossible to realize, it galvanized people to work toward its promise—and made them believe that that promise was realizable.* Endgame, the ICE Office of Detention and Removal's 2003–12 strategic plan, struck a similar note: "As the title implies," wrote DRO director Anthony S. Tangeman, "the endgame to immigration enforcement . . . is the removal of all removable aliens . . . We must strive for 100% removal rate."[206]

---

* I'm riffing off Lauren Berlant's concept of *cruel optimism*, which refers to the set of affective dispositions ordinary people must cruelly adopt to strive for an unobtainable good life under neoliberalism. (Lauren Berlant, *Cruel Optimism*, Durham: Duke University Press, 2011.)

Did any of it work? By the time construction on the new border fence was underway at the tail end of Bush's second term, the era of mass undocumented Mexican migration that had begun in the 1970s was ending. DHS has found that the stepped-up enforcement increased the odds that migrants will give up attempting to cross.[207] But as the Congressional Research Service put it, "Disentangling the effects of enforcement from other factors influencing migration flows is particularly difficult . . . because many of the most significant new enforcement efforts—including a sizeable share of new border enforcement personnel, most border fencing, new enforcement practices at the border, and many of the new migration enforcement measures within the United States— all have occurred at the same time as the most severe recession since the 1930s."[208]

What militarization certainly accomplished was rendering the border region into something of a police state. For many in Texas, Arizona, New York and other states abutting Mexico and Canada, Border Patrol checkpoints have now long been a daily reality on local roads. Federal agents stop, search, and even assault drivers going about their daily lives even when they are not crossing an international boundary, and they do so without much regard for reasonable suspicion or probable cause. Checkpoints have seemingly had more success seizing motorists' marijuana than they did detaining unauthorized migrants.[209]

Border Patrol agents have long regularly boarded trains and buses heading to and from domestic destinations to quiz people on their legal status. Between 2006 and 2011, Border

Patrol agents based out of Rochester erroneously arrested nearly 300 people with legal status—including citizens, permanent residents, foreign students, and tourists—as part of its program targeting bus and train riders. [210] In 2017, CBP officers questioned passengers disembarking a domestic flight from San Francisco at New York's John F. Kennedy Airport.[211]

The border is not just a place: it is a laboratory and a pretext. As far as the Border Patrol is concerned, it has the authority to conduct vehicle searches within one hundred air miles of any border, and the right to question individuals and detain them anywhere within the United States—New York, Los Angeles, Washington, DC, Boston, Chicago, Miami. Roughly two-thirds of Americans live inside of an area that the Border Patrol treats as a "Constitution-free zone," according to the ACLU.[212] So much for norms and institutions.

Obama's change

Obama inherited Clinton and Bush's entanglement of civil immigration enforcement and criminal justice and took it to new heights. All, once again, to placate nativists and pave the way for comprehensive reform.

In 2014, Mexico launched Programa Frontera Sur, a US-backed operation to stop Central American migration to the United States. It forced migrants to "traverse longer segments of the route by foot through the wilderness, leaving them even more exposed to the elements and criminal preda-tion," as Noelle K. Brigden writes.[213] That route had already become strikingly more dangerous since 2006, when Mexico launched its bloody drug war with strong US support.[214] Domestically, Obama rolled out Secure Communities, a program initiated at the end of the Bush administration that uses local criminal justice systems to identify and deport immigrants, which I address in chapter 4. Obama also continued a shift toward formally deporting more migrants apprehended at the border who previously would have simply been returned to Mexico. The upshot was that those migrants would be barred from entering the country legally for years and subject to prosecution for the federal felony of illegal reentry if they tried to cross again. Tens of thousands of border crossers were behind bars at any given moment—in civil detention centers pending deportation but also in federal penitentiaries serving hard time for immigration-related criminal offenses.[215] In fiscal year 2012, formal deportations that had been rising rapidly since 2003 surpassed four hundred thousand. It was a record annual total and more than double the number carried out in 2002.[216]

In federal courts, prosecutions of immigrants charged with illegally reentering the country and rose steadily under presidents Clinton and Bush, then *skyrocketed* under Obama. Prosecutions for illegally entering the country, a misdemeanor, rose as well. In 2016, people convicted of immigration-related related offenses made up 8 percent of the federal prison population, or 13,300 inmates.[217] As immigration law became increasingly indistinguishable from criminal law, the court system was converted into a prosecutor-directed assembly line to prison and then deportation. As of 2016, *more than half* of all federal prosecutions were for these two migration "crimes."[218]

In 2009, Congress required that DHS maintain more than 33,000 detention beds, later increased to 34,000.[219] By the end of 2012, DHS had detained a staggering 477,523 immigrants for the fiscal year.[220] That was bad news for immigrants but great news for a system in which private prison companies have played a major role. In 2005, roughly a quarter of immigrants in DHS custody were detained by a for-profit enterprise. By 2015, private prison companies controlled 62 percent of those beds.[221]

The Trump presidency sent private prison stocks soaring.[222] Stocks for GEO Group and CoreCivic (formerly and more forthrightly known as Corrections Corporation of America) had fallen sharply after Obama's Justice Department announced that it would phase out using private prisons for federal inmates, even though it left the private detention of immigrants, where private companies play a much larger role, untouched.[223] Attorney General Jeff Sessions quickly reversed even that minor reform and Trump's nativist agenda promised a boom in immigrant detention.[224] "It's really an escalation of capacity need," GEO Group chief executive George C. Zoley told Wall Street analysts on a conference call, due to the president "redirecting the approach to border security."[225]

A central question animating this book is why Americans have become ever more committed to the notion that the border is insecure at the very time that it has become more militarized than ever. Every chapter explains one thread of the overdetermined story. This chapter told the story of how American anxiety over the vicissitudes of global capitalism, crime, and terrorism was often expressed as anger over people and drugs making their way across the border with Mexico. For many Americans, a more fundamental and visceral danger lurked behind the complex phenomena of vanishing jobs, elusive foreign enemies fighting an unconventional war, and the racial and cultural change that mass Mexican immigration signified. As Trump would later put it in a tweet, "A nation WITHOUT BORDERS is not a nation at all."

With Trump, the border security complex that took over American politics in the early 1990s reached its maximally disassociated conclusion: The entire country, racked by downward mobility and opioid overdose, was now a border crisis. Hundreds of miles of fencing were in place and nearly twenty thousand agents patrolled the line.[226] But many Americans felt less secure than ever.

One silver lining to Trump's rise has been that previously normal anti-immigrant policies have become toxic from center to left. Before Trump, centrist liberals considered a wall sound public policy—and voted for it. But Trump has made the wall a monstrosity. In her race for the Democratic nomination, Hillary Clinton suddenly found herself beset by criticism, compelled to explain to Univision's Jorge Ramos the difference between the 2006 Secure Fence Act she had supported "and Donald Trump's idea on building a wall with Mexico."[227] After less than two years of Trump's presidency, the very legitimacy of deportation was up for debate, with many on the left demanding, "Abolish ICE!" (Though it was unclear what some opportunistic Democrats who embraced the call meant by it.)

Even as enforcement won public support, the impossible pledge to secure the border under Presidents Clinton, Bush, and Obama legitimated the objective and raised the stakes, encouraging maximalist demands on the nativist right. Border enforcement inevitably stokes racism and xenophobia because the fences, walls, and army of agents are a monument to racist and xenophobic principles. And these principles have the structure of an infinite, unsatisfiable demand whose fulfillment only reinforces the desire for more. Trump has finally drawn a line that asks everyone: Which side are you on?

3
EMPIRE

As Whites see their power and control over their lives declining, will they simply go quietly into the night? Or will there be an explosion?

—Federation for American Immigration
Reform founder John Tanton, 1986[1]

When Justice Department lawyers defended Trump's Muslim ban, their briefs neglected to mention one of its most favorable judicial precedents. It was an 1889 Supreme Court decision affirming the federal government's right to single out Chinese people for exclusion from the United States. In *Chae Chan Ping v. United States*, the court ruled against a challenge to the Chinese Exclusion Act of 1882, which barred Chinese workers from entering the country, and its amendments of 1888, which expanded the Act by disallowing the reentry of resident Chinese immigrants who had left the country. The government, the court's majority ruled, had an incontestable power to exclude when it "considers the presence of foreigners of a different race in this country, who will not assimilate with us, to be dangerous to its peace and security."[2]

Immigration, the court found, was fundamentally a question of racial policy, foreign policy, and national security. Who came into the country and what status they were accorded once they arrived were constant dilemmas because they posed an impossible contradiction: the nation needed racialized others on the inside but desperately wanted them out at the same time. The inexorable push for territorial expansion and demand for cheap labor, in other words, have always had to contend with the exigencies of white demographic supremacy. Chinese exclusion would be law until 1943 and would only be substantively abolished in 1965.

From the American Revolution through the early nineteenth century, immigration was largely a matter of recruiting white migrants and coercing African ones. The story of American immigration, however, begins earlier still: not with Ellis Island but with settler colonialism, when one country gained control of foreign territory by populating it with its subjects. From Jamestown to the mid-seventeenth century, racism was not yet fully codified in law. There was not yet a sharp social distinction between indentured European and enslaved African laborers. It was only with the development of the plantation system and its institutionalization as a pillar of American political economy that whiteness became synonymous with freedom, and blackness with slavery.[3] In the interest of consolidating territorial control and securing economic gains, British America required more white migrants than England alone could provide—and increasingly, the system demanded enslaved Africans. Enslaved people made up an estimated 17 percent of the 198,400 migrants who arrived from 1607 to 1699, compared with the 49 percent who were indentured servants. From 1700 through 1775, enslaved people comprised an estimated 47 percent of 585,800 total migrants. Whereas English and Welsh people made up an overwhelming majority of seventeenth-century European migrants, Germans, Irish and Scots made up three-quarters of the pre-Revolutionary eighteenth-century total, anticipating an expansive definition of whiteness that would become law after the Revolution.[4] What we now consider to be *immigration politics* is rooted in and inseparable from what was originally considered *settlement politics*.

The American Revolution is conventionally understood as a revolt against monarchical tyranny. Settlers, too, understood their rebellion in such terms: they consistently described their subjection to British rule as a form of "slavery."[5] But settler elites in no sense rejected an unequal political order. The economy, after all, was in large part powered by enslaved labor, the slave trade and dispossessed Native land. The basic dispute behind the Revolution was not over the persistence of settler colonialism—and the tyrannical uses of power it necessitated—but over whether settlers would claim the prerogative to direct its march across the continent.[6]

King George, the Declaration of Independence complained, "has endeavoured to prevent the population of these States; for that purpose, obstructing the Laws for Naturalization of Foreigners; refusing to pass others to encourage their migrations hither, and raising the conditions of new Appropriations of Lands." What's more, it complained, he "has excited domestic insurrections amongst us, and has endeavored to bring on the inhabitants of our frontiers, the merciless Indian Savages." The Crown had barred settlement west of the Appalachians. For settlers, any imperial conciliation with Native people was a declaration of war on the colonies.

After winning independence in 1783, the United States proceeded to conquer vast stretches of a continent under the control of Native people, European empires, and Mexico. The United States then had to make choices about what made an American, and who had the right to become one. In a constitutional republic where citizens enjoyed civil and political freedoms, including in limited cases the right to elect representatives to rule on their behalf, it was imperative to designate the boundaries of citizenship. Government by "we the people" forced Americans to decide who the people were. The country's first naturalization law, enacted in 1790, answered that question by opening citizenship to most any "free white person." US citizenship was thus notably expansive, including a wide variety of Europeans beyond the confines of Anglo Protestantism. Yet in doing so, it further sharpened the color line facing those who remained on the other side of it.

Old-stock Protestants, of course, expressed ambivalence and hostility toward non-British and Catholic immigrants. In 1798, President John Adams, a Federalist, signed the Alien and Sedition Acts, targeting immigrants perceived to be supportive of the opposition Democratic-Republican Party, and of the radicalism of revolutionary France, at a moment when war seemed probable. The Acts authorized the deportation of aliens deemed "dangerous to the peace and public safety of the United States," increased the years of residency required for naturalization, and gave the government new censorship powers.

But war did not come, no immigrants were deported, and in short order the Acts were mostly repealed or expired* because Thomas Jefferson's Democratic-Republicans, who had a strong base among immigrant workers, won power. Because European immigrants could easily gain citizenship, many could vote—though by no means all, since all women and many poor men were barred from doing so.[7] European immigrants could and did protect European immigration through exercising the franchise.[8] Anti-Catholic nativism was constant. But European settlement was mostly not only tolerated but encouraged, with massive amounts of free or cheap land provided across the expanding frontier.[9] White settlement and the forced relocation of enslaved Africans were necessary for holding territory and staffing factories and fields.

But the absence of federal immigration policy against Europeans didn't mean that the United States had open borders. While the federal government exercised power over territorial expansion, it was the states that regulated

---

* Save for the Alien Enemies Act, which remains on the books. President Franklin Delano Roosevelt used the law to detain Japanese, German and Italian "enemy aliens" during World War II, alongside the larger Japanese internment.

immigration until the late nineteenth century: Northeastern states, drawing on colonial-era British poor laws that allowed for excluding paupers and banishing beggars, targeted the poor; their Southern counterparts wanted to control the movement of free blacks, including sailors; many states excluded convicts. "There can be no concurrent power respecting such a subject-matter," said Friedrich Kapp, New York City commissioner of emigration, in 1870. "Such a power is necessarily discretionary. Massachusetts fears foreign paupers; Mississippi, free negroes." There weren't immigration laws so much as a collection of policies governing freedom of movement into and across multiple domestic jurisdictions.[10]

The United States' territorial ambitions imposed the familiar dilemma of managing the admission of racial others while ensuring their domination. In 1848, United States victory over Mexico set into motion a process by which an estimated sixty thousand Mexicans became Mexican Americans, now "strangers in their own land."[11] The United States had annexed Texas after a rebellion by slaveholding Anglo settlers. Then president James Polk launched the nakedly racist, imperialist, and ruthless Mexican-American War. Some clamored for the United States to seize the entirety of Mexico. But those who warned against incorporating what they deemed to be unassimilable racial others prevailed.

The result was the seizure of roughly half of Mexico's territory. Later, even as courts crafted legal rationales to determine whether Afghans, Asian Indians, or Syrians were white and thus eligible to naturalize,[12] Mexican Americans were reverse engineered as white because they were, by way of the war-ending Treaty of Guadalupe, citizens.[13] But that was only in narrow legal terms: in practice, racist ideology framed Mexicans as a backward "hybrid race," both Spanish and indigenous.[14] They were met with widespread discrimination, violence, and segregation. New Mexico would not be admitted as a state until the late date of 1912 precisely because too many Mexicans and Natives resided there—and too few whites.[15]

An immigration boom helped triple the US population between 1820 and 1860, when nearly one-half of New York City's population was foreign born.[16] It was commonplace for states to accord non-citizen European immigrants the right to vote. They were presumed to be what legal scholar Hiroshi Motomura calls "Americans-in-waiting," people whose arrival would inevitably result in citizenship. Even still, in the 1850s a powerful nativist movement, the "Know Nothings," achieved huge electoral success fulminating against the Romanist peril posed by Catholic migrants; amid an intensifying debate over slavery, nativism united North and South in nationalistic opposition to aliens.

Nativists derided Irish immigrants as drinkers and criminals and believed they posed a manifold threat to "free labor": they were supporters of the slaveocracy, dependent wage workers, paupers, and a base of corrupt big-city Democratic machines.[17] From the 1830s through the 1880s, Massachusetts targeted Irish paupers, disproportionately women with children, deporting fifty thousand people—including citizens— to Ireland, Britain, and Canada and also to other states in the

United States. "Deportation was therefore a policy intended to ensure that the United States was a nation of self-sufficient workers by eliminating foreigners who deviated from this vision," writes historian Hidetaka Hirota.[18] Government saw Catholics and paupers as security threats and used its powers to treat them as such.

The growing sectional conflict over slavery, however, eclipsed the nativist movement's appeal and caused it to split along sectional lines. But migration politics never went away, as the possibility of abolition also meant the possibility of black migration out of the South. Fear of the latter dominated antebellum debate over emancipation and made the colonization—forced or voluntary emigration—of black people to Africa or elsewhere a mainstream position among anti-slavery white Americans.

Black colonization was a political fantasy, albeit a widely held one: eliminating the racialized bottom caste of American capitalism so as to create a homogeneously white republic. Abraham Lincoln remained an adherent of it well into his presidency.[19] But whites across the North and West sought to stop black in-migration; Oregon came into the Union barring both slavery and the presence of black people.[20] The unfeasibility of black colonization nevertheless had the consequence of marginalizing non-whites, cheapening their labor, and undermining the possibility of mass solidarity. In other words, exclusion politics, whatever their aim, functioned not just to keep people out but to bolster the power structure within. The same population politics governed policy toward indigenous people, who amid the continuation of long-running genocide were confined to reservations, their freedom of movement restricted as their territory was systematically dismantled and handed over to settlers.

After the Union victory, free blacks and Radical Republicans for the first time expanded the bounds of citizenship beyond total white supremacy. With the Fourteenth Amendment, citizenship was opened to "all persons born or naturalized in the United States," referring especially to African Americans and emancipated slaves, with some exceptions—most notably indigenous people—read into the law later on. Naturalization law, theretofore limited to whites, was also opened to "aliens of African nativity and to persons of African descent." But efforts to universalize naturalization were frustrated: White supremacist politics, including rising anti-Chinese sentiment in California, checked the Radical Republican agenda.[21] Despite protests from race egalitarians, Republicans moved to embrace Chinese exclusion in 1876—anticipating their agreement to withdraw troops from the South a year later and the 1882 passage of the Chinese Exclusion Act.[22] Famed abolitionist William Lloyd Garrison condemned the "demagogical, partisan rivalry between Republican and Democratic Senators as to who should the most strongly cater to the brutal, persecuting spirit which for the time being is so rampant in California."[23] The same thing could have been said in the mid-1990s.

The nation continued its push westward, providing millions of acres of cheap land to settlers, including 96 million acres over forty years through the Homestead Act—a program that excluded Asians because they were ineligible for citizenship.[24] Rather than a heroic frontier epic, writes political scientist Paul Frymer, westward expansion was a set of "laws . . . explicitly recognized for the way they could help manufacture racial demographics by incentivizing white Americans and Europeans to settle the West."[25] Government actively recruited across Europe, promising, in Secretary of State William H. Seward's words, "active, industrious, and intelligent men . . . abundant means of support and comfortable homesteads."[26] In the South, massive violence and federal acquiescence brought an end to Reconstruction, re-imposing white supremacist government.

White supremacists sought to defeat Reconstruction to crush black political power, frustrate populist cross-racial alliances, and protect the exploitation of black labor. Their methods included vagrancy laws, convict-lease labor, and peonage. "Southern political elites," write political scientists Michael C. Dawson and Megan Ming Francis, "wanted to secure a subservient and captive black labor force by driving blacks who were becoming economically independent— figuratively and actually—back onto the plantation."[27] In other words, Southern elites meant to *keep black people in their place*, an appropriately spatial metaphor for a system that used the control of black movement to enforce economic and racial hierarchies. White reactionaries also, however, created the conditions for the next stages of black struggle: the black freedom movement and the long-feared mass migration of black people from the South.

The race foe

It was only after the Civil War that a nation of settlers began to look upon new arrivals as what we today call *immigrants* rather than *emigrants*. Whereas *emigrant* had been commonly used to refer to a settler, as historian Donna Gabaccia writes, *immigrant* had a largely negative connotation.[28] Amid the rise of industrial capitalism, the United States violently subdued the last major armed indigenous rebellions and consolidated its transcontinental dominion, closing the mythic frontier. The rise of corporate power, however, also undermined the basis for white settler egalitarianism: independent free labor. Newly arriving immigrants from Asia were not considered co-participants in the project of American empire and so were scapegoated for the unfolding economic plight.[29]

In response to the economic turbulence brought on by industrialization, the late nineteenth-century Populist move-ment of the people against corporate rule overlapped with a separate nativist movement for limiting who constituted "the people" so as to exclude Asians. As Teddy Roosevelt described it, Chinese exclusion renewed the American prom-ise of a free labor empire of white settlers that African slav-ery, by creating an alien domestic black population, had threatened: "The democracy, with the clear instinct of race selfishness, saw the race foe, and kept out the dangerous alien. The presence of the negro in our Southern States is a legacy from the time when we were ruled by a transoceanic aristoc-racy. The whole civilization of the future owes a debt of grat-itude greater than can be expressed in words to that democratic policy which has kept the temperate zones of the new and the newest worlds a heritage for white people."[30] For many, slavery had created a race problem; after the Civil War, Chinese exclusion was the means to stop the creation of another.[31]

With the Spanish-American War, however, Roosevelt fought for and celebrated the creation of a transoceanic empire, the opening of a new frontier and new markets, as the United States seized the Philippines, Cuba, and Puerto Rico. In Hawaii, American sugar plantation owners overthrew Queen Liliuokalani in a coup and won the islands' annexation as a US territory. Imperialists justified military and economic expansion by appealing to American national and white racial exceptionalism, while many anti-imperialists opposed the war and annexation on the nativist grounds that it would bring non-whites into the country.[32] The new phase of American overseas imperialism, as historian Paul A. Kramer writes, drew new "lines of race [that] would separate and bind those who ruled and those who were ruled."[33] The imperial contact with foreigners and the figure of the great white man astride the world, however, also strengthened the nativist idea that the great white race was at risk of contamination and in need of preservation.[34] Fortification and expansion were both coterminous and in conflict. Both defined what it meant to be an American.

The ban on Chinese people was extended to bar them from the Philippines, now an American possession.[35] It was followed by bans on other Asian nationalities, including one creating the 1917 Asiatic Barred Zone, which prohibited entry to the United States of all but those from Japan and the Philippines. Filipinos were American nationals (to nativists' dismay) by virtue of their colonial subordination.[36] Meanwhile, Japanese were targeted aggressively for exclusion, indirectly in 1907 (as part of an agreement with Japan, whose government the United States sought to avoid angering) and by law in 1924.[37] Remarkably, white opposition was motivated in part by Japanese Americans' determination to pursue independent settler life, with families and farms. In response, Japanese people were targeted by alien land laws that barred them from owning farms.[38] Japanese American economic independence posed a direct threat to white supremacy because whiteness was in large part defined by economic independence.

Only white settlers, "who maintained productive control over labor through land ownership or artisanal work, were truly independent and thus capable of participating in politics," as legal scholar Aziz Rana writes. Other forms of labor were degrading, and those who performed them were deemed unworthy of free citizenship. But since such menial labor was necessary to the system, racialized groups like enslaved Africans and Chinese workers were required to perform that labor; indeed, it was precisely the consignment to menial labor that made those workers intelligible as racialized others. "This intrinsic connection between economic freedom and economic compulsion meant that for settlers to enjoy free labor, they had to compartmentalize degraded work along ethnic, racial, and gender lines. And once consigned to wage earning, tenancy, conscription, and various modes of peonage, social outsiders then found their status justified precisely because of their relationship to production"[39] writes Rana. Or as W.E.B. Du Bois summarized the white perception of race as class and class as race : "Negroes are servants; servants are Negroes."[40]

Beginning in the late nineteenth century, millions from southern and eastern Europe began to migrate into the booming industrial workforce.[41] They were targeted in part because their dependency on wage labor made them seem unworthy for free citizenship and thus not entirely white. During an era of incredibly violent labor conflict, political and union radicalism could likewise only be attributed to a racial other. "There is no such thing as an American anarchist," the journal *Public Opinion* intoned after the Haymarket riot of 1886. "The American character has in it no element which can under any circumstances be won to uses so mistaken."[42]

According to Hirota, it was Massachusetts and New York's immigration control targeting Irish paupers that "molded the legal and administrative frameworks of national policy for excluding and deporting foreigners," thus enabling Chinese exclusion.[43] Chinese exclusion, in turn, was a critical precedent, writes historian Erika Lee. It created "the models by which to measure the desirability (and 'whiteness') of other immigrant groups." Italians, for example, were called "the Chinese of Europe" and "padrone coolies."[44]

Chinese exclusion normalized racially targeted exclusion and created institutions to administer and enforce it. Indeed, the Immigration Act of 1882, passed the same year, was the first comprehensive federal immigration law.[45] It barred entry to "any convict, lunatic, idiot, or any person unable to take care of himself or herself without becoming a public charge." It was modeled on New York and Massachusetts immigration laws that had been struck down by the Supreme Court because they infringed on the constitutional power accorded to the president and Congress over international affairs.[46] The Immigration Act of 1891 then provided the federal government with its first general deportation powers and gave immigration inspectors the unchallengeable power to exclude those they deemed "likely to become a public charge."[47] As would be the case with the late twentieth-century war on crime, the spectacular punishment of stigmatized minorities built repressive institutions that would target many others. Racism provided legitimacy to a system that oppressed the majority.

A nation of immigrants

World War I nationalism provided critical fuel to the movement against southern and eastern European migration. It unleashed an extreme variant of patriotism under the banner of "100 percent Americanism," which rendered "hyphenated Americans" suspect. German language schooling was shut down. English was patriotism's exclusive mother tongue.[48] Assimilation rendered most European-descendant Americans white and thus Americans.

As the Russian Revolution excited fear of domestic insurrection, the new European migrants were viewed as a political threat. In 1920, Attorney General A. Mitchell Palmer launched raids to round up and deport alleged immigrant

radicals. The first Red Scare, writes political scientist Daniel
Tichenor, "encouraged the brief yet crucial defection of key
business groups from the pro-immigration camp," paving
the way for the national origins quotas' massive immigration
restrictions.[49]

But it was the Progressive Era's congressional Dillingham
Commission that first created "immigration as a 'problem'"
to be solved by government—in particular the "Jewish,
Italian, and Slavic 'new immigrants'" who were presumed to
"be less assimilable and more 'alien,'" as historian Katherine
Benton-Cohen writes. This model, she argues, implicitly
designated Mexicans and Asians as entirely "other," which
helped "produce a racial subtext about 'illegal aliens' to the
present day." It was "a fact-finding body of unprecedented
size and scale" whose reports, published in 1911, totaled
twenty-nine thousand pages.[50]

The era's elites held expertise in high esteem and many
turned to eugenics to make the case for restriction (though
the Dillingham Commission, Benton-Cohen writes, did
not).[51] Race science became conventional wisdom that shaped
not only academic scholarship and policymaking but also
popular political culture. At state fairs, eugenicists ran "fitter
family" competitions to celebrate exquisite human stock,
alongside the contests for livestock.[52] The grim obverse to
this form of "positive eugenics" was "negative eugenics,"
which emphasized limiting the immigration and reproduction of those purported inferiors.

The restriction movement had wide appeal, though organized immigrants, the politicians who represented them, and

business resisted it.[53] But in contrast to the lead role played by white workers in the campaign for Asian exclusion, the push for southern and eastern European restriction was spearheaded by Harvard-educated Anglo-Americans at the Immigration Restriction League (IRL), founded in Massachusetts, a stronghold of anti-Irish politics throughout the nineteenth century, and focused on lobbying and social scientific research.[54] Prominent Western nativists were often themselves immigrants, and they often targeted Asians on behalf of white people as a whole.[55] By contrast, the patrician nativists at the IRL worried over the immigration of and high birthrates among southern and eastern Europeans. It would, as IRL vice president, "self-proclaimed" anthropologist, and leading conservationist Madison Grant put it in his book *The Passing of the Great Race*, trigger Anglo-American "race suicide," a concept that his friend and fellow conservationist Teddy Roosevelt likewise embraced.[56] Mercifully, American racial stock might be upgraded "not by killing off the less fit, but by preventing them from coming into the State, either by being born into it or by migration."[57] The nativist environmentalists who launched the contemporary movement in the 1970s alleged that immigration harmed nature; the conservationist eugenicists of Grant's era believed that science could assist nature in making society more fit.[58]

Yet restrictionism was by no means an exclusive project of the Northeast elite. Some West Coast anti-Asian nativists offered their support. The AFL leadership, overcoming internal opposition, swung the organization behind restriction.[59] In the late nineteenth century, the anti-Catholic and nativist

American Protective Association had developed a mass base in the Midwest and Northeast.[60] And then, in the 1920s, the rise of the Second Ku Klux Klan saw millions of white Protestants nationwide, often middle-class, join the organization. They called for "the restoration of 'true Americanism' and offered members a platform that demonized blacks, Catholics, Jews, Mexicans, Asians, and any other non-white ethnic immigrants while also condemning Communism, most other forms of leftist politics, and 'base' cultural influences such as alcohol, birth control, and the teaching of evolution in public schools." The KKK unleashed murderous violence and counted governors and senators among its members—all as part of an organization that for its members was as wholesome and innocuous as today's Rotary Clubs.[61] In the South, elites had mounted a major campaign to recruit immigrants to settle in the region—an effort to economically modernize and solve labor shortage problems, replacing free black people and poor whites. But when that failed Southerners quickly embraced xenophobia on familiar racist grounds.[62]

The nativist campaign against disfavored Europeans soon won legislative victories. In 1917, a literacy test was adopted alongside the Asiatic Barred Zone, which didn't work well because too many targeted migrants were literate.[63] Far more consequentially, the Immigration Act of 1921 and the Johnson-Reed Act of 1924 created the national origins quota system to dramatically restrict immigration from eastern and southern Europe. The quota system was an astonishingly bureaucratic and statistically complex attempt to freeze US demography in place by using census data on Americans' immigrant backgrounds to determine the number of visas allotted to people from various European countries.[64] The more Americans who were classified as being from a given country, the more visas people from that country received. The Johnson-Reed Act extended the Asian ban to cover Japanese, excluding all "aliens ineligible for citizenship": unlike restricted Europeans, banned Asians were denied the right to naturalize because of their race. As a result, they were banned even if they came from a non-Asian country.[65] There were only a token number of visas issued to independent African nations, because black Americans were treated as though they had no national origins at all.[66] For the duration of the quotas' four-decade lifespan, immigrants from Great Britain, Germany and Ireland made up nearly three-quarters of the total.[67]

Race and immigration law were one and the same—with lethal results. In the face of Nazi terror, the US government actively restricted Jewish immigration, with the staunch support of the American Legion and other nationalist groups.[68] White leaders of settler societies as far away as Australia and southern Africa followed American immigration race law.[69] As did the Nazis. In *Mein Kampf*, Adolf Hitler praised American immigration law for "excluding certain races from naturalization," favorably comparing the United States against a racially defiled Latin America. He also called nativist and eugenicist Grant's *Passing of the Great Race* "his Bible."[70]

Racial bars to naturalization were not fully eliminated until the 1952 McCarran-Walter Act. Even then, Asians were assigned quotas based on both race and country of origin and provided only token quotas until 1965.[71] It also maintained the national origins quotas, barred communists and homosexuals, and protected growers against sanction for employing undocumented workers. The right to exploit Mexican labor was ardently defended by leading nativists in Congress.[72] The 1952 law was thus largely a reactionary one and was passed over President Harry Truman's veto. When white Americans today say that their ancestors "came the right way," this is, often unconsciously, the history they are referring to.

Chinese exclusion was only relaxed in 1943 when China became a World War II ally.[73] Americans of Japanese descent were collectively imprisoned because they shared a bloodline with the enemy, at times transported and guarded by Border Patrol agents.[74] The law that provided for the transition to independence of the Philippines simultaneously all but barred Filipino immigration; the 1910s mass migration of Filipino workers to Hawaiian sugar plantations and Western farms and canneries had prompted warnings of an "invasion" and a sexual threat to white women.[75] Meanwhile, the New Deal state performed a quietly systematic mass assimilation—a second Homestead Act of sorts. The social-democratic policy program that made the mid-century middle class (secure jobs, subsidized homeownership, social insurance) was systematically denied to non-whites, effectuating the neat trick of making "white ethnic" families seem naturally American in contrast to others who could or would not assimilate. The suburbia that the postwar order built became the social base for California's 1990s nativist revolt.

Organized white supremacists and nativists know the racist history of immigration law well, and take explicit inspiration from it. But most people have no clue: "colorblind" liberal immigration politics have taught most Americans that we have always been a "nation of immigrants." It was President Lyndon Johnson who accelerated this collective forgetting of racist population politics in 1965, when he signed the Hart-Celler Act, eliminating the quota system. "Our beautiful America was built by a nation of strangers," he proclaimed. "From a hundred different places or more they have poured forth into an empty land, joining and blending in one mighty and irresistible tide."[76]

The law's origins are complex. It was passed in part because targeting the nationals of would-be allies for exclusion, like the repression of black people in the Jim Crow South, was a geopolitical liability. Immigration law met the demands of a liberal Cold War order in which the United States struggled against the Soviet Union for the decolonizing world's affections.[77] Targeted groups like Italians had also made their way into white America and clamored for repeal.[78] The quota system was replaced with one prioritizing family unification. In doing so, it favorably remade the United States' image for the world, in the world's image: that immigrants chose America was part of what made it exceptional. Johnson pointed to the diversity of US troops fighting and dying in Vietnam, a war that he insisted was not imperialist, and announced that the United States was wide open to Cuban refugees. And he made a point of emphasizing that the law's significance was primarily symbolic and suggested that a white majority would remain unchallenged. "This bill that we will sign today is not a revolutionary bill," said Johnson at a signing ceremony before the Statue of Liberty. "It does not affect the lives of millions. It will not reshape the structure of our daily lives, or really add importantly to either our wealth or our power. Yet it is still one of the most important acts of this Congress and of this administration. For it does repair a very deep and painful flaw in the fabric of American justice. It corrects a cruel and enduring wrong in the conduct of the American Nation."[79]

More bluntly, Senator Ted Kennedy pledged that "the ethnic mix of this country will not be upset."[80] Both Johnson and Kennedy were wrong: the geographic origins of immigration changed dramatically and, as a result, so did anti-immigrant politics. Before Hart-Celler, the vast majority of immigrants came from Europe. In the years after its implementation, more than half came from Latin America and a quarter from Asia.[81] Critically, however, the law also coincided with the end of the Bracero Mexican guest worker program, and for the first time imposed a cap on immigration from the Western Hemisphere. The sudden restriction on Mexican immigration was exacerbated in 1976, when country-specific caps were made universal, allotting Mexicans the same low number of slots as Uruguayans or Belgians.[82] It inserted a time bomb into the very heart of American immigration policy and politics: Mexicans would continue to come but would be received as criminals.

With Hart-Celler, the country celebrated its commitment to being a "nation of immigrants," an idea that had been popularized by a martyred John F. Kennedy, the first Catholic president. The United States, however, was never that nation. A novel popular mythology with strong amnesiac properties, it relocated the nation's origin story from the settlers at Plymouth Rock to "huddled masses yearning to breathe free" at Ellis Island, as historian Matthew Frye Jacobson writes.[83] The celebration was overwhelmingly for a nation of "white ethnic" immigrants who "came the right way," obscuring the fact that migration policy had for much of American history been a white supremacist demographic project and absolving a white nation of the moral stain of Native genocide and African slavery.[84]

White ethnics had for four decades been not only restricted from immigration but excluded from full membership in whiteness. The 1965 reform accelerated an expansion of whiteness that included them at its core—a model of white virtue contrasted against black people who failed to strive their way out of the ghetto, and against Mexicans who snuck past the Border Patrol instead of undergoing inspection in New York Harbor.[85] This "nation of immigrants" belonged neither to the Native people rendered invisible in this "empty land," nor to the black people who had been forced to North America in chains, nor to the Mexicans who began to cross the southern border without authorization in enormous numbers because there was no other way.

The white right

In 1979, *U.S. News and World Report* warned of an illegal "invasion," contending that "the traditions of Mexican Americans remain undiluted, refreshed daily by an influx of illegal immigrants from another country." In 1983, *Time* sounded the alarm of "a staggering influx of foreign settlers," people "feeling as much like a migrant as an immigrant, not an illegal alien but a *reconquistador*."[86] There were even fears, as the *Los Angeles Times* put it in 1979, that "hundreds of thousands of Third World immigrants entering California and the rest of the United States are bringing with them a panoply of communicable diseases that could, according to health experts, move the country back toward nineteenth-century standards of public health."[87]

The white reaction to the black Great Migration and freedom struggle resisted black movement into previously white neighborhoods, schools, and jobs. It laid the groundwork for mass incarceration, a system emerging in the 1970s to take a people on the move and fix them in place. It also created a model for resisting immigration: a template of white identity politics organized for territorial defense against the fiscal, criminal, and demographic threats posed by racial others. It was this mass political moment that a new, violent white power movement tapped into. Its racist ideology eschewed liberal niceties, putting immigration and fertility at the center of its adherents' belief in an apocalyptic plan to replace the white race. The movement, which took root in the 1970s among radicalized Vietnam War veterans, declared that a

"Jewish Zionist Occupational Government" conspired to destroy the white race through abortion, interracial marriage, birth control, and immigration.[88]

In 1977, white power activists launched the "Klan Border Watch," an armed patrol on the Mexican border. "We will be here as long as it takes to meet the response of the illegal alien problem," said David Duke, the Ku Klux Klan's young Grand Dragon.[89]

In 1981, the Knights of the Ku Klux Klan took advantage of a local backlash against refugee shrimpers whose resettlement along the Texas Gulf coast prompted worries over competition from white fishermen. Robed and armed Klansmen patrolled the Galveston Bay with a human effigy hanging from the rigging.[90] Two Vietnamese were acquitted on self-defense grounds after a white fisherman was shot and killed in a dispute over crab traps; Vietnamese boats were burned; Vietnamese shrimpers were threatened and harassed.

For the far right, the campaign against hundreds of thousands of resettled Indochinese refugees was the continuation of a war on communism in Vietnam that government surrender had left unfinished. That many refugees fought alongside or supported the United States did not matter. Political threats, like economic ones, were racialized; in fact, that's how race was made, again and again.

In 1980, 125,000 Cuban asylum seekers arrived in Florida during the Mariel boatlift, which included some released prisoners.[91] "It seems to me the evidence is clear and overwhelming that Castro is emptying out his prisons and his mental institutions," said Colorado's nativist Democratic governor Richard Lamm, demanding that no Cubans be resettled in his state.[92] But Cuban asylum seekers—people fleeing a communist nation—were ultimately accommodated because doing so fit Cold War foreign policy aims. By contrast, their black Haitian counterparts were targeted for detention and exclusion. Indeed, the persecution of Haitians fleeing the Duvalier dictatorship, carried out by the Carter and then the Reagan administration, created the immigration detention system that we know today.[93]

The Refugee Act of 1980 had for the first time made US law consistent with international law: it codified the right to protection from persecution as a universal one rather than as merely a blunt tool for Cold War foreign policy that provided shelter to those fleeing countries governed by US adversaries.[94] But Reagan, whose dirty wars across Central America were waged in the name of securing the US southern border against communism and refugees alike, continued to deploy it as just that. Rallying support for the Contra war in Nicaragua, Reagan declared that if the Sandinista government were left unchecked, it would expand into "a sea of red, eventually lapping at our own borders."[95] Failure to wage war, he warned, would lead to a flood of refugees heading to the United States: "If the Communists consolidate their power, their campaign of violence throughout Central America will go into high gear, bringing new dangers and sending hundreds of thousands of refugees streaming toward our 2,000-mile long southern border."[96]

Reagan, of course, helped instead to cause a massive refugee exodus fleeing US-backed violence. As hundreds of thousands fled murderous US allied anti-communist governments in El Salvador and Guatemala, Reagan denied them asylum—accusing them of being unworthy "economic migrants." Reagan's actions, protecting murderous right-wing regimes by denying refuge to the people fleeing them, also sparked a sanctuary movement that, in tandem with left-wing solidarity organizations, became one of the largest social movements of the era.[97] The campaign, a new "underground railroad," used houses of worship to protect refugees and resisted intense US government repression. It also created an immigrant and refugee defense network that outlasted the dirty wars, and a model for the new sanctuary movement that would reemerge to fight deportations under Obama and then Trump.

Meanwhile, the white power movement was fighting Reagan's wars with official support that "ranged from inconsistent prosecution to tacit non-action to overt approval," as historian Kathleen Belew writes.[98] Across Central America, far-right US mercenaries trained military forces, including the Salvadoran military's Atlacatl Battalion, which had massacred nearly one thousand civilians in the village of El Mozote. At the southern border, the mercenary organization Civilian Materiel Assistance mounted an armed foray that went two and a half miles *into Mexico* in 1986. They set traps for migrants, shot at them, and stopped and detained sixteen at gunpoint. Instead of prosecuting the mercenaries, the United States deported their migrant captives.[99] Ironically, the far right decried the militarization of domestic security—precisely what their desired war on immigrants would help accomplish.[100]

As the Cold War drew to a close, the two-way contest that had defined its politics collapsed into a unipolar world order. For many Americans, however, the victory seemed empty and even foreboding. It was the beginning of a now familiar state of affairs: an empire in crisis, conjuring up new enemies in a futile quest to give meaning to a rudderless national identity.

Delivering his 1991 State of the Union Address, as American troops led the First Gulf War's coalition against Iraq's annexation of Kuwait, George H.W. Bush declared it the first of a new kind of war and of "a new world order" under enlightened American leadership.[101] Bush announced that the United States had "kicked the Vietnam syndrome once and for all."[102] But for many on the right, the more substantive threat seemed to be the one posed by the American government itself—a pawn, conspiracists charged, of that "New World Order." Taking Bush's concept and redefining it as nefarious, the right declared that the United States had ceded its sovereignty to the forces of globalism. Their fight would be to secure the border with Mexico.

The language of race

After the civil rights revolution, a colorblind liberal ethos rendered mainstream racism into racially neutral language. Language, a proxy for culture that was itself a proxy for race, would be at its center. The latest immigrants, nativists contended, would or could not assimilate. A campaign to protect the English language by making it the country's official language—something that in legal terms the United States has never had—was a palatable surrogate for ethnonationalism. The fear that English was so imperiled was, like much nativist politics, a fantastical projection: English had long since become the indisputable lingua franca, not just of the United States, but the entire world.

The contemporary English-only movement was born in 1983 when nativist movement godfather John Tanton founded the group U.S. English, whose advisory board included luminaries like Arnold Schwarzenegger, neoconservative sociologist Nathan Glazer, and Walter Cronkite. Legislation to amend the Constitution to make English the official language was repeatedly introduced beginning in 1981, when US senator S. I. Hayakawa, a California Republican who helped Tanton found the group, first introduced it.[103] The group also called for an end to bilingual ballots, which would necessitate repealing the Voting Rights Act provision requiring them in areas with significant non-English-speaking populations—one of many cases when anti-immigrant politics entailed attacks on victories won by historic freedom struggles.[104]

"White ethnic" European heritage was widely celebrated. But the invocation of black and Latino cultural difference, whether regarding Ebonics or bilingual education, elicited scorn and suspicion. Right-wing leader Howard Phillips described bilingual education as "a semantically appealing cover slogan for liberal activists who wish to emphasize those things which divide Americans . . . rather than those which unite us." White ethnics were celebrated for surviving the melting pot. Latino and Asian immigrants were portrayed as refusing to melt.[105]

"Experts," as a *Christian Science Monitor* story put it, worried that a near-majority of immigrants speaking one language—Spanish—might lead to "a bilingual, bicultural strain that could tear at a national cohesion based, in large part, on English as a common language."[106] The focus was on immigrants' failure to assimilate rather than the nation's refusal to integrate; cultural and racial difference, rather than racism, was blamed for undermining national unity.

U.S. English had a more unabashedly right-wing counterpart, English First, run by Larry Pratt. A former anticommunist mercenary in Central America, Pratt was the executive director of the more-right-wing-than-the-NRA Gun Owners of America, and would later be an agitator within the 1990s white power militia movement as well as Pat Buchanan's campaign co-chair.[107] English First complained that "tragically, many immigrants these days refuse to learn English" and warned that "the next American president could well be elected by people who can't read or speak English!"[108]

Official English legislation was taken up in most states and passed in many—including in California, where a large majority of voters backed Proposition 63 in 1986 after a campaign that received nearly all its funding from U.S. English–related sources.[109] Afterward, Filipino nurses in Pomona, east of the city of Los Angeles, reported being told that they could not speak to each other in Tagalog, even on breaks.[110] The city also passed an ordinance, later struck down in court, requiring that at least 50 percent of store signs be in English. In the San Gabriel Valley suburb of Monterey Park, officials objected to a donation of Chinese-language books to the public library. To the south in Huntington Park, a municipal court clerk was barred from speaking Spanish.

Prop 63's direct impact was largely symbolic—at least in the short term. In the 1980s, Tanton had failed in a major effort to build a membership base in Southern California. Official English provided a means to inject xenophobia into the discourse by portraying their agenda as in part a liberal one concerned with immigrants' ability to meaningfully participate in society; a campaign to free immigrants from "linguistic ghettos" by turning up the melting pot's heat was a pretext to build support for immigration restriction.[111] As historian Carly Goodman notes, official English was politically successful because it appealed to "the idea of multi-ethnic inclusion, and therefore fulfilled rather than fought the nation of immigrants mythology." It evoked "cultural threat without being explicitly linked to race or immigration."[112] That simultaneous appeal to both overt racists and those committed to assimilating immigrants, however, fell apart when Tanton was exposed as a white nationalist.

The year that California voters approved Prop 63, Tanton penned a memo to movement leaders warning of a "Latin onslaught." Citing the settler dictum coined by nineteenth-century Argentine intellectual Juan Bautista Alberdi—"to govern is to populate"—he asked, "Will the present majority peaceably hand over its political power to a group that is simply more fertile?" When Tanton's memo was exposed in

1988 in a widely publicized scandal, U.S. English president Linda Chavez, a Hispanic Reagan administration alumnus whose public profile had helped make the organization safe for moderates, resigned.[113]

The nativist movement, however, would only become more overtly right-wing. And while overpopulation had disappeared as a major concern, anti-immigrant politics remained fixated on the threat posed by Latina reproduction—and increasingly, not in environmentalist language but in civilizational terms that resonated with the conservative base. As Tanton wrote to a major donor, he was concerned "about the decline of folks who look like you and me," and argued to Garrett Hardin that "for European-American society and culture to persist requires a European-American majority, and a clear one at that."[114] Throughout the 1990s, these arguments gained remarkable mainstream legitimacy.

Reconquista

In the 1990s, Pat Buchanan warned that "our Western heritage" would be "dumped onto some landfill called multiculturalism." He warned of "demands for Quebec-like status for Southern California," a possibility echoed by Stanford historian David M. Kennedy in *The Atlantic*.[115] The issue for Buchanan was cultural. And by cultural, he meant racial. "I think God made all people good, but if we had to take a million immigrants in, say Zulus, next year, or Englishmen, and put them in Virginia, what group would be easier to assimilate and would cause less problems for the people of

Virginia?" he asked.[116] Buchanan didn't buy Clinton's war on undocumented immigrants, accusing him of leading a "revolution to overturn our ethnic and racial balances."[117]

In California, Prop 187 leader Barbara Coe said that she converted to hard-core xenophobia after visiting a social services center in Orange County, viscerally repulsed by the presence of people not speaking English. "I walked into this monstrous room full of people, babies and little children all over the place, and I realized nobody was speaking English," said Coe. "I was overwhelmed with this feeling: 'Where am I? What's happened here?'"[118] Glenn Spencer said that he founded his pro-187 group Voice of Citizens Together (initially called Valley Citizens Together and later also known as American Patrol and American Border Patrol) after he witnessed rioting Mexicans in 1992 Los Angeles "tearing down" his "old neighborhood." Spencer would ultimately take his fight to the borderlands in Arizona. But he first became radicalized in the affluent San Fernando Valley neighborhood of Sherman Oaks, which had led the region's suburbanite revolts against school busing and property taxes.[119] For California suburbanites, "illegal immigration" was only the latest assault on their fragile utopia. Mexico, Spencer warned, "is purposefully sending drugs into our nation to destroy us. It is sending its people to occupy our land. It is involved in 'Reconquista,' the retaking of the American Southwest."[120]

Spencer concluded that Mexican immigration was a war on white people. It was a parable of demographic threat that shaped the organized nativist movement and ordinary

nativist sentiment alike. It was, writes anthropologist Leo
Chavez, fueled by a fixation on Latina reproduction: "Their
fertility," the theory goes, "is out of control, which fuels both
demographic changes and the alleged reconquista."[121]
Congress, after the passage of Prop 187 and Republican
Revolution, was listening. In 1995, House Speaker Newt
Gingrich's Congressional Task Force on Immigration
Reform called for denying birthright citizenship to the chil-
dren of undocumented immigrants—a direct assault on the
Fourteenth Amendment, a pinnacle of Reconstruction-era
black struggle.[122]

The "reconquista" conspiracy was amplified by talk radio,
an ascendant conservative mass media that bypassed traditional arbiters of political debate. California taxpayers, said
talk radio host J. Paul Emerson in 1995, should have the right
to "be a bounty hunter . . . go out there and shoot illegal
immigrants who come across the border, and . . . shoot killers, robbers and rapers and drag them down to the police
station and collect a reward."[123]

Emerson was speaking on KSFO, that year rechristened as
the San Francisco conservative talk radio station that gave a
novice host, Michael Savage, his breakout show. An embit-
tered Savage had moved to talk radio after publishers rejected
his manuscript for a book entitled *Immigrants and Epidemics*—
which argued that immigrants spread disease.[124] Conservative
AM talk had emerged in the 1980s, after music stations shifted
to FM format and the FCC Fairness Doctrine, which had
required stations to provide time for opposing views, was
repealed. For years, small magazines had spoken to

conservative elites. Now, talk radio targeted and helped call into being a broader public.

But it wasn't just the far-right fringe. In 1995, just a few years after Cold War triumph, the Senate voted 99–1 on a resolution denouncing proposed history teaching standards, calling for programs receiving government support to "have a decent respect for United States history's roots in Western civilization."[125] And throughout the decade, mainstream publications and publishing houses eagerly courted nativist contributions. In 1994, *The Atlantic* published an anti-immigrant essay by Roy Beck, an editor of Tanton's racist journal the *Social Contract*.[126] Two years later, W. W. Norton published Beck's anti-immigrant book.

Meanwhile, the conservative movement was integrating nativism into the core of its culture war. This was an easy shift, given the movement's long-standing opposition to black civil rights. As *National Review* founder William F. Buckley put it in his infamous 1957 editorial defending segregation: "The White community is so entitled because, for the time being, it is the advanced race."[127] *National Review* also had a long history of racist immigration politics—defending the principle of nationality-based restrictions on the eve of their repeal in 1965, in 1977 warning of a Mexican reconquista and insisting that the United States "gain control of its demographic fate," and in 1990 declaring that Muslim immigrants were "brown-skinned peoples cooking strange foods and maintaining different standards of hygiene."[128]

In 1992, the *National Review* published a lengthy cover story by senior editor Peter Brimelow decrying "so-called

Hispanics" as a "strange anti-nation inside the U.S."[129] In 1995, Random House published Brimelow's unapologetically racist argument at book length: *Alien Nation: Common Sense about America's Immigration Disaster*. "The American nation has always had a specific ethnic core," wrote Brimelow, "and that core has been white." He continued: "It is simply common sense that Americans have a legitimate interest in their country's racial balance. It is common sense that they have a right to insist that their government stop shifting it. Indeed, it seems to me that they have a right to insist that it be shifted back."[130] In a memo, John Tanton wrote that he had "encouraged Brimelow to write his book" and "provided the necessary research funds to get it done."[131]

The book, openly nostalgic for the national origins quotas, was a white nationalist anti-immigrant screed published by a major house, widely and positively reviewed in the mainstream press. In 1995, writer Jack Miles praised Brimelow in (of course) *The Atlantic* for having "the courage to admit that the matter can have no economic resolution and the greater courage to step forward as an apologist for the received Euro-American culture."[132] *New York Times* book critic Richard Bernstein gushed that it was to Brimelow's "credit that he attacks" what he called "the strong racial element in current immigration" without flinching—"head on, unapologetically."[133] For Bernstein, Brimelow's violation of political correctness seemed to hold a transgressive appeal. Indeed, it was Bernstein who in 1990 first popularized the term "politically correct" as a pejorative, warning in a *New York Times* article that universities were in thrall to "a growing intolerance, a closing of debate, a pressure to conform to a radical program or risk being accused of a commonly reiterated trio of thought crimes: sexism, racism and homophobia."[134]

In 1999, however, Brimelow would transgress even that era's rather capacious tolerance for bigotry, founding the openly white nationalist website VDare, unsubtly named for the girl said to be the first English child born in the New World. Tanton referred to the site as "our enterprise."[135] Between 2006 and 2008, Tanton's journal the *Social Contract* dedicated the entirety of two issues to VDare material. In 2009, the *New York Times* called VDare white supremacist and "extremist."[136] Yet Brimelow's views had been perfectly clear in 1995.

Though Brimelow was ultimately pushed out of *National Review*, openly racist anti-immigrant politics were not. In 2004, Buckley praised *The Camp of the Saints*, a racist French novel that depicts a flotilla of "cholera-ridden and leprous wretches" from India that, thanks to liberal guilt and fecklessness, take over France, precipitating Third World conquest of the entire West.[137] Buckley mused, "What to do? Starve them? Shoot them? We don't do that kind of thing— but what do we do when we run out of airplanes in which to send them back home?"[138] Tanton's Social Contract Press published an English language translation of the book, a text that Tanton described as "prescient"—which it was.[139] The novel became a bible of the alt-right, an early warning against "white genocide" praised by Steve Bannon and white nationalist Republican representative Steve King.[140]

In the 1990s, racism found mainstream respectability amid a political culture dominated by questions of welfare, crime, and immigration—all in the name of revolt against liberal elites. Allan Bloom's 1987 bestseller *The Closing of the American Mind* had lamented the denigration of the Founders as racist killers motivated by class interests, complaining that "cultural relativism" had dethroned "reason" in universities governed by an "intellectual minority" who "expected to enhance its status" by depicting "a nation of minorities and groups each following its own beliefs and inclinations."[141] Dinesh D'Souza followed in 1991 with *Illiberal Education: The Politics of Race and Sex on Campus*, parts of which appeared in *The Atlantic* as a cover story.[142] D'Souza deplored "the ideological claims of the minority victims' revolution on campus," which threatened to bring the "lurid bigotry, intolerance, and balkanization of campus life" to "society at large." Bloom, D'Souza and others decried the liberal establishment and were praised for doing so in liberalism's leading publications; they claimed to speak from the margins while receiving funding from "networks of conservative donors—particularly the Koch, Olin and Scaife families—who had spent the 1980s building programs that they hoped would create a new 'counter-intelligentsia.'"[143]

The problems purportedly posed by black and Latino people were the subject of high-profile debates among self-professed serious people, exemplified not only by *The New Republic*'s 1994 publication of an excerpt of the notoriously racist book *The Bell Curve* but by *The Atlantic* and *New York*

Times's friendly reviews of *Alien Nation*. Murray Rothbard, who led a segment of neoliberals toward alt-right libertarianism, remarked that "until literally mid-October 1994 [when *The Bell Curve* was published], it was shameful and taboo for anyone to talk publicly or write about, home truths which everyone, and I mean everyone, knew in their hearts and in private: that is, almost self-evident truths about race, intelligence, and heritability."[144] Some neoliberals explained inequality by way of racial proxies like culture, but others did not bother.

Nativists tapped into the often-unstated racial anxiety at the core of post–civil rights era race and immigration politics. And nativists were right: the new immigration did pose a threat to the US order, and it was different from immigration in other periods. From settlement through the arrival of Italians, Jews and others in the late nineteenth century, European immigrants weren't "immigrants" at all: they were *emigrants* who in general (but not always, as made clear by Massachusetts's persecution of Irish paupers) automatically received the status accorded to European settlers as they arrived from the metropole to take part in a burgeoning settler-colonialist project. An overriding and explicit goal of this project was engineering white majority and supremacy. By contrast, as Rana writes, immigrants since 1965 had often been from the periphery of the global political-economic order—the very sorts of groups that had forever been brutalized and excluded—traveling to its new center and metropole, the United States.[145]

Nativists, in a neurotic projection, believe that immigrants will do to them what their European settler forbearers had perpetrated against indigenous America: a new settler-colonialist project to impose foreign cultures, ideologies, and institutions. Immigrants, Glenn Spencer warned, had come to "occupy and colonize us and take away our nation."[146]

In August 2019, a gunman massacred shoppers at an El Paso Walmart popular among visitors from both sides of the border. At least eight Mexican nationals were among the twenty-two killed.[147] Shortly before the attack a manifesto written by the killer appeared online decrying "the Hispanic invasion of Texas." For liberals, celebrating a nation of immigrants is premised on the erasure of settler colonialism. For the far right, defending America is openly premised on securing its victories. "Some people will think this statement is hypocritical because of the nearly complete ethnic and cultural destruction brought to the Native Americans by our European ancestors," the shooter continued, "but this just reinforces my point. The natives didn't take the invasion of Europeans seriously, and now what's left is just a shadow of what was."[148]

The shooter made a point of emphasizing that his "opinions . . . predate Trump and his campaign for president." In truth, that is entirely plausible. Right-wing nativists have understood what liberal pablum obscures, though in grotesquely racist terms. Since 1965, immigrants have indeed posed a threat to the racist settler ideal. And as Tendayi Achiume argues, this transformation contains an anti-racist emancipatory potential: migration from a Global South pillaged for centuries by colonial powers is in fact, in many ways, an act of decolonization.[149]

The inevitability of what is described as a minority-majority America was crystallized in the far-right conspiracy theory that Mexicans were engaging in a reconquista of the United States, the prefix *re-* betraying a recognition that the land was not "ours" to begin with. A form of this theory was ultimately embraced by the president of the United States. "When Mexico sends its people, they're not sending their best," said Trump, announcing his presidential campaign. "They're sending people that have lots of problems . . . They're bringing drugs. They're bringing crime. They're rapists." He would later make it clear that he literally believed that immigration was the policy of a hostile Mexican state: "The Mexican Government is forcing their most unwanted people into the United States."[150]

For Trump, immigration and the great game of inter-state economic competition with countries like China are inseparable. And this is in a sense true: the drive for empire in the name of American exceptionalism has always prompted immigration, which in turn excited nativism because the presence of racialized others challenged what Americans believed made them exceptional.

"The fundamental question of our time is whether the West has the will to survive," Trump said in a 2017 speech in Warsaw, drawing a line from Poland's casting off of Soviet domination to present-day xenophobia. "Do we have the confidence in our values to defend them at any cost? Do we have enough respect for our citizens to protect our borders?

Do we have the desire and the courage to preserve our civilization in the face of those who would subvert and destroy it?"[151]

The battle for Laredo

The September 11 attacks and the official state violence of the global war on terror marked the beginning of the new nativism's final sequence, incorporating Islamophobia into a politics long defined by anti-Mexican racism. Initially, the attacks displaced anti-Mexican politics. Soon thereafter, however, immigration politics reemerged. Nativism was strengthened by national security state politics, and increasingly merged with it.

In 2004, Bush renewed the push for legalization that 9/11 had suddenly and emphatically deferred. Tellingly, Bush made his case in the language of security, contending that "illegal immigrants" posed a terrorist threat because their illegal status made their identity illegible to the security state. Bringing them out of the shadows, the argument went, would make them known and thus safe.[152]

The right reacted with fury. "People who are here illegally—they need to be deported," said Representative Tom Tancredo, the far-right House nativist leader. "People who hire them need to be fined. If they keep doing it, they need to be sent to jail."[153] John Kobylt, a host of *The John and Ken Show* on KFI-AM in Los Angeles, said that Bush's proposal had made immigration his callers' central focus. "That speech, where the president announced he was for amnesty, really set us off . . . Our listeners savaged their congressmen with calls and e-mails, and it was running 1,000 to 1 against Bush's proposal."[154]

Bush and other establishment politicians wanted a reform that included legal status for undocumented immigrants. But those efforts would repeatedly false-start and implode. In the meantime, establishment politicians called for increased enforcement. In August 2005, two Democratic border state governors, New Mexico's Bill Richardson and Arizona's Janet Napolitano, declared states of emergency to redirect more law enforcement to the border. Richardson called it "an act of desperation" that would be necessary "until Congress and the feds deal with this issue," a clear echo of Californians' arguments for Prop 187 a decade prior.[155]

Hillary Clinton, now a senator from New York, told an interviewer in 2003: "I am, you know, adamantly against illegal immigrants," lamenting the sight of day laborers waiting for work in the Bronx and Westchester. Conservative commentator and former Newt Gingrich press secretary Tony Blankley praised her rhetoric as "Pat Buchanan-esque."[156] "She's not a dumb woman," said a spokesperson for Tancredo. "She's got a great liberal base, and she realizes there's no better way to draw in more conservative voters. She has really come out to the forefront on that."[157]

In a 2004 presidential debate, moderator Bob Schieffer told Bush and Democratic nominee John Kerry that he had received "more email this week on" immigration "than any other question."[158] Recall that in 2000, not a single debate featured *any* discussion of immigration. Bush, who had just that year proposed a legalization program, attacked Kerry for backing "amnesty."[159] Kerry responded by falsely asserting that "the borders are more leaking [*sic*] today than they were before 9/11" and that "we now have people from the Middle East, allegedly, coming across the border." Bush, buoyed by conservative Christians and enjoying his last moments of wartime president luster, won reelection. And he won with a striking 44 percent of the Latino vote.[160]

Once again, the right exploited a moment of public fear to reset the parameters of the debate over immigration. Establishment politicians quickly acquiesced, supporting proposals to legalize undocumented immigrants and expand guest worker programs while churning out alarmist hyperbole about border security in an effort to win credibility. Predictably, those efforts not only failed, but further stoked nativist sentiment, degrading politicians' standing among the anti-immigrant voters whom they had hoped to appease. Buchanan, issuing a reluctant and late endorsement of Bush's reelection, presciently warned of a coming war between Republican leadership and the far right: "I think he better wake up to the immigration invasion. I think that neoconservatism is the Aryan heresy of the American right," Buchanan said. "It has led to massive deficits, an unwise and unnecessary war in Iraq, open borders and an invasion of this country by millions of illegal aliens this year and a trade policy that has cost us one in six manufacturing jobs in the last three years."[161]

In 2005, the undocumented population reached an estimated more than 11 million, and volunteer members of the

Minuteman campaign, a new anti-immigrant border militia, took the war to protect the homeland into their own hands.[162] California Republican governor Arnold Schwarzenegger, hailed as a "supermoderate" by the *New Yorker*, praised them.[163] "I think they've done a terrific job," said Schwarzenegger, an immigrant from Austria who relied on Prop 187 champion and former governor Pete Wilson for advice. "They've cut down the crossing of illegal immigrants a huge percentage. So it just shows that it works when you go and make an effort and when you work hard. It's a doable thing." He continued: "It's just that our federal government is not doing their job. It's a shame that the private citizen has to go in there and start patrolling our borders." Schwarzenegger had been watching Fox News and was upset to see "hundreds and hundreds of illegal immigrants coming across the border." Democratic senator Dianne Feinstein's bold liberal retort? She criticized the governor for "praising efforts by untrained volunteers to patrol the borders. The best course," she said, "would be to add an additional 2,000 border patrol agents."[164]

Mid-2000s nativism was still expressed mostly in anti-Mexican rather than Islamophobic terms, though Islamophobia, tapping into long-standing Orientalist stereotypes, played some role in nativism even before 9/11. Ahead of the 2000 election, FAIR accused Senator Spencer Abraham, a Republican immigration moderate of Lebanese descent, of "trying to make it easier for terrorists like Osama bin Laden to export their war of terror to any city street in America."[165] After Bush's reelection, anti-Muslim sentiment was still in large part mobilized behind the government's war on terror and had yet to fully emerge as an independent power on the right. But that was changing. The evolving character of nativism was perhaps best represented by Representative John Culberson, a Houston Republican, in an October 2005 "Border Security Alert."

"Al Qaeda terrorists and Chinese nationals are infiltrating our country virtually anywhere they choose from Brownsville to San Diego," he warned, and "a large number of Islamic individuals have moved into homes in [the Mexican border city of] Nuevo Laredo and are being taught Spanish to assimilate with the local culture." Fears of immigrants, old and new, were being remade into a total worldview with apocalyptic overtones. "Full scale war is underway on our southern border, and our entire way of life is at risk if we do not win the battle for Laredo."[166]

The right-wing populism pioneered by Buchanan in the 1990s, tying immigrants to a globalist economic threat, thrived too. Onetime business enthusiast Lou Dobbs in the early 2000s refashioned himself into a warrior for downtrodden Americans, using his popular CNN show to take simultaneous aim at greedy corporations and immigrants that were squeezing the everyday worker. Foreigners were threatening American jobs, he said, and may even be spreading frightening diseases like leprosy.[167] He even suggested that "the White House" was "using amnesty to create a North American union."[168]

"The invasion of illegal aliens is threatening the health of many Americans," said Dobbs, a proud populist who dined at the Four Seasons among the New York elite.[169] After September 11, he affixed an American flag pin to his lapel and never looked back, decrying corporations that sent jobs abroad and the immigrants who took them at home, the Dubai-based company seeking to take over American ports, and the injustice of convicting Border Patrol agents for shooting a pot smuggler dead.[170] He broadcast from FAIR's annual "Hold Their Feet to the Fire" anti-immigrant talk radio broadcast marathon and celebrated the valor of the Minutemen border vigilantes.[171]

Dobbs was the most high-profile anti-immigrant demagogue with a mainstream perch. By then, in the 2000s, a right-wing mediasphere, stitching AM talk radio, Fox News and the internet into a potent web of outrage and conspiracism, stoked fears over a changing nation and sowed distrust of any mainstream outlet that contradicted its doomsday message. CNN's embrace of Dobbs, controversial among journalists inside the company, reflected the right-wing's dominance of the airwaves and the mainstream's bid to catch up. Nativism sold.

Sensenbrenner

The resurgent post-9/11 nativism won a gigantic victory in December of 2005, when a harsh enforcement bill authored by Wisconsin Republican representative James Sensenbrenner passed the House, largely with Republican votes. The Border Protection, Antiterrorism, and Illegal Immigration Control Act of 2005, popularly known as the

"Sensenbrenner bill," proposed to criminalize both unauthorized presence in the country (then and now a civil offense) and the provision of assistance to undocumented immigrants.

Rights activists nationwide denounced the bill, a radical escalation in the war on immigrants. Millions filled the streets in a wave of historic demonstrations the following year, spurred on by unions, clergy and Spanish-language DJs. I helped organize demonstrations that year in Portland, Oregon. At the time, I was the coordinator of the Portland Central America Solidarity Committee, which had been formed in 1979 as the Portland Nicaragua Solidarity Committee to defend the Sandinista Revolution, and which fought against Reagan's dirty wars throughout the 1980s. We worked alongside Voz, a day laborer organizing group; Portland Jobs with Justice, a coalition of the city's progressive unions; the statewide immigrant rights group Causa; and many others.

From an organizer's perspective, it was unreal: the people arrived and it was our job to facilitate the sign-and-flag-waving masses. That year's protests included enormous May Day protests, including an estimated 500,000-plus in Los Angeles. That mass mobilization pointedly reclaimed May Day as a global day for working-class protest—in the country where late nineteenth-century labor activists had given birth to the holiday and where nationalist anti-communism had then scrubbed it from the calendar and replaced it with Loyalty Day. The action, "A Day without Immigrants," used a labor strike to assert that immigrants were at the core of the American working class and its struggle; it simultaneously mocked the fantasy of mass deportation by demonstrating precisely what the absence of immigrant labor would mean.[172]

The bill and the protests against it signaled a new era. On the right, business interests had long held sway, advocating for the admission of authorized immigrant workers and against interference with their employment of undocumented workers—even as they tolerated border militarization and demagoguery about immigrant criminality. Now, the Republican Party was clearly in thrall to right-wing nativists nakedly hostile to Mexicans and to Bush's efforts to legalize them. Among establishment liberals, the bill was too far to the right of the bipartisan anti-"illegal" consensus, anticipating a growing partisan polarization over the issue. On the left, the protests initiated the contemporary fight for immigrant rights as a mass movement.

The nativist movement's congressional efforts were matched by a flurry of state and local action. In 2003, Alabama, with Senator Jeff Sessions's help, had been the second state to sign a 287(g) agreement with the federal government, deputizing state troopers to detain undocumented immigrants under draconian legislation signed by President Clinton in 1996.[173] Soon thereafter, Hoover, a white-flight suburb of Birmingham, created a city "Department of Homeland Security and Immigration" as part of a crackdown on Latino day laborers.[174]

In 2004, Arizona voters approved Proposition 200, dubbed "Protect Arizona Now" in a clear echo of California's "Save Our State" Proposition 187. Like 187, it restricted access to public benefits and required state employees to report any unauthorized immigrant who dared apply. It also required that voters provide proof of citizenship to cast a ballot, which the Supreme Court later ruled could not be applied to federal elections.[175] In the following years, the conservative voter suppression and anti-immigrant movement would only continue to fuse and gain steam.

Other laws targeting unauthorized workers passed in Arizona, Utah, Colorado, and Georgia, while Alabama, Georgia, and South Carolina moved to bar unauthorized immigrants from public colleges and universities.[176]

In 2006, Hazleton, Pennsylvania, implemented a harsh local ordinance that served as a model for other jurisdictions nationwide, barring landlords from renting to undocumented immigrants.[177] It was based on a measure that nativists had failed to get on the ballot in San Bernardino, California. Though the Hazleton ordinance was ultimately struck down in court, the fight became a rallying point for the nationwide right and ultimately catapulted its mayor, Lou Barletta, into Congress. In Philadelphia, Joey Vento, the owner of the legendary Geno's cheesesteak shop, posted a sign reading, "*This Is* AMERICA: WHEN ORDERING, *Please* 'SPEAK ENGLISH'"—though Vento's grandfather, an immigrant from Sicily, struggled to do so.[178] Looking ahead to his presidential run, Massachusetts governor Mitt Romney signed a 287(g) agreement so that state troopers could enforce immigration law.[179] The next year, he cited that agreement in a campaign ad attacking John McCain.[180] In Danbury, Connecticut, the mayor requested that state troopers enforce immigration laws as local police cracked down on Ecuadorian immigrants' backyard volleyball games.[181]

"Immigration is now a national phenomenon in a way that was less true a decade ago," said Mark Krikorian, executive director for the Center for Immigration Studies, a core node in Tanton's nativist network. "In places like Georgia and Alabama, which had little experience with immigration before, people are experiencing it firsthand. Immigrants are working in chicken plants, carpet mills and construction. It's right in front of people's faces now."[182]

Ironically, writes sociologist Douglas Massey, it was border militarization that helped precipitate the geographic dispersal of Mexican immigration (away from the traditional receiving states of Texas, California, and Illinois) because it disrupted established migration routes. Between 1992 and 1998, the portion of unauthorized migrants heading to nontraditional destinations tripled, increasing from 15 to 45 percent, as they sought out jobs in industries like meatpacking, construction and poultry processing across the Northeast, Midwest and South.[183] But nativism is not bound by some law of nature to automatically emerge in response to immigrants' arrival. It was national media (conservative and otherwise) and bipartisan national politics that had made immigration a national problem.

Blowback

Six days after the 9/11 attacks and less than a month before he launched the first bombing runs over Afghanistan,

President Bush visited a mosque and said, "Islam is peace."[184] He insisted that "we don't fight a war against Islam or Muslims."[185] Just as overt racism had threatened Cold War foreign policy aims, overt Islamophobia would complicate a global war on terror that just happened to target Muslim-majority countries in the name of liberating them. "Instead of proclaiming a 'clash of civilizations'," Nikhil Pal Singh writes, "the administration defaulted to the vocabulary of cold war American universalism."[186] Bush's repeated insistence that the United States was not at war with Islam, however, suggested that many Americans thought just that. After all, the only thing that secularist-governed Iraq had in common with the 9/11 attackers or the Taliban was that a majority of Iraqis were Muslim. The war on terror, despite its pledge of altruistic democratization, identified external and internal enemies that were linked by Islam alone. Yet initially, Bush's framing held: the percentage of Americans with a favorable view of Muslim Americans significantly *increased* after the attacks, with Republican favorability surging from 35 to 64 percent in just eight months.[187]

As the terror war expanded while failing to secure victory, however, hostility toward Muslims rose, particularly among Republicans.[188] Hostility then reached a new peak during the 2008 presidential election, which featured a Democratic nominee named Barack Hussein Obama running in the midst of a Wall Street–driven economic meltdown. The crisis shook Americans' sense of security and their confidence in government. False rumors circulated online, including through a viral chain e-mail: Obama had attended a madrassa during his childhood years in Indonesia. Obama, maybe, was something other than what he seemed. Polls showed that 12 percent of Americans believed Obama was a Muslim, and the candidate went to great lengths to assure voters that he was not.[189] His campaign rejected an offer from Representative Keith Ellison, the first Muslim elected to Congress, to campaign on Obama's behalf, and Obama did not visit a single American mosque.[190] And though the campaign later apologized, many in metro Detroit, the heart of Muslim America, were insulted when campaign volunteers told two women in hijab that they could not stand behind the candidate during a rally at the Joe Louis Arena.[191]

Obama's campaign characterized the charge that he was a Muslim as a "smear."[192] His opponent, John McCain, did likewise. "No, ma'am," he replied when a woman at a Minnesota town hall accused Obama of being an Arab. "He's a decent family man, citizen, that I just happen to have disagreements with on fundamental issues, and that's what the campaign's all about. He's not."[193] The emphatic bipartisan refutations of the charge that Obama was a Muslim or an Arab, of course, were premised upon the notion that there was something very wrong with being a Muslim or Arab. And this conflation of Arab and Muslim identity—many Arabs are not Muslims and most Muslims are not Arab—played a key role in the racialization of Muslims.[194]

The rise of the Tea Party in 2010 accelerated Islamophobia's rise—and the portion of Americans who believed that Obama was a Muslim, which rose to 18 percent and almost a third of Republicans.[195] Like California's 1990s fiscal nativism, the Tea

Party was at its core a tax revolt; a movement against the redistribution of wealth to invading and dangerously fecund non-white people. This movement charged that Obama was among those foreign others, insisting that he was born outside the United States—making him, in essence, an immigrant illegally occupying the White House. In 2011, Fox News chief Roger Ailes provided Trump with a regular appearance on *Fox & Friends*.[196] He used his time to advance the "birther" conspiracy, becoming its most high-profile popularizer and the issue— merging anti-black racism, nativism, and Islamophobia— launched what would become his presidential bid.[197]

Protests against mosque construction sprang up from Tennessee to California. By 2011, nearly one-third of Americans believed that Muslims were intent on imposing Sharia law. Former representative Tom Tancredo proposed bombing the holy city of Mecca if "fundamentalist Muslims" used nuclear weapons on the United States. (In an attempt to explain himself, he added that "much more thought would need to be given to the potential ramifications."[198]) In 2010, Obama called off a planned visit to the Sikh Golden Temple in India, reportedly because of concerns that he would have to cover his head with a cloth to enter.[199]

But a novel polarization emerged on the ground: Republican hostility toward Muslims rose while Democratic hostility waned.[200] The two parties' social bases were radically diverging, and ordinary liberals recoiled as naked anti-Muslim politics became a conservative staple.

Arsons and bombings targeted mosques, and recorded hate crimes against perceived Muslims surged by 50 percent in 2010 alone.[201] In 2011, Representative Peter King held hearings on the "radicalization" of American Muslims.[202] Federal and local law enforcement's surveillance of Muslim communities reached scandalous proportions, including a vast NYPD spy operation that tragicomically extended to a group of Muslim college students on a whitewater-rafting trip.[203] Representative Michele Bachmann warned that American judges have "usurp[ed], and put Sharia law over the Constitution" and suggested that Huma Abedin, an aide to Secretary of State Clinton, had ties to the Muslim Brotherhood.[204]

Paradoxically, Bush had led what many considered to be a modern-day crusade but in doing so held the far right in check by simultaneously intensifying and sublimating its violence into state-sanctioned war and police repression. This is something that Obama was unable to do: as a black man with an Arabic middle name whose father was a Kenyan migrant from a Muslim family, Obama was suspect no matter how energetically he continued to wage the war on terror across the "Muslim world." As support for war was supplanted by mass cynicism, Islamophobia emerged as an unbridled force in domestic politics. The number of Americans who thought Obama was a Muslim only increased in the two years after his election, and the percentage of Republicans who said that Islam is more likely than other religions to encourage violence rose from 33 percent in 2002, to 62 percent in 2013, to 70 percent in 2016.[205]

Neoconservatives declared that they brought democracy and freedom to the "Muslim world." But the Bush administration sharply restricted the resettlement of Iraqis—including many who had at great risk worked for the American invaders—because resettling refugees would confirm that there was a refugee crisis and thus that the Iraq War had been a disaster. "Our obligation," said former Bush UN ambassador and militarist John Bolton, "was to give them new institutions and provide security. We have fulfilled that obligation. I don't think we have an obligation to compensate for the hardships of war."[206] After the end of the Vietnam War in 1975, by contrast, more than one million refugees and immigrants from Vietnam, Laos and Cambodia came to the United States.[207] In a never-ending war that could neither be decisively won nor lost, "compassionate conservatism" found its limits.

By the end of Bush's second term, the neoconservative dream had become a nightmare. Islamophobia, temporarily channeled into state violence in the wake of the attacks, escaped its prescribed bounds. It was no longer constrained by the ostensible tolerance and high purpose that had served an interventionist foreign policy regime until that regime had hopelessly discredited itself. It was this second wave of post-9/11 Islamophobia—the proximate consequence not of the September 11 attacks but rather of the war on terror expanding even as it sank into quagmire and disrepute—that helped catapult Trump into office.

In the early 1990s, US victory in the Cold War undermined the moral purpose that had united a bipartisan political establishment behind NATO and the US-led international security regime, opening space for isolationists on the far right like Pat Buchanan to emerge. After September 11, neoconservatives used Bush's "Freedom Agenda" to revivify American purpose in the world: an exceptional nation's zealous drive to deliver democracy to a backward Orient. In the absence of a strong anti-war movement—what existed had fizzled by 2006—disillusionment with war caused people to blame Islam rather than imperialism. In 2003, 75 percent of Americans supported the war in Iraq. In April 2008, just 36 percent did.[208] The failure to win the war was recast as Muslims refusing the priceless gift of freely offered American blood and treasure. The United States was no longer seen as fighting a war for Iraqi liberation but rather a civilizational struggle against Islam. Just as they did after Vietnam, conservatives blamed defeat on liberal betrayal. The empire's battlefield failure required scapegoats.

Bring the war home

"Donald J. Trump is calling for a complete and total shutdown of Muslims entering the United States until our country's representatives can figure out what the hell is going on," Trump told supporters at a December 2015 rally. The war on terror had been sold on idealism. Its glaring failure bred a deep pessimism and even nihilism, which abetted both opposition to foreign military entanglements and hostility toward foreign-born people.

Under Obama, the war on terror continued to spiral into a growing set of global conflicts. In 2014, the Islamic State of Iraq and Syria, or ISIS, seized full control of the Syrian city of Raqqa, then took Mosul in Iraq, and proclaimed an Islamic caliphate, disregarding the national borders that World War I's European victors had imposed on a defeated Ottoman Empire.[209] Thanks to the war on terror, what had been a relatively small and dispersed cohort of militant Islamists was thirteen years later a spectacularly violent and thoroughly mediatized state, governing millions of people and providing a framework to violently connect local grievances from Brussels to Baghdad.[210]

As of early 2015, the war on terror had killed an estimated minimum of 1.3 million people in Iraq, Afghanistan, and Pakistan.[211] More salient for most Americans were the thousands of US troops dead, the trillions of dollars spent, and the Muslim world's perceived lack of gratitude for American sacrifice.[212] After the invasion, Bush had repeatedly told Coalition Provisional Authority head Paul Bremer that Iraq's new leader should be "someone who's willing to stand up and thank the American people for their sacrifice in liberating Iraq."[213] As his time in office drew to a close, Bush ruminated upon American disaffection with his war. "That's the problem here in America. They wonder whether or not there is a gratitude level that's significant enough in Iraq."[214]

Gratitude, of course, was not what most Iraqis felt. It was this violently narcissistic amnesia that made it possible for Trump vice-presidential nominee Mike Pence to charge in 2016 that it was Obama's troop drawdown in Iraq that allowed ISIS to be "literally conjured up out of the desert," portraying the president as some sort of genie.[215] And it was what allowed Trump to declare that Obama had founded ISIS.

Literally. "No, I meant he's the founder of ISIS," Trump said, when an interviewer assumed he had meant it metaphorically. "I do. He was the most valuable player. I give him the most valuable player award. I give her, too, by the way, Hillary Clinton."[216]

In 2015, a series of spectacular attacks resulted in the massacre of staff at the offices of the French magazine *Charlie Hebdo*, and later of scores of civilians at multiple sites across Paris. (The *Charlie Hebdo* attack was claimed by al-Qaeda in the Arabian Peninsula and the subsequent attacks were claimed by ISIS.) After the *Hebdo* attack, Trump and others on the right fixated on Obama's refusal to say the words "radical Islamic terrorism," terminology that he believed counterproductively antagonized ordinary Muslims.[217] Obama's diplomatic language, critics believed, was a sign of politically correct cowardice—or even complicity. For many Americans, the origins of the war on terror and Islamist militancy remained hazy, buried amid the World Trade Center's rubble. Osama bin Laden's actual 1996 declaration of war or his 2002 letter to the American people, which exhaustively detailed grievances against US imperialism, was rarely reported or read and remained largely unknown.[218] What many did know was that Americans had sacrificed "blood and treasure" for Muslims who wanted to kill them—and liberals like Obama bafflingly refused to acknowledge that reality and act upon it. By 2016, Americans believed that 17 percent of people in the United States were Muslims, when in fact they numbered just 1 percent.[219]

"I think Islam hates us," Trump said in 2016, speaking to the popular amnesia.[220] What's most new about Trump isn't that the federal government is perpetuating Islamophobia but rather that it is doing so in nakedly racist terms rather than in the lofty rhetoric of global policing and democracy promotion. "Islamophobia is," as Khaled Beydoun writes, "a systemic, fluid, and deeply politicized dialectic between the state and its polity: a dialectic whereby the former shapes, reshapes, and confirms popular views or attitudes about Islam and Muslim subjects inside and outside of America's borders."[221] Trump made the official and popular versions of Islamophobia one and the same.

Trump's zero-sum vision of global affairs prevailed because foreign policy mandarins' grand strategies proved disastrous on their own terms. "I've always said—shouldn't be there, but if we're going to get out, take the oil," said Trump in September 2016.[222] The gaping chasm between neoconservative promise and reality nurtured a pervasive cynicism about foreign military interventions and foreign-born people alike. The economic crisis and the government's Wall Street–coddling response compounded the sense that government was not protecting "our people."

Trump's America First foreign and immigration policy promised to make a white America secure against both domestic invasion and foreign entanglement yet strong enough to take on the world economically and militarily. But it was Trump's predecessors who primed Americans to believe that the nation was under siege from Muslims and Latinos. To many, Trump's extremist politics seemed like solutions to the very "problems" that the establishment had for decades made a reality. Trump exploited Latino and terrorist threats created by others, further merging them into a unitary menace.

Exporting violence

In April 2017, Attorney General Sessions made a stop on his immigrants-are-killing-Americans tour in Long Island to present the Trump administration's case that open borders had abetted the rise of the gang Mara Salvatrucha, or MS-13, members of which were charged with brutal murders in the area.[223] He declared that "transnational criminal organizations ... enrich themselves by pedaling poison in our communities, trafficking children for sexual exploitation and inflicting horrific violence." The solution? "Securing our border and restoring a lawful system of immigration."[224]

After taking office, Trump falsely proclaimed that his government was "actually liberating towns" from MS-13 and that he had deported half of the gang's US-based membership.[225] He blamed "weak illegal immigration policies" under Obama for allowing the gang to spread, calling it "a serious problem" that "we never did anything about."[226] But Obama and Trump's immigration policies were more alike than either of their supporters might understand. Obama had called for the deportation of "felons, not families" and claimed to target "violent offenders and people convicted of crimes," all while deporting hundreds of thousands each year.[227] Obama unsurprisingly gave the impression that huge numbers of immigrants were indeed criminals and posed a unique security threat. His policies helped Trump make sense.

For Trump, MS-13 had become an obsession ever since he came across a story about the gang in *Newsday* in November 2016: "'EXTREMELY VIOLENT' GANG FACTION" blared the headline he brandished in front of the writer composing his *Time* Person of the Year profile.[228] "They're coming from Central America. They're tougher than any people you've ever met," Trump said. "They're killing and raping everybody out there. They're illegal. And they are finished."[229] For Trump's purposes, MS-13 was a Latin American ISIS.

The origins of MS-13, however, are in the United States: the gang was formed in Los Angeles among refugees from Reagan's dirty war in El Salvador. Only after gang members were deported back to El Salvador as part of the bipartisan crackdown on "criminal aliens" did MS-13 and other gangs take root in Central America, where they rapidly created a new social order atop societies wrecked by conflict and underdevelopment. The violence and government repression unleashed a new movement of refugees heading north. The United States, twice over, created MS-13—and then an influx of refugees to be demonized by Trump. Reagan's dirty wars had not only defeated the left across Central America but laid the groundwork for reactionary security politics well into the future.

The tragic upshot is that, thanks to flashy headlines about international gang violence, many are primed to support the same sort of policies that created this spiraling crisis in the first place: those of deporting Central Americans, refugees and alleged gang members alike, while funding the law-and-order crackdowns and promoting the business-friendly economic reforms in the region that only make things worse.[230] The United States is not importing problems from Central America. Rather, it is *exporting* violence, time and again, to Central America.

It's part and parcel of the larger mystifications that under-gird US nativism in general: that we can have violent military interventions without the people touched by the violence ever making their way to this country; and that we can maintain an incredibly unequal global economic order without seeing labor moving to the places where it is demanded. Despite establishment professions of innocence, it was a promised salve to these contradictions that made Trump's Fortress America so appealing to so many.

4

REACTION

Felons, not families. Criminals, not children. Gang members, not a mom who's working hard to provide for her kids. We'll prioritize, just like law enforcement does every day.
—President Barack Obama, November 20, 2014.[1]

On December 12, 2006, the Bush administration orchestrated the largest workplace raid in US history,[2] rounding up nearly 1,300 immigrants at Swift and Company meatpacking plants in six states.[3] The government prosecuted and sentenced many to federal prison for identity theft; as unauthorized immigrants often must, they had to use fraudulent Social Security numbers to secure employment.

A year prior, the House passed Representative Sensenbrenner's bill to criminalize the very presence of undocumented immigrants and anyone who might "assist" them, sparking historic protests. It was never addressed in the Senate, and the Senate's comprehensive immigration reform (CIR) bill was never taken up in the House.[4] The Sensenbrenner bill was too extreme. Like Prop 187, it marked a fracture in the bipartisan consensus behind the war on "illegal immigrants." It also signaled that politics had changed in a way that establishment reformers have disastrously failed to understand ever since: conservatives in Congress had become radicalized nativists who would *never* vote to support "comprehensive immigration reform." CIR was meant to include measures to please all: "a path to citizenship," border militarization, and a guest worker program. But for much of the Republican Party it was simply "amnesty": the mass pardoning of criminals. No concession would do.

Perversely, Bush's crackdown aimed to convince legislators like Sensenbrenner to support CIR. It was common sense because most everyone in Washington save for the nativist right believed that it was the exclusive and pragmatic way that the immigration "problem" would be "solved." "I've made no secret about the fact we need a comprehensive program," said DHS secretary Michael Chertoff at the time.[5] An enforcement crackdown "clarifies the choices we have . . . The choices are clear, and the consequences of the choices are clear." The Bush administration was using undocumented workers as leverage to win CIR, treating them like hostages. It was a doomed strategy; the right wing he needed to convince were happy to see the hostages shot.

The widely shared belief was that CIR's three-legged stool could win the necessary bipartisan consensus between various interests. It followed the model set out by the Immigration Reform and Control Act of 1986 (IRCA), the historic legislation signed into law by Reagan. In principle, CIR was supported by a broad consensus of Democrats, establishment

Republicans, and business, labor, and DC-based immigration reform groups. There was disagreement on specifics, including between unions and business on guest worker programs. These were the sorts of differences, however, that had for decades been overcome through ordinary bipartisan negotiation: crafting bills that reflected a coalition of divergent interests to win broad bipartisan support from legislators who represented those interests.

But the enterprise was premised on a failure of or resistance to understanding. The right-wing radicalization of the Republican Party was changing politics in part because vitriolic opposition to immigration was changing the Republican Party. Even though Reagan and Republicans of the Gingrich Revolution were radicals, they were radicals who governed on behalf of the institutionalized power of business and the wealthy. And still, many establishment Republicans, albeit with increasing timidity, continued to support CIR, first under Bush and then under Obama. They did so for different reasons: on economic grounds, out of religious principle, or to win over Latino voters. But the extremist politics that allowed Republicans to maintain a mass base had also nurtured a more hardline nativism, which refused to do the new Republican establishment's bidding. The populist right did not care, in other words, that Grover Norquist or the US Chamber of Commerce wanted CIR.

When right-wing members joined the left to shoot down the first attempt at a bank bailout in September 2008, it shocked observers (and global markets).[6] People were shocked again when the Tea Party took over

Republican politics in 2010. And again when Trump was elected. But they shouldn't have been. The successful right-wing Republican campaigns to defeat "amnesty" throughout the Bush administration were the early but often ignored evidence that the populist right was immovably opposed to bipartisan compromise. The system was undergoing what political scientists call "asymmetric polarization," but the center didn't realize it. Bush's experience with CIR should have made it clear that the old rules were no longer in place. One of Obama's greatest failings—on immigration and more generally—was that he refused to recognize this reality even as it became abundantly clear. Indeed, it was this failure to understand the significance of right-wing defeats of "amnesty" that helped make a Trump victory seem impossible until the moment that he won.

Bush and then Obama tried to pass CIR through Congress, only to be repeatedly frustrated by the nativist right. From the vantage point of Trump's presidency, the two are often remembered as pro-immigration moderates. But that conventional story line is an *ex post facto* distortion. It elides both presidents' roles in dramatically escalating the persecution of undocumented immigrants and militarizing the border— and, in doing so, facilitating radicalization on the right. During the CIR years, the establishment helped shift immigration politics to the hard right, just as Republicans and New Democrats had done throughout the 1990s. Establishment politicians didn't just offer to trade enforcement for legalization; Bush and Obama repeatedly pursued stand-alone enforcement measures as a goodwill gesture to win support for a CIR that would never come.

The year 2005 marked the beginning of a decade-long fight between the establishment and the nativist right that culminated in Trump's election.

Incomprehensible reform

After the Sensenbrenner bill's 2005 passage and amid the 2006 mass protest movement against it, the Senate considered a CIR bill. Bush used a primetime television address to bolster the effort, announcing the deployment of thousands of National Guard troops to the border as a stopgap measure until he could increase the size of the Border Patrol. "We do not yet have full control of the border, and I am determined to change that," he declared.[7]

Bush had made similar pledges and ratified the notion that the border was out of control before. On March 29, 2005, the administration announced that it would send five hundred additional Border Patrol agents to Arizona.[8] The announcement took place just three days before the Minuteman Project vigilante group was set to begin a mass citizens' patrol of the state's border with Mexico. "President Bush called the Minuteman Project a bunch of vigilantes—but if it's the case that this did start because of the Minuteman Project, then the project is a success," said Minuteman spokesperson Bill Bennett.[9] Later that year, Minuteman activists selected Houston[10] and Herndon, Virginia,[11] as sites for the launch of Operation Spotlight to target day laborers—among the most visible and marginalized undocumented immigrants and the subject of increasing persecution nationwide.

Border militarization created the Minutemen. It pushed migration routes away from California and into Arizona; this created a spectacle of lawlessness that was consistently amplified by political leaders pledging to secure an out-of-control border. And it was also yet another instance of blowback from the nation's never-ending wars, a cycle of foreign intervention and domestic radicalization dramatically escalated by Bush's terror war. Many Minutemen were Vietnam and Iraq vets, retired white men continuing a long war.[12] "I don't want this country to end up like they did, dead on that battlefield," said Minuteman Project founder Jim Gilchrist. "Too many immigrants will divide our country. We are not going to have a civil war now, but we could."[13]

It was, more basically, a chance to make the country great again by redeeming a lost war. "This gives me the opportunity to get the 1945 homecoming that I didn't get in 1968," said one Minuteman leader who lost his left eye in Vietnam. "In my hometown, people are very, very supportive. They tell me 'Good job. Way to go!'" Vets were, he said, "trying to rectify what had become a love-hate relationship with the country."[14]

Representative J. D. Hayworth, a right-wing Arizona Republican, said that the mobilization demonstrated that "the federal government can do something about illegal immigration other than to raise a white flag and surrender to the invasion on our Southern border."[15] But Bush was not surrendering at all; instead, he was waging a war of a far larger magnitude. In October 2006, he signed the Secure Fence Act, winning votes from many establishment Democrats. The law led to the construction of hundreds of miles of border fencing—and gave incumbents a border security victory to campaign on in the midterms. Meanwhile, the administration implemented Operation Streamline, facilitating the criminal prosecution and deportation of migrants who had illegally entered the country. Customs and Border Protection increasingly utilized a provision called "expedited removal," which made it easier to deport recently arrived migrants by limiting judicial review. It had been authorized by Clinton's Illegal Immigration Reform and Immigrant Responsibility Act of 1996 (IIRIRA) but used only in a limited fashion in the past.[16] ICE initiated its campaign of jobsite raids, causing the number of workplace criminal and civil arrests to surge from fiscal years 2006 through 2008.[17] ICE also launched Operation Return to Sender, a crackdown resulting in nearly nineteen thousand ICE arrests in under one year's time.[18]

In a 2016 interview, Chertoff confirmed to me that DHS intended the workplace raids "to establish credibility with respect to enforcement, which would then enable reforms in a more comprehensive way." When that effort fell apart in 2006 and again in 2007, the crackdown continued. "It was pretty clear there wasn't going to be legislation, but we still felt it was important to establish that, one way or the other, the government was going to apply the law," said Chertoff. "And we're not going to back down on enforcement. Because there had been a sense that somehow enforcement in the past had been relaxed because of political pressure."

What Chertoff refers to as "a sense that somehow" is in effect what the theorist Antonio Gramsci called hegemony: border militarization politics had made it the conventional wisdom that the border was "insecure." As linguist George Lakoff and Sam Ferguson write, this fueled the anti-immigrant politics that border militarization was intended to tame. The narrow framing of the "immigration" debate "has shaped its politics, defining what count as 'problems' and constraining the debate to a narrow set of issues . . . and hence constrains the solutions needed to address that problem." Politicians and the media define the "problem" of "illegal immigration" by "the illegal act of crossing the border without papers," and so "the logical response to the 'wave' of 'illegal immigration' becomes 'border security.'"[19] The framing had deep roots in the early days of immigration restriction. Beginning with the Dillingham Commission, policy-makers had represented immigration as a "problem" to which the federal government could provide a "solution."[20] This technocratic approach, however, couldn't function within the new nativist politics that exploded in the 1990s and then, in the early twenty-first century, took over the Republican Party.

This is the Alamo

In November 2006, Democrats tapping into a backlash against Bush and the war on Iraq won back the House. Yet immigration permeated the campaign. Republicans emphasized anti-immigrant themes to drive the base to the polls.[21]

Democrats often responded by trying to outflank them. Indeed, Illinois representative Rahm Emanuel, the chair of the Democratic Congressional Campaign Committee and former Clinton advisor, encouraged right-leaning Democrats to back the Sensenbrenner bill to, in *The Intercept*'s words, "burnish their conservative credentials."[22]

Jim Kessler, vice president for policy at the Clintonite group Third Way, urged Democrats to attack Republicans for being weak on illegal immigration.[23] The plan was embraced by Emanuel and New York senator Chuck Schumer, his counterpart at the Democratic Senatorial Campaign Committee. In Arizona, Democrat Harry Mitchell ousted J. D. Hayworth, one of the most hard-line xenophobes in Congress. Mitchell's campaign focused on corruption, but it also made a point of holding Hayworth responsible for border insecurity. One ad for Mitchell declared: "The number of illegal immigrants in our state has increased 400 percent during his tenure in Congress."[24] This approach was typical for purple-seat Democrats.

North Carolina Democrat and former NFL player Heath Shuler and Nebraska Democratic senator Ben Nelson both ran ads decrying "amnesty." In Tennessee's Senate race, Democratic representative Harold Ford Jr. declared in a debate, "I'm the only person on this stage who has ever voted for an anti-illegal-immigration bill, matter of fact the strongest in the country."[25]

In June 2007, another Bush-backed reform bill spectacularly failed in the Senate after pro-labor Democrats critical of guest worker programs (SEIU supported the bill but the

AFL-CIO opposed it)[26] and conservative Democrats joined most Republicans in opposition. Nearly two decades of establishment pledges to lock down the border had enabled the right to insist that they follow through. Pairing legalization with harsh enforcement measures was unacceptable. Only enforcement would do. "The message is crystal-clear," said Louisiana Republican senator David Vitter. "The American people want us to start with enforcement at the border and at the workplace and don't want promises. They want action, they want results, they want proof, because they've heard all the promises before."[27]

Alabama Republican senator Jeff Sessions accused reformers of having tried to pass the bill "before Rush Limbaugh could tell the American people what was in it."[28] But "tell the American people" is precisely what talk radio did. "We're not giving away the sovereignty of America," Michael Savage told listeners, "This is the Alamo right now!"[29] Limbaugh, Sean Hannity and Savage, along with Dobbs on CNN and Bill O'Reilly on Fox News, rallied the faithful.[30] Dozens of talk radio hosts gathered in Washington for a broadcast marathon against "amnesty" organized by John Tanton's FAIR.[31]

At one point in 2007, according to a Pew Research Center study, immigration became the most discussed story on talk radio.[32] "See, we don't live in Africa where people settle arguments with machetes," Savage railed in response to a presumably African caller who had criticized his ignorance of Africa. "Couldn't use the machete so his mind went blank . . . There's multiculturalism for you. There's immigration for you. There's the new America for you. Bring them in by the millions. Bring in 10 million more from Africa. Bring them in with AIDS. Show how multicultural you are. They can't reason, but bring them in with a machete in their head. Go ahead. Bring them in with machetes in their mind."[33]

CIR was dead for the remainder of the Bush administration. But the crackdown, ostensibly a means to an end, had taken on a life of its own. On May 12, 2008, ICE raided Agriprocessors, a kosher meatpacking plant in Postville, Iowa, detaining 389 workers in one of the largest workplace raids ever. Hundreds were sentenced in makeshift courtrooms set up at nearby Waterloo's National Cattle Congress fairgrounds in what the ACLU called a "guilty-plea machine."[34] Two hundred ninety-seven served five-month prison sentences before deportation.[35]

Making Arpaio

Facing repeated defeats at the hands of the right, Bush empowered state and local law enforcement to play a growing role in immigrantion enforcement. In 2007, ICE signed twenty-seven new 287(g) agreements, deputizing local law enforcement and jails to identify and detain undocumented immigrants. The agency signed twenty-eight more in 2008. The statute was part of Clinton's 1996 IIRIRA law but was first employed in 2002 as an anti-terrorism measure.[36] Instead of defusing nativism, Bush's move increased its local salience—including in Arizona, which had become for anti-immigrant politics what California was in the 1990s.

ICE signed an agreement with Democratic governor Janet Napolitano's Department of Public Safety and one with the Maricopa County Sheriff's Office. The sheriff was Joe Arpaio, notorious for running an abusive desert jail camp, arresting critical journalists, persecuting political enemies, investigating Obama's place of birth and, of course, for using his deputies to hunt down undocumented immigrants across greater Phoenix.[37] "Let them go to California," he swaggered, echoing the right-wing belief that an increasingly liberal and Latino California was an object lesson in what happens when borders fail.[38]

Arpaio had made harsh, brazenly racist immigration enforcement his calling card, which in turn made him a right-wing folk hero. But until the mid-2000s, Arpaio, a former DEA agent, hadn't evinced much interest in the subject and was seemingly content to revel in the media attention paid to his chain gangs and Tent City jail, where prisoners were issued pink underwear, fed bologna, and suffered rampant violence.[39]

Remarkably, it was Governor Napolitano who helped make Arpaio.[40] During her time as US attorney in the mid-1990s, Napolitano protected Arpaio from a Justice Department investigation into abuse at his Tent City jail. In 1995, she emphasized that the investigation should not be construed as reflecting poorly on Arpaio, who was providing her with his "complete cooperation." "We run a strict jail but a safe jail, and I haven't heard from anyone who thinks that this is a bad thing," she said.[41] In 1997, Napolitano declined to file civil rights charges against Arpaio. Standing alongside the sheriff, she announced that the lawsuit, which she called a "technicality," had been settled with what she called "lawyerly paperwork." "Nothing changes," Arpaio assured the public.[42] When Napolitano ran for governor in 2002, he returned the favor by recording a campaign ad declaring her "the Number One prosecutor of child molesters in the nation." It may have proved decisive in an election she won by fewer than twelve thousand votes—an election in which Arpaio had considered running as a Republican.[43]

After taking office, Napolitano mostly looked the other way as complaints of Arpaio's abusive and racist practices mushroomed and as the sheriff turned to a more explicitly anti-immigrant agenda.[44] The turning point was 2005, when army reservist Patrick Haab held up a group of men he thought were undocumented at gunpoint in a self-styled citizen's arrest.[45] Arpaio's deputies arrested Haab and the immigrants were taken into custody by Border Patrol.[46]

"You don't go around pulling guns on people," said Arpaio, not yet alert to the power of right-wing anti-immigrant sentiment. "Being illegal is not a serious crime. You can't go to jail for being an illegal alien . . . You can only be deported." But Maricopa County Attorney Andrew Thomas, who had run for office with signs blaring "STOP ILLEGAL IMMIGRATION!," refused to press charges against Haab, who had become a folk hero.[47] Arpaio took notice, recrafting his publicity-driven, law-and-order sadism to fit the prevailing mood. "You could almost see a light bulb go off as Arpaio watched the positive reaction from the public," said Paul K.

Charlton, who was US attorney for Arizona at the time. "From that point on, we lost him."[48]

But the feds hadn't lost Arpaio at all. In October 2007, he claimed that deputies trained to enforce immigration law under his newly signed 287(g) agreement had arrested 349 undocumented immigrants. Those swept up in Arpaio's crackdown included at least forty-nine day laborers and corn vendors.[49] "Ours is an operation where we want to go after illegals, not the crime first," said Arpaio. The Bush administration had no problem with that. "I saw nothing that gave me heartburn," said ICE Office of State and Local Coordination head Jim Pendergraph, as Arpaio's deputies and posse members swept through Hispanic neighborhoods. Pendergraph, who signed his own 287(g) agreement during his time as sheriff in Mecklenburg County, North Carolina, wasn't an unbiased observer. Touting the program at a law enforcement gathering, he declared: "If you don't have enough evidence to charge someone criminally but you think he's illegal, we can make him disappear."[50] By 2010, Arpaio's office had held more people on ICE detainers than any other 287(g) jurisdiction, a full 16 percent of the nationwide total.[51]

Napolitano bolstered Arpaio in other, little-noticed ways. In 2005, she wrote a letter to DHS secretary Chertoff laying out her plan to have state police work with Border Patrol to identify undocumented immigrants, including those identified during "routine traffic or other law enforcement activities," to be jailed by Arpaio.[52] Then, in 2006, facing a reelection campaign that would feature Republican attacks that she was weak on "illegal immigration," she and Arpaio co-authored a letter to Chertoff complaining that ICE's outgoing Special Agent in Charge in Phoenix had shown "hostility to state and local law enforcement." In particular, they charged that "ICE cooperation has been so lacking that the agency even has refused to pick up and deport undocumented immigrants who have been convicted under Arizona's human smuggling statute."[53] Already, Arpaio was being widely criticized for using that state law (signed by Napolitano)[54] to arrest and charge the clients of those "smugglers": ordinary undocumented migrants.[55]

Secure Communities

In 2008, Barack Obama defeated John McCain, who had tried to win right-wing support by backing away from the kind of reform legislation that had once borne his name. Business conservatives increasingly shied away from "amnesty." It fell to Obama to adopt Bush's mantle—and, along with it, the principle that harsh enforcement was the prerequisite for securing CIR. It's also possible, however, that Obama knew CIR might not pass and simply thought that simultaneously enacting tough enforcement while calling for legalization was good politics.

In 2009, Napolitano moved to Washington to take over at Obama's DHS. As governor, she had vetoed the most extreme anti-immigrant legislation.[56] But by voluntarily vacating the office, she recklessly turned over unified control of Arizona government to Republican Jan Brewer and right-wing colleagues like former Arpaio chief deputy and state senator Russell Pearce, ensuring that such legislation would become law.[57] Immediately, the Obama administration distanced themselves from Arpaio. In March, the Justice Department announced that it was investigating the Sheriff's Office. In October, DHS terminated Maricopa County's "task force" 287(g) agreement that allowed deputies in the field to enforce immigration law, drawing complaints from Arizona senators McCain and Jon Kyl.[58] DHS, however, left in place the consequential authority to enforce immigration law at Arpaio's jails.[59]

In November 2009, Napolitano gave her first major immigration speech at the Center for American Progress (CAP), the center-left Washington think tank tethered to the Obama White House. She declared that reform "begins with fair, reliable enforcement." IRCA had been a failure, she argued, because it was "one-sided reform" that never led to the promised enforcement, which "helped lead to our current situation, and it undermined Americans' confidence in the government's approach to this issue." Indeed, she said that CIR had collapsed in 2007 because of "the real concern of many Americans that the government was not really serious about enforcing the law." The dramatic increase in enforcement since, by contrast, "makes reform far more attainable this time around."[60]

In her speech, Napolitano touted 287(g) agreements like the ones that her Arizona Department of Public Safety and Arpaio had signed as "effective force multipliers in our efforts to apprehend dangerous criminal aliens." She also lauded a program called Secure Communities, which changed immigration politics and policy forever. Initiated under Bush during his final months in office, it revolutionized enforcement by merging a DHS biometric database with an FBI database of fingerprints entered by law enforcement after an arrest. Now, every local police department booking a suspect into custody was a proxy ICE force ascertaining their immigration status. The program had in its first year of operation "identified more than 111,000 criminal aliens," she said. Touting her experience in Arizona, she praised Bush's militarization. "Border Patrol has increased its forces to more than 20,000 officers, and DHS has built more than 600 miles of border fencing. Both of these milestones demonstrate that we have gotten Congress' message."

CAP, which would play a key role in CIR efforts under Obama, loved it. Founder and president John Podesta, Clinton's former chief of staff, called CIR "a pragmatic solution that recognizes the impracticalities of driving a large number of people from the United States."[61] CAP's lead on the issue, National Immigration Forum veteran Angela Kelley, declared that "DHS has driven the issue to the threshold of Congress' door. Congress must open the door and we all must join together to pass legislation that restores our identity as a nation of immigrants and a nation of laws."[62] Polling had led CAP and other Democrats to conclude that reformers must refer to "illegal immigrants" whom CIR would force to "obey our laws, learn our language and pay our taxes."[63]

But National Day Laborer Organizing Network (NDLON) legal director Chris Newman was listening to the speech, and it didn't make sense. Secure Communities identifies undocumented immigrants at the point of arrest, not conviction. It couldn't have identified that many "criminal aliens" in a year. In response, NDLON launched an investigation of the program, which had quite suddenly become the centerpiece of federal immigration enforcement.

Secure Communities plugged federal immigration enforcement into the core of the state and local law enforcement information network. ICE received a flood of positive identifications on deportable immigrants; if ICE wanted them in custody, they would issue a "detainer," or request that police hold a suspect until ICE could pick them up. It was embraced as a subtle, targeted, and cost-effective force multiplier. Secure Communities also seemed to promise better public relations, targeting "dangerous criminal aliens" instead of sympathetic low-wage workers.[64] And unlike the 287(g) program, which deputized local law enforcement to directly enforce immigration law, it wouldn't involve signing deals with controversial figures like Arpaio.

In reality, Secure Communities targeted a broad swath of migrants by creating an unprecedented, computerized deportation machinery linking local police to ICE. "The scale in just the number of people who were being checked against these databases increased tremendously," Faye Hipsman, then a Migration Policy Institute analyst, told me. "It became essentially the main pipeline . . . into the deportation process." And the number of deportations exploded, even though unauthorized immigration had already plummeted after 2007 with the onset of the devastating recession.[65]

Secure Communities was the culmination of a decades-long process of linking civil immigration and criminal law enforcement, and framing immigration as fundamentally about crime. The program's dragnet was remarkably wide, identifying immigrants everywhere at the point of arrest—which, in a country that arrests so many people, included a massive and diverse set of immigrants. It soon became clear that many of those being deported had either no criminal record or had been convicted of only minor crimes.[66]

In 1994, California governor Pete Wilson campaigned against "illegal immigration" by contrasting it with immigrants who come the "right way." In 1996, Clinton had signed IIRIRA, targeting "illegal immigrants" and "criminal aliens," while a bill to cut legal immigration was scuttled. Establishment reformers did the same, emphasizing "this good immigrant, bad immigrant binary," immigration law scholar César Cuauhtémoc García Hernández told me, and were "repeatedly willing to sacrifice the so-called criminal aliens in order to move the CIR ball forward."[67] Obama's stated plan was the same as Bush's: tough enforcement to win CIR.[68] Protecting some immigrants by demonizing others, however, is a strategy that sows the seeds of its own opposition. Praising *good immigrants* for restoring America, as political theorist Bonnie Honig writes, also suggests its opposite: the specter of the *bad immigrant* who will do us harm.[69]

Raising Arizona

By the late 1990s, the immigration wars had waned in California. At the border near San Diego, once-ubiquitous and highly visible illegal crossings had fallen in response to

rising militarization. The migrants, however, did not disappear: they were pushed east into the Arizona desert. In 1991,
just over half of Border Patrol apprehensions in the Southwest
took place in the San Diego sector. In 2000, only 9 percent
did; 36 percent were made in the Tucson sector, an area
stretching 262 miles from Yuma County to the New Mexico
state line.[70]

Crossing into Arizona, migrants had to traverse lethal
desert conditions. They also walked into a state that, unlike
California, remained majority white. That was in part thanks
to a migrant influx of a different sort: people from across the
United States—including from places like Joe Arpaio's
native Massachusetts—flooded into the state's cheap and
sun-soaked exurban developments, many of them retirees.[71]
Americans riding the easy-credit housing boom migrated
from the Northeast and Midwest, and also from California,
whence an estimated more than 186,000 arrived between 1995
and 2000 alone.[72] Many moved to Maricopa County, which
had among the largest net gain of elderly people of any
county nationwide.[73]

The California exodus included Voice of Citizens
Together/American Patrol founder Glenn Spencer, a far-
right, Tanton-funded Proposition 187 activist;[74] and Chris
Simcox, who would go on to found the Minuteman Civil
Defense Corps, an outgrowth of the 2005 Minuteman Project
border mobilization.[75] Many Californians were likely fleeing
high housing prices and in search of a low-tax haven.[76]
Spencer moved because his state had lost what he called a
"demographic war" to Mexico.[77] "California has been

destroyed by illegal immigration," Spencer wrote in 2003. "Americans, especially white Americans, should get out of California—now, before it is too late to salvage the equity they have in their homes and the value of their businesses."[78]

In 1998, California voters had passed Proposition 227, restricting bilingual instruction in public schools.[79] But it was the movement's last gasp in a state that was shifting decisively left. For people like Spencer, the white supremacist Golden State dream was over. Arizona, then, was the state to secure the conquest of 1848, a last stand for an Anglo and English-speaking Southwest. "I moved from Los Angeles because of illegal immigration," said a Scottsdale woman in 2004. "Now the problems are following us to Arizona."[80]

Arpaio's Arizona passed a raft of anti-immigrant bills in the 2000s. Proposition 200, passed in 2004, required proof of citizenship for public services and to register to vote (the latter was blocked by federal courts), and required that state employees report any undocumented immigrants who tried to apply for services anyway.[81] In 2006, Proposition 100 (also ultimately struck down in court) denied bail to undocumented immigrants charged with "serious" crimes.[82] That same year, Proposition 102 barred awarding civil damages to undocumented immigrants;[83] Proposition 103 made English the official language;[84] and Proposition 300 denied in-state higher education tuition and state financial aid to undocumented students, and childcare funding to undocumented parents.[85] According to the National Institute on Money in Politics, six anti-immigration groups, including Tanton's FAIR and U.S. English, provided the vast majority of funding behind the measures.[86] "The political and emotional landscape [of Arizona] is almost identical," remarked Dan Schnur, a former aide to Governor Wilson. "History doesn't repeat itself, it just moves east."[87]

In April 2010, Republican governor Jan Brewer signed the anti-immigrant Senate Bill 1070 into law. Among other things it directed law enforcement to search out people suspected of being undocumented immigrants, imposing the Maricopa County model statewide.[88] It also targeted day laborers and their employers, which in Arizona and elsewhere had become a flashpoint in the anti-immigrant reaction.[89] The law, entitled the Support Our Law Enforcement and Safe Neighborhoods Act, was the most significant moment in popular immigration politics since the Sensenbrenner bill. It was drafted by state senator Russell Pearce with help from the most consequential legal activist in the nativist movement: Kris Kobach, the lawyer with FAIR's Immigration Reform Law Institute who helped develop Bush's post-9/11 crackdown on immigrants from Muslim-majority countries.[90] Kobach also helped develop the overall strategy behind SB 1070 and the rush of other state and local laws: "attrition through enforcement," or compelling immigrants to "self-deport" by making life in the United States too difficult.[91] Pearce also had input from the private prison company Corrections Corporation of America, according to an NPR investigation, through their joint participation in the American Legislative Exchange Council (ALEC), which brings conservative state legislators and business together.[92]

Eighteen days later, Brewer signed a law (this one also

later blocked in court) banning ethnic studies and any instruction that sought to "promote the overthrow of the United States government" in state public schools. It was an effort to shut down Tucson's Chicano studies program. State superintendent of public instruction Tom Horne complained of one Chicano history book that taught "kids that they live in occupied America, or occupied Mexico."[93] As the right denounced an imaginary immigrant reconquista, they attempted to ban teaching about the actual history of settler-colonial conquest.

Arizona's nativist revolt took root throughout the 2000s and was then turbocharged by and merged with the Tea Party.[94] Arizona's nativist movement shared the profile of California's suburban 1990s revolt. Arpaio's base included the outer Phoenix suburbs, places like Sun City, a massive retirement community where deputies in 2008 conducted an immigration sweep after the sheriff received a letter complaining that employees at a local McDonald's spoke Spanish.[95] The domestic migrants that comprised much of Arpaio's base, however, had helped create the demand for immigrant labor because their arrival sparked an enormous housing boom. Maricopa County added more housing units than any county nationwide in the 2000s.[96] That boom, combined with border enforcement's rerouting of migration routes away from California, drew in more Mexicans. By 2006, foreign-born Hispanics made up more than a third of the state's construction workforce.[97]

In 2008, that real estate boom exploded in a spectacular bust. By 2009, Arizona registered the second-highest foreclosure rate nationwide.[98] At year's end, the state's unemployment rate reached nearly 11 percent.[99] By 2011, home prices had fallen by half in Phoenix, nearly double the national average.[100] The stampede of Americans relocating to the area slowed to a crawl.[101] Arizona's boomtown future was suddenly beset by doubt. The white, retired middle-class Tea Party base was far from the hardest hit. But the "threats to these investments convinced many Tea Partiers that hard work is no longer fairly rewarded in America," as Theda Skocpol and Vanessa Williamson write.[102] One study found that the crisis accompanied a major deterioration of attitudes toward undocumented Mexicans, particularly though not exclusively among whites.[103] The study was limited to state university students in Arizona, and so likely found levels of anti-immigrant sentiment much lower than existed within a general population that included older whites.

It was a state founded on seized Mexican territory with a long history of segregation and racism, in explicit contrast to a heavily Mexican-descended New Mexico.[104] A governing class of conservative developmentalist elites had transformed the desert outpost into the sprawling conurbation that produced Barry Goldwater—right-wing senator, Civil Rights Act opponent, and 1964 Republican presidential nominee.[105] Phoenix was touted as a "romantic, urban, Anglo metropolis" with suburban homes for "the new metropolitan cowboy conservative."[106] But the conservative, elite-led growth machine created a reactionary constituency of white middle-class homeowners that would revolt against it.[107]

The decline of the high-tech industry in the 1970s made Phoenix increasingly reliant on real estate and services.[108]

"As long as new blood and new business kept heading into the state, Arizona met its budget."[109] The crisis struck deep. White transplant retirees worried that their rapidly depreciating homes were paying taxes for educating Latino youth.[110] Latina reproduction was targeted. "The birth rate among illegal immigrants is substantially higher than the population at large," wrote senator and 1070 sponsor Russell Pearce in exposed e-mails. "Battles commence as Mexican nationalists struggle to infuse their men into American government and strengthen control over their strongholds. One look at Los Angeles with its Mexican-American mayor shows you Vicente Fox's general Varigossa [*sic*] commanding an American city."[111]

Shortly after SB 1070's passage, Pearce led a failed effort to deny birthright citizenship to the children of undocumented immigrants,* saying that kids "are citizens of the country of their mother . . . That's why they are called in some cases 'jackpot babies' or 'anchor babies.'"[112] The state's economy demanded immigrant labor to build its homes and to staff its hospitality industry. But just as in California, many Arizonans consuming the fruit of immigrant labor found the presence of Mexican workers to be intolerable.

In California, immigrants had been portrayed as both an economic and criminal threat, and Prop 187 emphasized the denial of public services. By contrast, the politics around SB

---

* Pearce has a major interest in reproduction. He was recalled in 2011 but in 2014, as state Republican Party vice chair, proposed requiring that women on Medicaid take birth control.

1070 fixated on the criminal threat posed by Mexicans, and the law emphasized expanding law enforcement powers. Ever present was the fear of drug cartels shaped by the widely publicized violence of Mexico's drug war, which had exploded in 2006. "We cannot afford all this illegal immigration and everything that comes with it, everything from the crime and to the drugs and the kidnappings and the extortion and the beheadings and the fact that people can't feel safe in their community. It's wrong! It's wrong!" Brewer said, defending the law on Fox News.[113]

There had been no beheadings. A paranoid Brewer had projected US-driven drug violence in Mexico to north of the border.[114] The threat was crystalized for many in the shooting death of Rob Krentz, a prominent southeast Arizona rancher, less than a month before the passage of SB 1070.[115] The murder was popularly attributed to Mexican drug smugglers, though the killer has never been identified.[116] There was no border, nativists insisted, and so the border was everywhere.

Which of two sovereigns

The Obama administration sued Arizona and in 2012 won a Supreme Court ruling that struck down much of SB 1070, which was later further winnowed down by a 2016 settlement with rights groups.[117] But notably, Obama's lawyers did not argue against the law on the grounds that it violated civil rights but rather because it unconstitutionally "preempted" federal immigration law.[118] In short, they contended that the

Constitution made it the federal government's job to detain and deport immigrants, not Arizona's. The federal government, Solicitor General Donald B. Verrilli Jr. noted, already used the Secure Communities and 287(g) programs to do much of what Arizona was attempting to accomplish by allowing local police to enforce immigration law.[119]

Famed Supreme Court reporter Linda Greenhouse wrote that she found oral arguments in the case "utterly depressing," noting "the failure of any participant in the argument, justice or advocate for either side, to affirm the simple humanity of Arizona's several hundred thousand undocumented residents." The two sides sparred over "which of two sovereigns, the United States or the state of Arizona, has the right to make the immigrants' lives difficult." Arizona was right, she concluded, to suggest that the state "was simply following Washington's lead."[120]

Obama's strategy worked in court but failed politically. The activists mobilized against Arizona's law seized on its unpopularity among liberals as an opportunity to draw attention to Secure Communities, its more consequential federal counterpart—managed by President Obama, who had been elected as a liberal hero. By 2013, according to the Transactional Records Access Clearinghouse at Syracuse University, Secure Communities was responsible for a majority of interior deportations nationwide.[121] The problem for Obama was that SB 1070—declared odious by Obama and a broad swath of mainstream opinion—substantively resembled Obama's policies, so much so that they argued that federal policies made the Arizona law redundant.

"This is the manifestation of all the repressive laws that the Obama administration has been promoting," said Sal Reza, then a leader of Puente Arizona, as he and other activists blocked an entrance to the Maricopa County Sheriff's Fourth Avenue Jail.* "Obama is hiding behind the lawsuit [against SB 1070] while 287(g) and Secure Communities are empowering people like Sheriff Joe."[122]

Secure Communities had initially received little public attention even as DHS announced enormous numbers detained under the program.[123] Arizona's "show me your papers" law, however, energized immigrant activists and Democratic voters wary of the Tea Party's rise. The grassroots activists were determined to link the Arizona law to White House policy, and turned to city halls and state legislatures nationwide in an effort to thwart Secure Communities at its entry point, warning that the law would harm police-community relations and incentivize racial profiling.

"The passage of S.B. 1070 in Arizona should be proof enough of the dangerous and disastrous nature of ICE-police collaboration programs like the so-called Secure Communities program," said NDLON executive director Pablo Alvarado in April 2010, announcing a lawsuit against the federal government seeking the disclosure of information about the federal program. "The President should heed his own advice and act responsibly by reclaiming the federal

---

* It was a movement that would launch other movements, as Opal Tometi, who worked with Puente and other migrant justice groups, would go on to cofound Black Lives Matter.

government's exclusive authority over the nation's immigration laws. By terminating all police and ICE partnerships, the President can help restore community safety and protect civil rights and due process for all."[124]

Soon thereafter, the City Council of Washington, DC, unanimously announced its support for the nationwide movement to boycott Arizona, and called on police to thwart Secure Communities by refusing to share arrest data with DHS.[125] Other cities, like Arlington, Virginia, and Santa Clara, California, tried to block Secure Communities as well. In 2011, Illinois, New York and Massachusetts announced that they were pulling out of the program.[126]

Obama charged that measures like SB 1070 "threaten to undermine basic notions of fairness that we cherish as Americans." He blamed Congress, saying that "our failure to act responsibly at the federal level will only open the door to irresponsibility by others."[127] Yet in May 2010 Obama responded by announcing the deployment of 1,200 National Guard troops to the border and visited Republican lawmakers to make the case that he was outdoing Bush on border security. He hoped that, in return, they would support CIR. By this time, however, it wasn't just immigration extremists in Tom Tancredo's mold standing in his way but also ostensible Republican moderates like Senator Olympia Snowe. Onetime CIR champion John McCain asserted that a deployment of *six thousand troops* was required. "I said we needed to secure the border first," said McCain, recounting his meeting with Obama. "I pointed out that members of his administration who have not read the [Arizona] law have mischaracterized the law."[128]

In August 2011, as Obama fought the law in court, his administration suddenly informed states and localities that their rebellion against Secure Communities was futile: DHS tore up their agreements and asserted that the program was, despite all misdirection to the contrary, essentially mandatory.[129] All along, ICE had sent mixed messages about whether localities could opt out, suggesting at some points that it was voluntary, at other times that it was compulsory. Now, ICE was on the defensive. The public records lawsuit filed on behalf of NDLON by the Center for Constitutional Rights and others had surfaced internal government discussions about how to handle the local rebellion. One takeaway, according to the federal judge handling the case, was that there was "ample evidence that ICE and DHS have gone out of their way to mislead the public about Secure Communities."[130]

Activists had exploited the backlash against SB 1070 to embarrass the federal government, forcing it to reveal that its mass deportation campaign had always been premised on a lie. The program had been sold as federal cooperation with localities; in reality, it was a negotiation-free imposition that commandeered local law enforcement. ICE was happy for localities to believe Secure Communities was voluntary only so long as everyone volunteered.

Even as Obama ramped up deportations, his administration attempted to differentiate its policies from Republican extremists, fighting SB 1070 in court and, in September 2010, suing Arpaio for refusing to cooperate with a civil rights investigation.[131] The president was protected on his left flank by his close ties to major establishment immigration reform groups like the National Council of La Raza, the National Immigration Forum, and the Center for American Progress. According to Ana Avendaño, who led immigration policy at the AFL-CIO, there were constant White House attempts to "get us to tow the CIR line . . . most nefariously, over ending the deportations."[132] The Obama-tied establishment coalition, as political scientist Alfonso Gonzales writes, worked "to pacify the migrant movement and channel the popular demands of migrant workers" toward CIR.[133] But the radical movement wouldn't be checked. The awkward convergence between Obama and the nakedly right-wing Arizona law surfaced a divide in the immigrant rights movement and opened space for grassroots organizers to mobilize against the president.

Real America

The Tea Party movement had taken off in February 2009 in response to a mainly imaginary government bailout of "loser" underwater homeowners.[134] Both grassroots-driven and Koch brothers–funded, the movement was a right-wing fiscal revolt and, as with California's in the 1990s, it made nativism "central to [its] ideology."[135] It was a reactionary politics waged on racial, generational, and economic grounds, a rebellion against government redistributing the wealth of older white Americans to subsidize the rise of a diverse younger generation that would replace them.

The movement evaluated "entitlement programs not in terms of abstract free-market orthodoxy, but according to the *perceived deservingness of recipients.*" And "two groups of people [were] unambiguously included in the 'nonworking' population: young people and unauthorized immigrants."[136] Obama, they worried, would legalize the undocumented to create a vast new pool of Democratic voters. Obama's banal campaign call for "change" likely suggested something entirely sinister.

In 2010, hundreds of Tea Party activists rallied at the border southeast of Tucson with nativist luminaries including Arpaio, Arizona state senator Pearce, and former Republican congressman J. D. Hayworth, who was running a nativist primary challenge against McCain. "Instead of finding bugs in our beds, we're finding home invaders," said Tucson radio host Tony Venuti, attaching a sign to the border fence directing migrants away from the demographically fragile white utopia of Arizona and toward a Los Angeles presumably lost to the Mexicans.[137] Fox News launched a series of stories about the border entitled "America's Third War," summoning the specter of the "Third World" while also riffing off Hayworth's declaration on *Fox & Friends* that, "It's not so much that we're losing a war. We're failing to fight it."[138]

McCain released a campaign ad of himself walking along the Nogales border with the county sheriff. "Drug and human smuggling, home invasions, murder," McCain mused. "Complete the danged fence." "It'll work this time," the sheriff responded, instantiating the amnesia that pervades border control politics. "Senator, you're one of us."[139] The "us" was telling. Right-wing nationalism drew a bright line around a national "us" that excluded not only immigrants but also any American who didn't share their views. The sentiment had reached its lyrical apex in 2008 when McCain running mate Sarah Palin praised small towns for being the "real America . . . you hard working very patriotic, um, very, um, pro-America areas of this great nation."[140]

Fox News and the website Breitbart News warned that unauthorized immigrants might bring Ebola. Or, said right-wing radio host Laura Ingraham, they might spread drug-resistant strains of tuberculosis.[141] YouTube provided a platform for everyday people to launch viral conspiracy theories, including at least one positing that Mexico was hatching a long-term plan to subjugate the United States to a new Mesoamerican empire.[142] Under Obama, right-wing concerns about the loss of sovereignty were personified by a black president middle-named Hussein born to an immigrant father, and with an aunt, Zeituni Onyango, discovered to be living in Boston public housing while fighting deportation. "Obama's Aunt: An Illegal Alien, Getting Government Benefits, Who Donated to Barry's Campaign," the right-wing blog *Ace of Spades* wrote in 2008. "Sort of sums up his entire candidacy, doesn't it?"[143]

As president, Obama rarely invoked being the son of an immigrant father while discussing immigration. John F. Kennedy, Ronald Reagan, and Michael Dukakis had all highlighted their white ethnic immigrant roots to prove their Americanness. Tellingly, Obama decided that this wouldn't work in the case of an African father.

Glenn Beck, whose stream-of-consciousness conspiratorial ramblings transplanted the talk radio format to cable television, condemned government for failing to secure the border and business for hiring the migrants who crossed it. "We just think we're like everybody else," Beck said. "But we're not. We're not citizens of the world. We're citizens of the United States. At least—at least right now we still are."[144]

Alfonso Aguilar, the director of US Citizenship Office under George W. Bush, joined a group of reform supporters on the right to "unmask" Tanton-network groups like FAIR, NumbersUSA, and the Center for Immigration Studies (CIS) as "radical environmentalists"[145] who were "anything but conservative."[146] Aguilar was right about the movement's origins but in denial about what it had become: the core of a Republican right obsessed with demographic change. The wrong people were having too many babies, and the right kind too few. "Mass immigration is social engineering," said CIS director Mark Krikorian. "It is Congress second-guessing American moms and dads, saying they're not having enough children."[147] It was, nativist rhetoric suggested, white genocide.

Yes, you can

Republican extremism had since the mid-2000s begun to break apart the popular support for the bipartisan war on "illegal immigrants": while Republican hostility became yet more vitriolic, a Democratic electorate increasingly composed of liberals and non-white people pushed back, adopting more favorable views toward immigration.[148] Arizona's and Obama's enforcement crackdowns accelerated the split.

In the lead-up to the 2010 mid-term elections, Obama continued to deport people in far higher numbers than Bush ever had.[149] Immigrant rights activists were infuriated. But the Republican right was too, making it clear that Obama's deportation campaign would be met only with derision and calls for escalation. Representative Hal Rogers, a Kentucky Republican, accused Obama of practicing "selective amnesty."[150] That November, Republicans riding the Tea Party wave won control of the House and gained ground in the Senate in a campaign suffused with nativist rhetoric.

"We have gone above and beyond what was requested by the very Republicans who said they supported broader reform as long as we got serious about enforcement," Obama complained in a 2011 El Paso speech. "All the stuff they asked for, we've done. But even though we've answered these concerns, I've got to say I suspect there are still going to be some who are trying to move the goal posts on us one more time . . . They said we needed to triple the Border Patrol. Or now they're going to say we need to quadruple the Border Patrol. Or they'll want a higher fence. Maybe they'll need a moat. Maybe they want alligators in the moat. They'll never be satisfied."[151]

Obama didn't seem to realize that his analysis amounted to an astute indictment of his own approach, and that of the rest of the establishment reformers. Nativists were indeed shifting the goal posts time and again, but Obama didn't grasp that it was mainstream, immigration moderates like him who had helped them do so. In March 2010, the establishment Reform Immigration for America coalition organized a mass march on Washington—*with* rather than *against* Obama, whose speech was transmitted via jumbotron.[152] Organizers passed out American flags and told those waving flags from Latin American countries to conceal them.[153] That December, the DREAM Act failed to clear the Senate.[154] It would have provided a way to grant legal status to DREAMers, the undocumented immigrants who came to the country as kids, portrayed as the sympathetic poster children for reform.

In June 2011, with an eye on his reelection fight, Obama finally began to shift gears when ICE released a memo directing the agency to deprioritize the deportation of immigrants such as longtime residents, DREAMers, and veterans.[155] And yet in fiscal year 2012, DHS deported 418,000, breaking his previous record.[156] In July, activists interrupted Obama's address at the NCLR conference with chants of "Yes, you can!," demanding that he bypass obstructionist Republicans and take executive action to stop the deportations.[157]

In June 2012, Obama shifted further, announcing the new DACA program to protect hundreds of thousands of DREAMers from deportation. While establishment groups were focused on CIR, it was militant youth activists on the Trail of Dreams cross-country march and groups like DreamActivist and Dream Team Los Angeles who won the fight for DACA.[158] The month before, the Justice Department filed a federal civil rights lawsuit against Arpaio alleging widespread discrimination against Latinos.[159] Democrats needed the Latino vote, and grassroots immigrant groups were increasingly organized.

Obama, however, emphasized DREAMers' noble exceptionalism, claiming that ICE was "focusing on criminals who endanger our communities rather than students who are earning their education."[160] Deportation protections for a minority would function as a smokescreen to obscure a crackdown on the majority. Just after DACA was announced, lawyers and advocates gathered at the White House to strategize over the coming Supreme Court decision on SB 1070. Napolitano said that "DACA was essentially an extension of the Secure Communities policy," NDLON legal director Chris Newman recalls, and that felons get deported so DREAMers can stay.[161]

Last gasp

Obama's greatest asset among Latino voters in 2012 was his Republican opponent, Mitt Romney, who declared that "the answer is self-deportation." Romney had won the Republican primary by refashioning himself as an immigration hard-liner and all-around "severely conservative" guy to make his way through a clown-car field packed with bizarre extremists.

He accused Newt Gingrich of supporting "a form of amnesty" and attacked Governor Rick Perry for defending a Texas law that allowed undocumented immigrants to pay in-state tuition, calling it a "magnet [that] draws people into this country to get that education." Perry was booed by the primary debate crowd when he meekly replied, "We need to be educating these children because they will become a drag on our society."[162] Perry in turn hit Romney for having hired a lawn care company that employed undocumented workers. Meanwhile, Bachmann called for a fence along "every mile, every foot, every inch" of the border.[163] Herman Cain, an avid defender of legal immigration during his time as a pizza magnate, said he might "put troops with real guns and real bullets" on the border and that the fence should be electrified, with a (bilingual) sign declaring, "It will kill you—Warning."[164]

Romney's cynical adoption of hard-core nativism made it easy for Obama to present himself as a friend to immigrants. "You know, there are some things where Governor Romney is different from George Bush," Obama said in a debate. "George Bush embraced comprehensive immigration reform. He didn't call for self-deportation." Obama did not, however, explain why "self-deportation" was any worse than his mass government deportations.*

Obama bragged that he had "put more border patrol" agents on the border than at "any time in history." But the contrast between him and Romney was apparently clear enough.[165] Obama won with nearly three-quarters of the Latino vote.[166] An autopsy report produced for the Republican National Committee, at the time received as a very important document, was unsparing: "If Hispanic Americans perceive

---

* In January 2019, Romney, shortly before he was sworn in as senator from Utah, would pledge to "speak out" against Trump's "anti-immigrant" politics. Every new nativist radicalization appears as though out of the blue.

that a GOP nominee or candidate does not want them in the United States (i.e. self-deportation), they will not pay attention to our next sentence."[167]

Both parties' positions were untenable. Republicans were caught between the hard right and a general electorate put off by extremism. For Obama, the political downside of enforcement had risen, costing him credibility with Latinos, while the upside, in the form of Republican cooperation, remained illusory. In December 2012, DHS announced that 287(g) task force agreements, which deputized local police as enforcement agents, would be phased out. But they left the agreements authorizing inspections in local jails in place.[168] And Secure Communities continued, remaining more efficient at accomplishing much the same thing nationwide.

In June 2013, a new CIR bill passed the Senate with sixty-eight votes after a last-minute amendment adding spectacular border enforcement measures.[169] It was crafted by a bipartisan "Gang of Eight" with support from the US Chamber of Commerce and a united labor movement (a deal was struck over the guest worker program), anti-tax crusader Grover Norquist, and the coalition of establishment immigrant reform organizations like NCLR, CAP, and the National Immigration Forum.[170]

The legislation included a "path to citizenship," a mandatory employment verification system, $44.5 billion to roughly double the number of Border Patrol agents to at least 38,405, and the construction of more border fencing.[171] It "practically militarizes the border" to the fullest extent, "short of shooting everybody that comes across," Republican senator Lindsey

Graham exclaimed.[172] The bill created a new guest worker visa for industries like construction and hospitality.[173] Also, in response to a massive campaign led by Facebook and other tech companies, the bill would dramatically increase skilled worker visas, and eliminate diversity visas and visas for some family-based immigration categories. It would become a "merit-based" system that aimed to supply business with workers.[174]

Establishment immigrant rights groups nonetheless supported the Senate effort, with NCLR saying that it wasn't "perfect" but "delivered a real solution to our broken immigration system."[175] The goal was to make it so spectacularly punitive that it would win over House Republicans.[176] "The glee over 68 votes was sickening," Avendaño told me. "People treated the bill as if it were a candidate, not a piece of public policy."[177] "Republicans have finally stumbled upon Democrats' dirty secret on immigration," MSNBC's Benjy Sarlin reported. "As long as the GOP is willing to concede a path to citizenship for immigrants residing here illegally, Democrats will meet any demand on border security—no matter how arbitrary and misguided."[178]

By contrast, a number of grassroots organizations condemned the bill as doing "more harm than good to the cause of fair and humane immigration reform." The bill, they wrote, would "increase discrimination and racial profiling of people of color through nationwide mandatory E-verify" and "create a virtual police-state and create environmental disasters in the 27 border counties by militarizing the US-Mexico border."[179]

The nativist Center for Immigration Studies, however, saw the measure as mere theater to distract the right from "amnesty." "They just pulled that 20,000 number [of additional Border Patrol agents] out of a hat," said CIS executive director Mark Krikorian. "They should have just said we're going to add a million border patrol agents and arm them with photon torpedoes."[180] For the nativist right, escalations in enforcement were also a means to another end: pushing undocumented people out and sharply restricting legal immigration.

For the right as a whole, "amnesty" was unacceptable no matter how much enforcement it was paired with. "The anger is more intense now than it was in 2010," said Tea Party Nation founder Judson Phillips. "They are more upset about the amnesty bill than they were about Obamacare."[181] And why should they have traded legalization for enforcement when establishment politicians had consistently escalated enforcement as a stand-alone policy? In November 2013, comprehensive reform issued its last gasp in the House as Speaker John Boehner capitulated to right-wing opposition and announced that there would be no negotiations with the Senate over a major overhaul.[182]

That year, Obama marked a milestone, deporting more than 438,000, up from 359,795 in 2008 and 165,168 in 2001.[183] Some would quibble with this figure, noting that many of the people counted as "removed," meaning formally deported, were the sort of recent border crossers who would have previously been "returned," meaning allowed to "voluntarily" leave the country. A widely circulated *Los Angeles Times* story, for example, cast doubt on the "deporter in chief" moniker, stating: "The portrait of a steadily increasing number of deportations rests on statistics that conceal almost as much as they disclose." Deportation numbers appeared to go up, according to the story, "primarily as a result of changing who gets counted in the US Immigration and Customs Enforcement agency's deportation statistics."[184]

This was a distortion: between fiscal year 2010 and 2015, the portion of apprehensions that resulted in a "voluntary" return, typically of someone detained soon after crossing the border, plummeted from 59 percent to just 4 percent as CBP intensified a "Consequence Delivery System" designed to deter repeated border crossing attempts. The *Los Angeles Times* reporter was wrong to suggest that this was the result of a terminological shift, or a change in the way that data was categorized: being "removed" rather than "returned" is a legal distinction with a big difference—which is precisely why the Obama administration emphasized removals. A removal is a formal deportation, which typically bars a deportee from entering the United States for a number of years, and if they do so anyway without authorization, they face prosecution for the federal felony of illegal reentry. Indeed, prosecutions for that and other immigration crimes surged, packing federal prisons with immigrants convicted of nothing but crossing the border illegally.[185] Deportations from the interior did fall beginning in 2012, thanks to activist pressure. But the border deportations were real deportations, too.

By Obama's second term, it had become abundantly clear that intransigent Republicans would not be moved and that

Obama was presiding over deportations that were tearing families and communities apart. And so the president became the subject of increasing protest. In August 2013, nine undocumented youth were released from custody after boldly entering the country from Mexico after departing the United States.[186] Three, including National Immigrant Youth Alliance organizer Lizbeth Mateo, had intentionally left the United States to reenter in protest.[187] "I waited 15 years to see my grandfather again, and to meet the rest of my family. My family is also one of the 1.7 million that have been separated by Obama's deportation 'monster,'" wrote Mateo.[188] The undocumented youth movement had been radicalizing since 2010, when members of the Immigrant Youth Justice League came out to declare that they were "undocumented and unafraid."[189] They weren't bluffing.

Deporter in chief

In November 2013, undocumented graduate student activist Ju Hong disrupted an Obama speech on immigration, telling the president: "You have a power to stop deportations for all."[190] Obama insisted, "Actually, I don't, and that's why we're here," saying they had to take "the harder path, which is to use our democratic processes to achieve the same goal that you want to achieve, but it won't be as easy as just shouting." Remarkably, he went so far as to suggest that taking unilateral action to stop deportations would "violate the law."[191]

Within the immigrant rights movement, the fissure widened between well-funded inside-the-Beltway organizations and grassroots groups frustrated at those groups' closeness to the White House.[192] Cecilia Muñoz, a onetime NCLR official, was promoted to run Obama's Domestic Policy Council, and one of Obama's central domestic policies was Secure Communities. "Her promotion is good for the White House and good for advocates of immigration reform," said Frank Sharry, once executive director of the National Immigration Forum and now head of America's Voice. "The White House senior staff will benefit from a 'wise Latina' who understands a community most of them clearly don't. And her understanding of immigration reform and her career as a lifelong advocate for it will surely elevate this issue within the White House."[193]

Activists on the grassroots left, however, weren't impressed by Muñoz's work in the White House. "Being Latina does not give you a license to advocate for, and spin around, policies that devastate Latinas," said Roberto Lovato, co-founder of Presente.org. "Muñoz is out there talking about immigrants like she's a Republican white man. The messenger has changed, but the message is the same."[194]

In 2014, the *New York Times* reported that foundations including the Ford Foundation, the Carnegie Corporation of New York, George Soros's Open Society Foundations, and the Atlantic Philanthropies had contributed more than $300 million over a decade to immigration organizations. Since 2003, Carnegie alone had contributed about $100 million. It was all, said Sharry, "about a movement that could win the grand prize: legislation that puts 11 million people on a path to citizenship."[195] Grassroots groups that decried border militarization and enforcement, NDLON's Chris Newman told me, got shut out.

The split between grassroots and Beltway organizations echoed history. The National Council of La Raza had been founded in 1968 in part to engage in the sort of advocacy that old-line Hispanic organizations like the League of United Latin American Citizens, or LULAC, at best shied away from.[196] Under Obama, DC-based establishment groups like NCLR were accused of selling out undocumented immigrants in a hopeless campaign to win CIR. The Washington-based organizations mistook access for influence—and in doing so offered Obama political cover for mass deportations.

In early 2014, the grassroots revolted against the CIR consensus and the establishment coalition led by groups like CAP, NCLR, and the National Immigration Forum. DREAM organizers joined a plethora of grassroots groups like NDLON to demand #Not1More deportation: *¡Ni una mas!* Major forces like the AFL-CIO and PICO coalition also got involved.[197] "The more dependent a group is on grassroots support, the more likely it is to pressure the White House to do something on deportations," *Politico* reported. "The more a group's influence relies on its access to power, the less likely it is to push back." The Obama administration still insisted that it could not act to halt deportations on its own. "It's becoming something that you can't control," Representative Luis Gutierrez said at the time. "People have tried to control it. This administration has put inordinate pressure on people not to criticize the president on his immigration policy and not to talk about prosecutorial discretion."[198]

The grassroots strategy was to put a face on individual immigrants and "show who Obama is actually deporting even though he says he's not deporting them," veteran DREAMer activist Mohammad Abdollahi told me. Obama promised to deport "felons, not families." But lots of "good" immigrants were being deported too. And how bad were the "bad" ones, given the vast number of individuals convicted of crimes in the carceral state?

With reform dead in Congress and intense pressure from the grassroots, NCLR president Janet Murguía in March 2014 declared Obama to be "deporter in chief," a term seemingly cribbed from NDLON.[199] Grassroots radicals, mobilizing on the ground in immigrant communities, outflanked the establishment camp in Washington and radicalized the latter's position. Frank Sharry told me that he and other immigrant rights advocates met with Obama in March 2014, just after NCLR's president had condemned Obama. "When Janet [Murguía] spoke up," he said, "it was the most intense silence you can imagine. It was clear [Obama] was composing himself . . . to not express how thoroughly pissed off he was."[200]

In April, protesters organized by NDLON's #Not1More campaign marched on the White House. "We are bringing the human suffering to the doorstep," said organizer Marisa Franco.[201] But even then, many White House–aligned groups continued to go so far as to ask the president to *delay* taking unilateral action to keep CIR alive. In May, major establishment groups called on Obama "to allow for this process to take place before issuing administrative action. We believe the President should move cautiously and give the House Leadership all of the space they may need to bring legislation to the floor for a vote."[202] That same day, Obama announced he would delay a review of deportation policies, suggesting close coordination with advocates.[203] Republican representative Raúl Labrador later warned that executive action "would see an all-out war here in Congress about him taking the law into his own hands."[204] Leading CIR advocates and the Obama White House seemed to agree.

In June 2014, Republican House Majority leader Eric Cantor lost a primary race to an upstart Tea Party–backed challenger who relentlessly accused him of supporting "amnesty."[205] His sin? Supporting not a widespread legalization of most undocumented immigrants but merely a path to citizenship for DREAMers.[206] Local law enforcement refusals of ICE requests for immigration holds surged in the lead up to the midterms.[207] Across the country, youth activists were frequently interrupting Obama, Hillary Clinton, and other Democrats during their speeches. "Unfortunately, that's why the president delayed administrative relief—they didn't think Latinos were as important as other folks who they needed," said Dream Action Coalition codirector Erika Andiola, a leading undocumented organizer. "I'm with you," Obama told hecklers in Bridgeport, Connecticut. "And you need to go protest the Republicans." One prominent Democratic operative told the press that "it's a little disturbing now days before the election to see so much focus on Democrats when it's still absolutely clear that the Republicans are the enemy."[208]

On the ground, Secure Communities was under unprecedented stress. In October 2013, California governor Jerry Brown signed the Trust Act, limiting local law enforcement's cooperation with ICE—a sharp break from the nativist tide that had once roiled the state.[209] But just a year prior, he had vetoed the legislation in the lead-up to the election under pressure from the Obama administration.[210] In March 2014, the US Court of Appeals for the Third Circuit ruled that ICE detainers were not mandatory.[211] The next month, a federal judge in Oregon ruled the same, finding that Clackamas County had violated a woman's Fourth Amendment rights by detaining her without probable cause.[212] Cooperating with ICE wasn't just bad policy; it exposed localities to heavy civil damages. Almost immediately, counties across Oregon announced that they would no longer honor ICE detainers.[213]

The decades-long enforcement crackdown had not only shattered millions of immigrant lives but also helped create and sustain a popular narrative about dangerous, murdering, raping, and drug-dealing criminal aliens.[214] In 2013, the Remembrance Project, highlighting the stories of "families whose loved ones were killed by illegal aliens," began to receive media attention beyond right-wing outlets.[215] The organization was founded in 2009 by Texan Maria Espinoza, who declared that her family had come from Mexico "the right way" and boasted of growing up in a home with no Mexican flags. "It was just America and the Bible." She wrote things like "child molestation and rape are very numerous in this illegal alien demographic!" and posted a link to an article on the neo-Nazi Daily Stormer site entitled "Family Furious as Illegal Alien Let Out of Jail to Kill White People." "Every state," Espinoza declared, "is a border state."[216]

The Remembrance Project received funding from U.S. Inc., an organization run by John Tanton, the Michigan activist who founded the contemporary nativist movement in 1979.[217] The dominant anti-immigrant message had become that immigrants were systematically murdering Americans. This framing both innovated upon and synthesized the various forms of nativism that had developed since the 1970s—populationist, linguistic, cultural, fiscal, economic, anti-crime, and anti-terrorism—into an existential nativism fixated on death and demographic change that would become the core of Trump's presidential campaign. All these themes had been present in previous eras. But as sociologist Kitty Calavita writes, "If immigrants serve as scapegoats for social crises, it stands to reason that the specific content of anti-immigrant nativism will shift to encompass the prevailing malaise."[218] That malaise was now existential, the fear of what white nationalists call "the Great Replacement."

Detained and sent back

In the spring and summer of 2014, thousands of unaccompanied minors and families fled across the border, escaping poverty and violence in El Salvador, Guatemala, and Honduras. Rather than welcoming the migrants—who, after all, were departing countries thrown into chaos in significant part by decades of US proxy wars, deportations, and economic policy—the Obama administration responded harshly, moving to detain them while their asylum claims pended.[219]

The Obama administration opened one facility to incarcerate asylum-seeking families in southeastern New Mexico, far from most lawyers who could represent them in asylum proceedings, as Wil S. Hylton detailed in a February 2015 *New York Times Magazine* story. In response, lawyers began to travel to the small town of Artesia. What they found when they arrived were "young women and children huddled together. Many were gaunt and malnourished, with dark circles under their eyes." "Kids vomiting all over the place." "A big outbreak of fevers." "Pneumonia, scabies, lice." A school that often seemed to be closed.[220]

Such detentions would serve, the Obama administration hoped, as a deterrent. "It will now be more likely that you will be detained and sent back," DHS secretary Jeh Johnson forebodingly warned while presiding over the opening of a massive detention facility for women and their children in Dilley, Texas. The for-profit Corrections Corporation of America* operated the facility.[221] The same day Johnson visited the detention center in Artesia, according to a Hylton source, ICE deported seventy-nine people back to the US-tilled killing fields of El Salvador. Of this group, ten youth were later reported to have been killed.

------

* Their name has since changed to the more antiseptic CoreCivic, which pledges to "better the public good."

One reason that Obama may have instituted family detention of asylum seekers, immigration law scholar Juliet Stumpf told me, was to protect DACA—which is the same rationale Napolitano had reportedly given to justify Secure Communities. Conservative critics had asserted that the asylum seekers had been lured by DACA's deportation protections, a rationale that Attorney General Jeff Sessions would later cite when he announced in 2017 that Trump was ending the program.[222] Once again, Obama saw draconian immigration policy as a means to reform. And, perhaps, he also saw minor reforms as a way to protect enforcement.

In November 2014, Republicans took control of the Senate and successfully cut into Democrats' advantage among Latino voters—who, after all, are a diverse constituency in terms of race, nationality, class, religion, and ideology.[223] But instead of welcoming those voters to the party, incoming Senate majority leader Mitch McConnell responded to the racist base that had long since become Republicans' indispensable constituency. He warned Obama that unilateral action on immigration would be like "waving a red flag in front of a bull," a surprisingly fitting metaphor. Obama, however, had a restive base of his own to attend to.[224]

After the election, Obama addressed the nation during prime time to announce major executive actions to further limit deportations.[225] The centerpiece was a new program to protect millions of undocumented parents of US citizens from deportation, called Deferred Action for Parents of Americans and Lawful Permanent Residents (DAPA).[226]

Though Obama didn't mention it, Secure Communities would, at least in name, be replaced by the Priority Enforcement Program (PEP).[227] Fingerprint sharing, the technological basis for Secure Communities, remained. But ICE would limit enforcement mostly to people convicted of a narrowed set of crimes, and typically request notification of a prisoner's release instead of requesting that their detention be extended, easing localities' liability concerns.

Secure Communities was in crisis, DHS secretary Johnson acknowledged. In September 2014, the percentage of individuals targeted by a detainer who were taken into ICE custody had declined to 41.2 percent while the portion of detainers marked as refused had risen to 10.1 percent—up from zero in 2008.[228] "The reality is the program has attracted a great deal of criticism," Johnson wrote. "Governors, mayors, and state and local law enforcement officials around the country have increasingly refused to cooperate with the program."[229]

The Tea Party, which by that point had "become a movement largely against immigration overhaul," erupted with anger.[230] But it had long since become clear that they would react that way regardless of what Obama did. These three victories—DACA, DAPA, and PEP—demonstrated that the grassroots radicals were right: political independence and militancy protected immigrants while seeking access in pursuit of compromise facilitated their deportation.

DAPA was blocked by a right-wing federal judge, a ruling that was upheld by the Supreme Court in a split decision thanks to Senate Republicans refusing to allow Obama to fill a vacant seat. In a painfully revealing irony, the

Republican-led states that filed the challenge against DAPA made a point of citing Obama's prior statements that he did not have the legal power to act unilaterally. PEP's reforms did turn out to be substantial, with ICE arrests and deportations from the interior each falling by about two-thirds between fiscal years 2011 to 2016. The reforms, however, also succeeded in luring resistant localities back into cooperation with ICE.[231] But it was too little, too late to decisively challenge the powerful immigrant-threat narratives that the bipartisan establishment had for decades co-authored with their enemies on the nativist right. The right-wing story line was set. All it needed was its orange-hued hero.

When Mexico sends its people

On June 16, 2015, Donald Trump announced his presidential campaign. From the beginning, immigrant criminality was without question his most salient message. "When Mexico sends its people, they're not sending their best," he warned. "They're sending people that have lots of problems, and they're bringing those problems . . . They're bringing drugs. They're bringing crime. They're rapists. And some, I assume, are good people."[232]

Much of the country was outraged by Trump's comments. But they should not have been surprised. Americans had been digesting a steady stream of right-wing news highlighting immigrant crime alongside mainstream political rhetoric that long portrayed the border as a violent threat. By the time Trump announced, what had begun as an amalgam of fears over drugs and immigration's economic, criminal, cultural, and demographic impact had transmogrified into the specter of a raping and murdering criminal army, fed by lurid anecdotes whose dots right-wing media connected into a total monstrosity.

Just over two weeks before Trump announced, Ann Coulter had published her book ¡*Adios, America! The Left's Plan to Turn America into a Third World Hellhole*. In it, she argued that "the rape of little girls isn't even considered a crime in Latino culture" and that "Mexicans specialize in corpse desecration, burning people alive, rolling human heads onto packed nightclub dance floors, dissolving bodies in acid, and hanging mutilated bodies from bridges." By one reviewer's count, a full six chapters are focused on immigrant rapists.[233]

Anxieties over sexuality, gender and reproduction have long served as justifications for racial and economic hierarchy. An immigrant man violating an American woman had become the counterpart to long-standing nativist preoccupation with Latina birth rates, and with Mexican women entering the United States to birth "anchor babies." The contemporary nativist movement was founded by overpopulation alarmists. But the alarm had become explicitly focused on the reproductive dynamics of Latinas, portrayed as fueling the reconquista, white genocide, and the "Great Replacement." As Tanton put it: "Those with their pants up are going to get caught by those with their pants down!"[234]

¡*Adios, America!* has been widely credited for shaping Trump's anti-immigrant politics.[235] Before announcing, he tweeted that it was a "great read." Though Trump doesn't read books, he picked up on its themes. "Where do you think all that spicy stuff about Mexican rape culture came from?" Coulter tweeted. "@realDonaldTrump got an advance copy." As for Coulter, she credited Peter Brimelow's 1992 *National Review* cover story—a touchstone for 1990s nativism—for sparking her interest in the subject.[236] Trump's pronouncements were met with understandable offense but also misplaced shock. Just two decades prior, Brimelow's book had been praised in the *New York Times* and *The Atlantic*.

Weeks after Trump announced, a real-life incident provided characters for his story line when an undocumented immigrant shot Kathryn Steinle, a young white woman, dead on San Francisco's Embarcadero.[237] The man was believed to be homeless, collecting cans along the pier.[238] He showed signs of mental illness, and said that he had found the gun, reported stolen from a Bureau of Land Management ranger's car, wrapped in a T-shirt.[239] Apparently, he shot the bullet into the ground and it then ricocheted, striking and killing Steinle. His defense argued that he did not even realize it was a gun and that he fired it by accident.[240]

The shooter had been transferred from prison, where he served a sentence for illegal reentry, to the San Francisco sheriff who then released him. He had a warrant out for a small-time marijuana offense. But since there was apparently nothing violent on his record, and he would never have been prosecuted for the old, trifling pot bust he was wanted for, the sheriff of the iconic liberal city refused to honor a request to hold him for ICE. It became and remains a cause célèbre on the right, and was sucked into a national discussion fixated on immigrants' violent criminality that Trump's announcement had inflamed like never before.*

Steinle's killing, Trump declared, was a "senseless and totally preventable act of violence" and "yet another example of why we must secure our border."[241] He talked about the killing constantly, referring to the victim as "beautiful Kate Steinle," making her into an icon of innocent white womanhood under threat from immigrant criminality. In August 2015, Trump released his first policy paper, a six-page proposal calling for, among other things, an end to birthright citizenship—targeting Latina reproduction as part of a campaign to protect white lives.[242] Anne Coulter called it "the greatest political document since the Magna Carta."[243] "I don't care if @realDonaldTrump wants to perform abortions in White House after this immigration policy paper," she tweeted. What she did not mention is that she, along with campaign aide Sam Nunberg, quietly helped write it.[244]

In September 2015, the Remembrance Project organized a meeting between Trump and the families of people who had been killed by undocumented immigrants. Maria Espinoza started speaking at his rallies, and Trump embraced her call for taxing remittances to compensate victims' families.[245] The Center for Immigration Studies published a map of so-called sanctuary cities that "protect criminal aliens from deportation." Mark Krikorian took to the *National Review* to declare

---

* Ultimately, the defendant was acquitted of murder but convicted on a gun charge, which at the time of this writing had been overturned on appeal.

that "San Francisco's refusal to turn over illegal aliens for the feds until they've been convicted of violent felonies (and the Obama administration's support for, and even promotion of such policies) is the only reason this poor woman was killed."[246] Breitbart likewise blamed the president, charging that "the only reason sanctuary cities like San Francisco get away with flagrant lawlessness is because the federal government and its degenerate bureaucracy allow them to do so. President Obama could have taken steps to end this 'sanctuary city' garbage long ago."[247]

The right's contention that Obama supported sanctuary cities, of course, had everything entirely backward. So-called sanctuary city policies, as I've detailed, were in fact the result of rebellions *against* Obama's Secure Communities and of federal judges' rulings suggesting that the program might violate the Constitution. Not only had Obama's harsh enforcement failed to placate the right, the right now associated Obama with those resisting him on the left. True to form, Hillary Clinton, once again a Democratic candidate for president, indicted San Francisco: "The city made a mistake not to deport someone that the federal government strongly felt should be deported."[248] Senator Dianne Feinstein, two decades after her anti-migrant rhetoric had smoothed Proposition 187's passage, declared that San Francisco should have "allowed ICE to remove him from the country."[249]

ICE likewise embraced the right-wing narrative, possibly owing to simmering anger at Obama within the agency's ranks.[250] A statement from ICE to the media lamented that "an individual with a lengthy criminal history, who is now the suspect in a tragic murder case, was released onto the street rather than being turned over to ICE for deportation."[251]

"Bottom line," the statement continued, is that "if the local authorities had merely notified ICE that they were about to release this individual into the community, ICE could have taken custody of him and had him removed from the country—thus preventing this terrible tragedy . . . ICE desperately wants local law enforcement agencies to work with us so we can work to stop needless violence like these [sic] in our communities."

Trump, the most anti-immigrant major party presidential candidate in modern history, twisted Obama's draconian policies to appear as though they were policies that coddled criminal aliens. Then, in a bizarre sleight of hand, Trump made the policies that Obama had curtailed under protester duress a centerpiece of his platform.

"We will restore the highly successful Secure Communities program. Good program," Trump said in August 2016, during a major speech on immigration in Phoenix.[252] Arpaio opened for Trump, and Trump ended the rally surrounded by so-called "angel moms," parents who spoke of losing children to undocumented immigrant crime.[253] "We will expand and revitalize the popular 287(g) partnerships, which will help to identify hundreds of thousands of deportable aliens in local jails that we don't even know about. Both of these programs have been recklessly gutted by this administration. And those were programs that worked." In September, Trump spoke at a private Remembrance Project luncheon. Espinoza praised him as the sole candidate "who reached out to our families, our stolen-lives families, America's most forgotten families." Kris Kobach also spoke, warning that "sanctuary cities" provided a haven for criminals and terrorists.[254]

Obama had claimed that his deportations targeted criminals rather than hardworking immigrants. When activists and then local officials resisted those deportations, they were, by Obama's logic, protecting criminals. Trump then contended that Democrats' policy was to coddle dangerous aliens, and he made Secure Communities and 287(g) his own.

The caravan

"The crime is raging, it's raging, and it's violent," Trump said in July 2015 on *Fox & Friends* when asked about Steinle's killing. "And people don't want to even talk about it. And if you talk about it, you're a racist. I don't understand it." Trump immediately pivoted to trade and then to ISIS. Steinle's death, he suggested, was just one piece of a multi-faceted national humiliation inflicted by bad deals. "Everything we do in this country is just off. Our trade deals are terrible, our border protection is terrible, our security is terr—you look at what ISIS is doing to us, they're laughing at us. You know, do we have victories any more in our country and the answer is really no."[255]

Trump's articulation of an interlocking threat complex struck a chord. No one could beat the pitchman's pledge of a "big, beautiful wall." During the general election, it left Hillary Clinton in a muddle. "I have been for border security for years," she professed, awkwardly honest. "I voted for border security in the United States Senate. And my comprehensive immigration reform plan of course includes border security."[256]

The wall, or at least roughly 650 miles of fencing, had already been built.[257] And Trump allies made a point of noting that Clinton had voted for it. They continued to make that point after his election, hypocritically hammering Democrats for hypocritically refusing to fund the very sorts of walls they once embraced.[258] At July's Republican National Convention, Trump slammed Clinton, asserting that "my opponent wants Sanctuary Cities. But where was the sanctuary for Kate Steinle? . . . Where was the sanctuary for all of the Americans who have been so brutally murdered, and who have suffered so horribly? These wounded American families have been alone. But they are not alone any longer."[259] In August 2016, he promised the Phoenix crowd deportations: "Day one, my first hour in office, those people are gone."[260]

Of course, Trump's White House has overwhelmingly marched in lockstep with the Republican Party's traditional powers: slashing taxes for the rich, enfeebling the Environmental Protection Agency, and packing the courts with courtiers of business and Christian conservatism who pledge to read the law through the eyes of eighteenth-century white settler society.

Trump, however, never lost sight of the nationalist message that had catapulted him to his primary victory. He launched tariff wars and a renegotiation of NAFTA. But

hyperbolic opposition to immigration remained the centerpiece of his politics. Initially, he declared victory. "You know,
the border is down 78 percent," said Trump in July 2017,
exaggerating a decline in apprehensions before making an
absolutely false statement. "Under past administrations, the
border didn't go down—it went up."[261]

Nevertheless, Trump was still no more capable of winning
the war on immigration than his predecessors. And besides,
"winning" the war wouldn't be advantageous, because
Trump's appeal required that he be a border-wartime president. As border apprehensions dipped, hard-core nativists
like Jeff Sessions, Steve Bannon, and Stephen Miller helped
craft a cascade of nativist provocations that ensured immigration remained constantly front and center.

In September 2017, Trump moved to end DACA. Holding
DACA hostage, he demanded his own brand of "comprehensive immigration reform" that combined billions for his
border wall and the sharp restriction in legal immigration
that had long been the nativist movement's most cherished
goal.[262] He mused that the United States should bring more
immigrants from places like Norway and fewer from
"shithole" (or, according to some present at the Oval Office
meeting, "shithouse") countries. That went nowhere.

Then came an uptick in irregular migration, which initially
infuriated Trump, prompting him to lash out at DHS secretary Kirstjen Nielsen.[263] But it was a failure that he quickly
remade for his own purposes, using legal tools finessed by his
predecessors to charge Central American migrants with illegal entry, thus separating them from their children—in some

cases perhaps permanently. While the child separations were widely seen as damaging to Trump, they also helped to consolidate the base that his political survival depends upon. As the 2018 midterms approached, Trump latched on to the steady progress of a thousands-strong caravan of Central Americans traveling together so as to protect themselves from the constant threats of assault, robbery, corruption, kidnapping, and rape—conditions that the US-backed drug and border wars had made a reality in Mexico. For Trump, their solidarity presented an opportunity.

Trump blamed Democrats for creating the policies that facilitated migrants' entry and even suggested that someone, perhaps liberal Jewish financier and philanthropist George Soros, was funding the caravan. "I don't know who, but I wouldn't be surprised. A lot of people say yes," Trump said, when asked to confirm the right-wing conspiracy theory.[264] "Criminals and unknown Middle Easterners are mixed in," Trump warned in a tweet. People supposedly so dangerous that the president deployed the military to confront them. If necessary, he suggested, soldiers might open fire.[265]

Trump's "caravan election" merged the MS-13 and ISIS threat into one. It also spectacularly ratified the far-right anti-Semitic conspiracy theory that Jews are organizing mass immigration to destroy the white race. With just under two weeks left before election day, a man walked into a Pittsburgh synagogue and massacred eleven Jews. Beforehand, he had posted an explanation on a far-right social media site attacking the country's leading Jewish refugee resettlement agency.

"HIAS likes to bring invaders that kill our people," he wrote. "I can't sit by and watch my people get slaughtered. Screw your optics, I'm going in."[266]

A bipartisan consensus had for decades made undocumented immigrants into a dangerous problem. Trump was elected because he offered the Wall, which had the cruel appeal of a comprehensive solution.

CONCLUSION

We want that stuff too—but we also want a wall . . . The chant at every campaign rally wasn't, "Enforce E-Verify!"[1]

—Ann Coulter

In July 2019, Trump tweeted that four Democratic congress-women are "from countries whose governments are a complete and total catastrophe." They are "viciously telling the people of the United States, the greatest and most powerful Nation on earth, how our government is to be run." Trump's proposed solution was that "they go back and help fix the totally broken and crime infested places from which they came."

Back to Puerto Rico, where Alexandria Ocasio-Cortez's family is from, seized at the height of white supremacist imperialism? To Palestine, the birthplace of Rashida Tlaib's parents, undergoing genocide at the hands of a US-backed occupation? To Africa, whence Ayanna Pressley's ancestors were kidnapped and enslaved? Or to Somalia, a country that the United States has helped throw into violent chaos and from where Ilhan Omar came as a refugee at age twelve?

That Trump's immigration crusade is racist population politics had long since been made clear. His threat to eliminate birthright citizenship would require eviscerating the Fourteenth Amendment, the Reconstruction-era victory that for the first time defined the people beyond the bounds of white supremacy.[2] He constantly recapitulates a long history of all-American nativism, promising that a country made white "again" will be great. Colonial settlement and westward expansion were explicit projects of ensuring white dominance over indigenous, black, and Mexican subjects, culminating in laws to exclude Asians from a closing frontier. The color line followed imperial expansion overseas and ricocheted back home in the form of massive immigration restriction. After overtly racist immigration laws were repealed in 1965, Cold War liberalism made the color line into a pretextual legal one, criminalizing Mexican labor migration. As Mexicans were rendered "illegal" and into a criminal threat, Muslims were fashioned into a terrorist one as a new war rebounded in the form of an insurgent Islamophobia.

It's a great analytical challenge, then, to describe what's old and new about Trump. Trump's policies have persecuted countless people by increasing deportations, attempting to end DACA protections for undocumented youth, separating families at the border, turning US Citizenship and Immigration Services into an enforcement agency, pardoning Sheriff Joe Arpaio for his crimes, easing the summary denial of asylum requests, slowing the naturalization process, attempting to terminate Temporary Protected Status for people from El Salvador, Haiti, Nicaragua, and Sudan, forcing Central American asylum-seekers to wait in Mexico and then requiring that they apply for asylum in the first country they enter on their journey, coercing Mexico and Guatemala into acting as proxy US border enforcers, sharply curtailing refugee admissions, and barring people from entry because their home nations are predominantly Muslim. Yet by his second year in office he had so far failed to match (not even close) the number of interior deportations overseen by Obama during his first term, or the border deportations undertaken during his second.*

Obama's methodical merger of immigration and criminal law enforcement was terrifyingly efficient until a Latinx-youth led movement forced him to retreat. But in the difficult circumstances that have defined his presidency, Trump always returns to the symbolic power of the Wall. The Wall, then, *is* a novel form of nativist politics. But given that 654 miles of "fencing" was in place when Trump took office, what's new about it is not what many think.[3]

Since the 1990s, the establishment attempted to use its wall to deter migration, forcing migrants into the desert, where thousands died. Their wall, however, more than anything was intended to convince Americans that government was solving the immigration problem. What it did instead was to help make immigration a problem and lay the political,

---

* A total of 237,941 people were deported from the interior in fiscal year 2009; in 2018, 95,360. (Alex Nowrasteh, "Trump Administration Continues to Expand Interior Immigration Enforcement," December 14, 2018, cato.org.)

institutional and physical foundations for Trump. Rather than slaking nativist demands, escalating enforcement measures only highlighted their own futility. They indicted government for inaction rather than convincing the public of its sovereign capacity to deliver security. Instead of placating xenophobes, it stoked them to the point where the ante could only be upped to a utopian vision of a hermetically sealed nation, at once autarchic and supreme.

Initially, Trump tried to make the Wall bigger than a racist metaphor or a mere physical extension of his predecessors' fencing. He proposed doing something truly revolutionary, using an escalation in the long-running war on "illegal immigrants" to support a full nativist agenda that sought to end *all* immigration as we have known it since 1965.

The Wall

In a campaign that included many startling pronouncements, Trump's pledge to *build the wall* in June 2015 became the iconic phrase that stitched together a right-wing nationalist tapestry of resentment, nihilism, and violent nostalgia.[4] Mexico would pay for it. A form of imperial tribute recast as reparations to a wronged and aggrieved America, whose sovereignty had been violated by unchecked "illegal immigration," unfair trade deals, and unfavorable inter-state alliances. Justice would finally be secured by a president with the boldness to reassert the rightful order among nations. The American people would remain composed of the white citizenry the founders envisioned.

Trump's embrace of the Wall as a big concept was new. On a policy level, however, Trump's wall as a physical barrier looked a lot like what the Republican and Democratic establishment had been building for years, though they had called it "fencing." But in August 2016, Trump, in his campaign's landmark immigration speech in Phoenix, promised that the Wall would go beyond the standard fare. Instead, it would be a metaphor for a comprehensive nativist agenda to not only crack down on "illegal immigrants" but also "control future immigration" so as "to keep immigration levels measured by population share within historical norms." He even referenced the year 1965, when President Johnson ended the racist national origins quota system.[5] It was a clear signal to the hard-core nativists in the powerful network founded by John Tanton in 1979. And they loved it.

"This kind of emphasis on dealing with legal immigration in this way is not something a major nominee has done in the last 60 years," said NumbersUSA head Roy Beck. "It was probably the best immigration speech any major party's political candidate has delivered," said Center for Immigration Studies executive director Mark Krikorian. White power activist Richard Spencer was thrilled too, reading the clear racial subtext of Trump's paean to national origins quotas and call to limit immigration to those who could achieve "success in U.S. society."[6] "Trump is returning to the ideas of the 1924 Immigration Act," he tweeted. "Immigrants will reflect the racial makeup of the country."[7]

After Trump won, Tanton-network nativists and their allies entered the administration. Jeff Sessions, the first senator to endorse Trump's primary bid, became his attorney general. Sessions, among Congress's most hard-line nativists, also provided Trump with his leading immigration strategist, former Senate aide and zealous xenophobe Stephen Miller. Many who had worked with FAIR joined too. One was Trump counselor Kellyanne Conway, its longtime pollster.[8] Another was Kansas secretary of state and Immigration Reform Law Institute attorney Kris Kobach, who led Trump's conspiratorial hunt for "voter fraud," continuing the long white supremacist tradition of doing everything possible to ensure the electorate's maximal whiteness.[9]

The war on "illegal immigrants" had thrived within rather than outside the reigning post-1965 liberal ideology that celebrated America as fundamentally a "nation of immigrants." This worldview took root amid the elimination of the racist national origins quotas and the mass criminalization of Mexican migration. The mainstream demonization of undocumented immigrants had been vicious but was waged in the name of defending the good legal immigrants who came the right way. For organized nativists, however, the goal was to smash that model and sharply curtail *all* immigration—to reverse the 1965 reform that today threatens the "white" majority. In 2017, Trump again lifted their hopes, announcing his support for legislation that would ultimately slash authorized immigration by an estimated 50 percent through cuts to family-based visas (stigmatized as "chain migration") and an end to diversity visas.[10]

Even though Democrats had made it clear that they would provide Wall money in exchange for protecting DREAMers,[11]

Trump seemed committed to a full nativist program. In his 2018 State of the Union, he laid out in detail a radical proposal to sharply limit legal immigration, build the Wall, and hire more ICE agents. All in exchange *not* for the major legalization of more than 10 million that was at issue under Bush and Obama but merely for protecting roughly 1.8 million DREAMers, many of whom so urgently needed protection because Trump's attempt to eliminate DACA (a move blocked by federal judges and heading to the Supreme Court at the time of this writing) had put them at risk of deportation.[12] Bush and Obama had responded with stand-alone enforcement escalations against undocumented immigrants after comprehensive immigration reform "grand bargain" proposals repeatedly failed. Trump rejected the bipartisan war on "illegal immigrants" and tried to replace it with a war on all immigration.

Ahead of the midterms, however, Trump reverted: the full nativist agenda receded, and scaremongering over the caravan of Central American asylum seekers and demands for the Wall took its place. Democrats then retook the House. The Wall delivered short-term political gains that consign Republicans to a strategic dead-end in their long-running battle to defend white America. Yet they cannot choose otherwise: the Republican base is diminishing but it's the only base they've got. Republicans can't pivot toward the center without committing suicide.

By late 2018, the full nativist agenda had mostly disappeared. Trump shut down the government, refusing to sign any budget that did not include $5 billion for the Wall, all the while falsely insisting that Mexico was indeed paying for it through a renegotiated NAFTA. True to form, Democrats instead offered $1.375 billion to fund border barriers that were somehow not the Wall.[13] Trump ended the shutdown, took those funds, and then signed an emergency declaration to raid the military budget to build the Wall anyway.[14] As of August 2019, the Supreme Court has greenlighted construction pending a lawsuit challenging the president's end run around Congress's power of the purse.[15] Trump will continue to rally his base: Build the Wall.

Trump, however, had initially blinked and sought to avoid a shutdown. In response Ann Coulter, Rush Limbaugh, Laura Ingraham and even Steve Doocy on Trump's beloved *Fox & Friends* attacked the television president. And harshly. "The chant wasn't 'SIGN A BILL WITH B.S. PROMISES ABOUT 'BORDER SECURITY' AT SOME POINT IN THE FUTURE, GUARANTEED TO FAIL!'" Coulter tweeted. "It was 'BUILD A WALL!'" If he failed to build the Wall, Coulter said, Trump's would be "a joke presidency that scammed the American people."[16]

FAIR, which developed a particularly close-knit relationship with right-wing media, joined the call.[17] But other Tanton-network leaders didn't care so much about the Wall. In fact, they worried about it.[18] "Note that better control over illegal immigration—walls, mass deportations, whatever— isn't going to fix this," Krikorian wrote in the *National Review*. "Most immigration is legal immigration, and that's where change is most needed"; otherwise, demographic change means "conservatism will be toast."[19] The shutdown over the Wall, NumbersUSA research director Eric Ruark lamented, "really isn't an immigration fight" at all.[20] What concerned Krikorian was that Trump might trade something that organized nativists care about (like stopping the DREAM Act) in exchange for his Wall fetish.[21]

Krikorian's fears were soon realized. In Trump's 2019 State of the Union Address, the president declared that he wants "people to come into our country in the largest numbers ever but they have to come in legally."[22] Trump, after flirting with legal immigration cuts, had returned to the "nation of immigrants" model: a war on "illegal immigrants" to protect the ones who *come the right way*.* "If the White House follows through on this it's going to blow up in his face," Krikorian said. "The president has said he could shoot someone on 5th Avenue and his base would stay with him, and that's probably true. But this is one thing that he won't be able to get away with." But what Krikorian thought was a secondary consideration at best. Nativist organizations didn't control nativist politics and never did. The right-wing media does. The day before launching his reelection campaign in June 2019, Trump played to the only audience that mattered, pledging not cuts to legal immigration but to begin mass deportations.

---

* Already in August 2016, candidate Trump hinted that he was open to some sort of legalization. At a Fox News town hall with Sean Hannity, he literally polled the audience on what he should do. "I'll ask the audience, you have somebody who's terrific, who's been here . . . long time . . . can we go through a process, or do you think they have to get out? Tell me. I mean, don't know. You tell me." (Dara Lind, "What the Hell Is Going on with Trump and Immigration, Explained," vox.com, August 25, 2016.)

Trump's right-wing presidency was seemingly not what nativist movement founders at first had in mind. In the 1980s, the Tanton network tried to build a nonpartisan coalition for anti-immigrant politics, winning support from Warren Buffett, Eugene McCarthy, and Walter Cronkite along with often friendly mainstream press coverage of restrictionism.[23] But the network's leaders ultimately found that mass nativist politics could be most powerfully mobilized through a right fired up to stop government from providing "amnesty" to "illegals." In doing so, they revolted against the bipartisan centrists who administered the long war on "illegal immigrants" but ultimately sought comprehensive reform. Ironically, however, nativists and the establishment both helped to narrowly and fanatically define the problem as one of migrant illegality. Today, the base isn't motivated by arcane legal immigration policy; in fact, many point to their support for people who *come the right way* as evidence that they're not racist. As Sheriff Joe Arpaio put it: "My mother and father came from Italy legally."[24]

The Tanton agenda has been supplanted by ambient, culture-war dysphoria. Coulter and Fox News don't prioritize wonkish restriction but rather right-wing mobilization, ratings, book sales, and a cornucopia of garish personal brands. The Wall, perhaps the most powerful synthesis of popular anti-immigrant sentiment ever, has become remarkably disconnected from actual immigration policy. The border has long since been more an idea than a place: militarization more than anything has moved the sites of unauthorized border crossings rather than stopped them, and many undocumented immigrants simply overstay their visas. Trump has eroded what little realism still adhered. The Wall is the now-indispensable tool for mobilizing white fear and grievance into an electoral force, scaring just enough ancient reactionaries out of their Fox News–facing recliners and into the polls to eke out popular-vote losing, electoral college victories.

The Wall is more than a monument to popular xenophobia. It's a symbol of Fortress America, the promise of total protection against not only a coming so-called majority-minority country but also terrorism and the ravages of corporate globalization. It is the smashed neocon dreams of the war on terror and dashed neoliberal promise of flat-world prosperity coming home to roost in the Garrison State. It is the Great Migration undone and the Civil War ended differently. It is the seizure of northern Mexico without Mexicans, the vast wealth produced by American capitalism without the people doing its most degraded labor. It's a country founded on Native genocide where the genocidaires' descendants native status goes unquestioned. It is the very impossibility of these fantasies that has always imbued them with such violence.

As Greg Grandin writes, the Wall is "a tombstone" to America's founding and recently deceased frontier myth, which can no longer even pretend to deliver on its promise of "perennial rebirth." "Instead of peace, there is endless war. Instead of prosperity we have intractable inequality. Instead of a critical, resilient and open-minded citizenry, a conspiratorial nihilism, rejecting reason and dreading change, has taken hold," Grandin writes. "Trumpism is extremism turned inward, all-consuming and self-devouring. There is no 'divine, messianic' crusade that can harness and redirect passions outward. Expansion, in any form, can no longer satisfy interests, reconcile contradictions, dilute the factions, or redirect the anger."[25]

The Wall is a structure of political feeling. It is a sadistic, gleeful performance of transgression against political correctness, a proud insistence on the very idea that Mexicans are "rapists" and "criminals." These are notions that draw much of their emotive force from the offense they cause to liberal propriety—even though it was liberal leaders who energetically helped to criminalize immigrants for decades. The Wall has come to stand in for Trump himself and thus for the entirety of the politics of white, nationalist grievance that he singularly embodies. By contrast, boring policy measures that might actually preserve a white majority are drowned out by soliloquies sung to a giant real estate development project. "We want that stuff too—but we also want a wall," said Coulter. "The chant at every campaign rally wasn't, 'Enforce E-Verify!'"[26] When it comes to nativism's popular appeal, what matters most is performance, not policy.

Polarization is good

With Trump in office, things can seem absurdly bleak. But after Republicans lost the House, it became clear that Trump's first two years were for nativists a critical opportunity to reshape the contours of the American *demos*.* And they blew it: Republicans had total control of government yet legislative cuts to legal immigration went nowhere. Meanwhile, Democratic voters are moving sharply left in the face of accelerating Republican extremism. The percentage of Americans calling for a decrease in legal immigration has plummeted since the early 2000s—particularly but not exclusively among Democrats. Indeed, since 2006 Democratic voters have swung from a strong plurality supporting legal immigration cuts to a stronger plurality backing increased legal immigration.[27]

In promoting attacks on "illegal immigration" and militarizing the border, establishment politicians from both major parties inflamed popular anti-immigrant sentiment. But they helped move the Overton window so far right that it snapped loose of its bipartisan frame, prompting vociferous resistance on the left. The war on "illegal immigrants" was based on a bipartisan consensus. It is becoming very partisan. That's good.

As nativists well know, immigration means that *we the people* is increasingly made up of people who don't look like Trump and his base. And they correctly worry that immigration is driving a large-scale demographic transformation that could ultimately doom the conservative movement—a prospect that the most honestly racist figures on the far-right call "white genocide." Non-white people disproportionately vote

---

* *Demos* is a Greek word that political philosophers use to describe "the people" and who gets included and excluded from it.

Democrat—a trend gravely exacerbated by unconstrained Republican racism that has alienated even wealthy and economically conservative non-white people. Demographics aren't destiny. But thanks to the foundational role that racism plays in American capitalism, they do mean quite a bit.

In August 2019, Trump finally implemented an aggressive attack on legal immigration, expanding the definition of what makes an immigrant "likely to become a public charge" and thus excludable from the country.[28] The rule further empowers immigration officers to deny entry to poor and working-class immigrants, particularly from Latin America, or to deny immigrants already in the country a green card. The rule radically expands a provision of US immigration law dating back to the Immigration Act of 1882 and, before that, to New York and Massachusetts's enforcement targeting Irish paupers. The Migration Policy Institute predicts that the rule "could cause a significant share of the nearly 23 million noncitizens and U.S. citizens in immigrant families using public benefits to disenroll."[29] And visa denials under Trump had already skyrocketed before the new rule was in place.[30]

It is unclear how profoundly the rule will reshape either the size or the class, national, and racial makeup of legal immigration. But regardless, the new rule is a reflection of Trump's inability to secure cuts or changes to legal immigration in Congress. The rule will very likely be rolled back under even a milquetoast Democratic president. The same holds true with Trump's deep cuts to refugee admissions, and the draconian proposal pushed by some in his orbit to cut admissions to zero. Trump is effectively terrorizing migrants in the present but failing to secure the enduring legislative change that would outlast his presidency.

There is no majority constituency today for enacting such legislation—nor any viable institutional vehicle for it. Whatever opportunity existed to leverage a white-grievance-fueled presidency toward a full nativist program has faded even as the right clings to power thanks to the system's profoundly anti-democratic features. The left is nowhere near winning. But it is at long last emerging as a real force in clear conflict with both the Trumpist right and the center that facilitated its rise.

For Bill Clinton, Hillary Clinton, Obama, Biden, Feinstein, Schumer, and a host of other Democrats, a measure of nativism was useful. Quite a bit more than that has proven necessary for Republicans. But too much nativism is a problem: no rational capitalist favors shutting out exploitable migrant labor. As Karl Marx wrote in *The Eighteenth Brumaire*, political stances that seem rooted in principle are in reality founded—if often in indirect, unconscious, and obscure ways—in "material conditions of existence." This is no doubt the case here.

The United States has undergone decades of enforcement escalation, fashioning a useful scapegoat for neoliberalism and empire while maintaining a segmented labor market. But business frequently lost too, most spectacularly with the repeated defeat of comprehensive immigration reform. Business wants the undocumented to be legalized and guest workers who provide the benefits of undocumented labor without the risk. But what perhaps best reflects—but by no means exclusively reflects—the power of business is what *hasn't* happened: deep legislative cuts to authorized immigration have been consistently off the table for more than two decades. This has been the case since the 1996 legislation to slash legal immigration was defeated in favor of a law to persecute undocumented immigrants and "criminal aliens." The immigration debate has taken on a bizarre and contradictory life of its own. The unspeakability of cuts to authorized immigration, and the failure to impose effective employer sanctions and employment verification systems reveal that immigration policy was still tethered, narrowly but firmly, to the interests of capital. With Trump, full nativism is spoken. But substantial immigration reductions still cannot pass Congress.

A full examination of the complex role of business, the rich, and their various factions during the past two decades of immigration politics is yet to be written. Some of its basic contours, however, are clear. For one, the capitalist class has become recklessly polyphonic. Lumpen-billionaires like the Mercer family and the Koch brothers have spent vast amounts to promote their ideologically distinct priorities rather than those of the collective.[31] The Tanton network is a case in point: it received more than $150 million since 2005 from the Colcom Foundation, founded by the late Mellon heir Cordelia Scaife May.[32] Ironically, independent right-wing oligarchs who pursue idiosyncratic agendas now rival the Chamber of Commerce for influence thanks to the policy achievements of groups like the Chamber of Commerce, which helped those oligarchs make and keep their billions. But does establishment big business even care about immigration anymore?

Political scientist Margaret Peters argues that productivity gains and globalization's facilitation of an overseas supply of low-wage labor has led to a lessening of business's need for immigrant workers, resulting in more restriction.[33] The evidence for this, however, is mixed. On the one hand, business has not won a major legislative expansion of immigration since 1990. But it has also not suffered a major defeat. What's clear is that business can tolerate border security theatrics and the demonization of "criminal aliens," and is content to exploit undocumented workers. As anthropologist Nicholas De Genova writes, "It is deportability, and not deportation per se, that has historically rendered undocumented migrant labor a distinctly disposable commodity."[34] Business opposes dramatic cuts to authorized immigration, effective employer sanctions, and mandatory employee verification. Business prefers legalization, but that doesn't rival priorities like tax cuts and deregulation; if it did, business would abandon the Republican Party. The roles played in immigration politics by business interests with various and often bipartisan attachments require further research, which will in turn help to clarify the woefully under-studied sociology of ruling class power more generally.

Meanwhile, business's hold on the Democratic Party has come under intense assault. The war on "illegal immigrants" that accelerated in the 1990s is facilitating a realignment of left-of-center politics in favor of a diverse, immigrant-inclusive working class in opposition to war, neoliberal oligarchy, and hard borders. The post–Cold War dominance of carceral neoliberalism had made such a popular coalition impossible; the exhaustion of that model signaled by the 2008 crisis has made it astonishingly credible. Record deportations and a radicalizing racist right triggered a revolt among the Democratic Party's young and increasingly diverse base. That base has along with much of American public opinion moved to perhaps the most staunchly pro-immigrant position in American history—and, in doing so, toward a radically inclusive vision of the American working class. Amid a post-Recession boom in labor militancy, that portends trouble for the entire political establishment and the racist and oligarchic order it protects.

Trump's election set that trajectory into overdrive, rendering opinions on immigration a basic proxy for one's partisan allegiance. Border militarization that once garnered bipartisan support is now the polarizing Wall. Obama's brutal migrant detention centers have under Trump been labeled "concentration camps." The number of Republicans who believe that the United States risks losing its national identity if the country welcomes immigrants from the world over has increased since Trump's election.[35] At the same time, Democrats have become more hostile to enforcement. In 2010, 47 percent of Democrats said that they equally prioritized a pathway to legalizing undocumented immigrants and "better border security and stronger enforcement of immigration laws," while just 29 percent prioritized a pathway to legalization alone. By 2018, the number prioritizing legalization alone skyrocketed to 51 percent.[36] As the war on immigrants kicked into high gear in 1994, just 32 percent of Democrats and 30 percent of Republicans agreed that immigrants strengthened the country. By 2016, the share of Democrats who said so had surged to 78 percent.[37]

Extreme polarization, the establishment's bête noire, is in fact the only solution to the long-standing bipartisan agreement that immigration is a problem for enforcement to solve. Demanded and rejected, oppressed and expelled, this country's many others have long insisted that the promise of American freedom, designed for if never truly delivered to white settlers, belongs to them too because they too are the people.[38] And contrary to what Trump's presidency might suggest, a growing number of Americans agree and are turning against nativism and war. Racism is, as the remarkable number of Americans embracing socialism understand, an obstacle to freeing everyone.

The issue of borders is, in turn, a simple one in principle for socialists: borders are a nationalist enterprise and thus incompatible with an internationalist workers' creed. Migration is a symptom of social violence when it is compelled by poverty, war, or climate change. But moving to faraway and strange places is often a beautiful journey too, one nurtured by love, adventure, and the drive for self-determination and realization. Migration should be free and the choice to migrate should be freely made. The border does not protect Americans against cultural change, economic insecurity, and terrorism. It bolsters a system of global inequality that harms people everywhere by dividing them.

Even with public opinion moving rapidly to our side, border controls will not fall anytime soon. To chip away at them, we must understand their historical particularity. The legal right to travel was, for most white people, a basic one for much of American history. It remains so for wealthy people, particularly those with passports from rich countries. Border controls arose in the United States not out of any neutral law enforcement principle but to exclude Asians, Jews, Italians, Latinos, blacks, Muslims, and other Others in the service of an exploitative and expansionist empire. Our land borders began to harden only alongside the rise of industrial capitalism, and were only militarized in recent decades.

If Democrats stick to the center on immigration, they will find themselves fighting on two fronts. A fight against Republicans, with the left at their back, will be far easier to win—and a more noble victory. Simple realism dictates that no legislation to grant citizenship to millions will be passed until Republicans are defeated. There's no use trying to appease them. The bipartisan consensus supporting harsh immigration and border enforcement has fractured. Democratic elected officials need to catch up or be defeated too. It's the task of the left to accelerate the nascent split, demanding radical reforms that correspond to our dream of a world where no human being is illegal. We must transform nation-states so that they no longer divide workers but instead are conduits for the democratic control of our social, economic, political, and ecological futures.

We must urgently develop demands for policies that will not create an open border overnight but a radically *more open* border soon. The border must be demilitarized, which would include demolishing the hundreds of miles of already existing wall and dramatically downsizing the Border Patrol. Criminal sanctions on illegal entry and reentry and the public charge rule must be repealed. Links between ICE and local law enforcement created by Secure Communities and 287(g) must be broken. Opportunities for legal immigration, particularly from Mexico and Central America, must be expanded. The right to asylum must be honored. And citizenship for those who reside here must be a stand-alone cause, unencumbered by compromises that are not only distasteful but also politically ineffectual—and that today would provoke opposition from both the nativist right and the grassroots left.

The nature of struggle

The most critical threat posed by xenophobia has not yet been examined so far in this book: unchecked climate change. Climate change, in turn, will ensure that immigration remains at the center of political conflict everywhere. Ecological catastrophe is already sending refugees fleeing within and across borders, and only movements that transcend borders can address it. The wealthy who are committed to maintaining the carbon-intensive status quo will need borders to impose a system of eco-apartheid, one fortified with new walls along external and internal boundaries guarding against ordinary people and rising seas. Militarization, segregation, incarceration, exclusion, and empire have all sought to ensure that the people who benefit most from the status quo are sheltered from its costs.

We face two possible futures. In one, we continue to live under a highly unequal system rooted in fossil fuels and private property, let nationalist politicians deny global warming, exploit natural resources, and, ultimately, construct workarounds to mitigate climate chaos for the wealthy, subjecting the majority, here and everywhere, to crisis, precarity, and death. In this future, nationalism, racism, and xenophobia are the only tools with which the rich can win over a cross-class alliance to their genocidal program. In the other future, we recognize our shared stake in climate safety and clearly identify our common enemies. Climate change is a planetary crisis; accordingly, we must confront it by embracing internationalism. Nationalism, symptomatized by war and xenophobia, poses a greater threat to addressing global warming than climate denialism. Or, alternatively put, nationalism *is* climate denialism. Defeating nativism and building a mass working-class movement to transform the world are the same thing and the stakes are unspeakably high.

The nativist movement strangely enough had its roots in the budding environmental consciousness of the 1970s. As the postwar consensus crashed, Americans paused to find their air and water filthy, and their future uncertain. Some identified population growth as a culprit. It was from this milieu that nativist godfather John Tanton emerged, warning that mass immigration posed a threat to the natural world. Yet nationalist environmentalism on an international planet never made much sense. In retrospect, hyperventilation about black and brown poor people having too many children was a smokescreen that obscured the existential threat posed by rich people emitting too much carbon.

The restriction of people's freedom of movement has been pursued in the name of protecting the environment, the economy, public safety, and a Euro-American majority. In every case, hardened boundaries have only served a ruling class whose hoarding of wealth visits ruin upon people on each side of every border. Freeing everyone will require that we tear down the Wall.

ACKNOWLEDGEMENTS

This book was a labor of love for the movement. But labor is a social relation, and I have many people to thank and, in doing so, briefly recount what led me to write this story.

I first decided to study the US–Mexican border in college, making lengthy visits to Ciudad Juárez, Mexico, in 2004 and 2005 to research my undergraduate thesis. This was a change in plan: I had initially tried to learn Arabic with the goal of studying the Middle East. The invasion of Afghanistan was launched with all-but-unanimous congressional support and a public mood pervaded by wild jingoism. Our tiny protests were lonely and too small to stop the war. Then the invasion of Iraq happened in the face of the largest global protests in history.

I joined the radical left in high school during the late 1990s. The global justice movement brought together a "Teamsters and turtles" labor-environmentalist protest alliance against the World Trade Organization meeting in Seattle, offering the possibility of a struggle against neoliberalism that would unite the vast majority against corporate rule. But September

11 provided the Bush Administration and its Democratic opponents alike with an opportunity to replace a nascent class conflict with civilizational war. A briefly vibrant anti-war movement, and my time with Chris Toensing and Catherine Clark of the Middle East Research and Information Project (MERIP), planted the seeds of this book's critique of empire.

Learning Spanish, however, was far easier. And Latin America's new "Pink Tide" governments and the social movements that catapulted them into power were, in all honesty, less depressing to study than the US-wrought carnage inflicted in Iraq. I learned about the region through the border, an in-between place that illuminated everything it divided. It helped me understand how Bill Clinton's beatifically flat world at the end of history had so quickly become George W. Bush's war on terror. Beneath the 1990s' plastic surface lurked the raw exploitation, violence, and racism that made Thomas Friedman's sunny pronouncements possible. And it was all most strikingly manifest at the border, where capital flowed freely and labor migration was criminalized.

The summer after my junior year at Reed College I headed to Juárez with the support of my advisor, anthropologist Charlene Makeley. She, along with Paul Silverstein and many other professors, taught me how to think critically about capitalism, nationalism, the state, race, and gender; they taught me how to make sense of the world by reading theory with and against concrete reality as people made it, if not under conditions of their own choosing.

In Juárez, I lived with Veronica Rosario Leyva and her family in Guadalajara Izquierda, a neighborhood built by migrants from across Mexico. Leyva's home was built by her mother, Margarita Leyva Burciaga, who moved to Juárez from the state of Durango in the 1960s to find work. Many moved there: the city's population nearly quintupled between 1960 and 2000 as workers sought jobs in the booming maquiladora industry. My temporary home offered a clear view of downtown El Paso, where the side of the Wells Fargo building was lit up as an enormous American flag at night. It was, I thought, an unsubtle illustration of Gloria Anzaldúa's classic line: "The U.S.-Mexican border *es una herida abierta* where the Third World grates against the first and bleeds."

Veronica had worked in maquilas and then as a labor organizer for the Labor Workshop and Studies Center (CETLAC), an effort by Mexico's Authentic Labor Front (FAT) to reach border factory workers and street vendors in a climate ferociously hostile to independent labor unions. It is to Veronica, *mi madre postiza*, and her colleagues Félix Leonardo Pérez Verdugo, Beatriz Eugenia Luján, and Daniel Rocha that I owe my introduction to the borderlands. And to Alejandro Pérez Ávila, a diehard troublemaker who spent so many days guiding me across his city. He is sorely missed. And also to Veronica and Alejandro's children José Alejandro "Alex," Claudia Angélica, and María Margarita Pérez Leyva. And a shout out to the Kasa de Kultura para Tod@s for welcoming this gringo to *punkero* Juárez.

My analysis of immigration would be impossible without the people in and around the Portland Central America Solidarity Committee (PCASC), where I inexplicably was hired as the sole staff member after graduating college in

2005. Founded in 1979 in solidarity with Central American revolutionaries, in 2006 we found ourselves at the center of the new mass immigrant rights movement. PCASC was a special place for the Portland, Oregon, left in the mid-2000s, uniting an unusual crew of young radicals, militants from El Salvador and Guatemala, Mexican *jornaleros*, and labor radicals from multiple union locals.

Thanks to everyone from those days in Portland. But I'd like to thank by name those who were at the core of immigrant rights work: Romeo Sosa from Voz; Deborah Schwartz, Megan Hise, Andreina Velasco, Maribel Gomez, Trillium Shannon, Shizuko Hashimoto, and Lolo Cutamay (of famed Salvadoran band Cutumay Camones) from PCASC; Aeryca Steinbauer from Causa; Chris Ferlazzo, Laurie King, and Dave King from Jobs with Justice; and Marco Mejia and Pedro Sosa at the American Friends Service Committee. And to the late David Ayala, a union organizer first in El Salvador, where he was detained and tortured by the US-backed regime, and then in the Pacfic Northwest. He was feared by bosses and oppressors on all sides of every border and is missed. And also to Wences, a working class organic intellectual from Oaxaca who frequented my messy PCASC office near the *jornalero* corner to discuss the machinations of global capitalism.

The analysis that informs this book is deeply indebted to the militant grassroots' immigrant rights movement. These fierce activists demanded so much more than their beltway counterparts could ever imagine—and they taught me that immigrant liberation is a struggle for everyone's freedom.

I wouldn't be a journalist at all if it wasn't for a ton of people who initially helped me pretend that I was one. Ben Dangl published my first reporting at *Upside Down World*. Christy Thornton, then executive director at NACLA, helped me publish my first investigative work. Everyone from Philadelphia *City Paper* and particularly the news team— Ryan Briggs, Emily Guendelsberger, Sam Melamed, Holly Otterbein, Isaiah Thompson—and Theresa Everline, for giving me my first reporting job. Journalism and this country are much worse off without alt-weeklies. And I am forever grateful to *Jacobin* editor Bhaskar Sunkara, who—after I was mercifully laid off from my brief stint at *Salon*—not only helped me secure this book contract but also (along with Micah Uetricht and Alex Press) welcomed *The Dig*, my podcast, into Jacobin's orbit.

My producer, Alex Lewis, makes *The Dig* possible every week, as have Logan Dreher and Julia Rock. Indeed, this book would have been impossible to write without the podcast: thank you to all the listeners who support the show. Jeffrey Brodsky, for crafting our signature tunes but even more so for being a great friend. The Taubman Center for Public Policy and American Institutions at Brown University's Watson Institute for International and Public Affairs provided me with a library card without which I could not have conducted this research. Portions of works that I published in *Jacobin* and the *New York Times* appear in chapter 4 and the conclusion—thanks to both.

This book would be a mess without my editor at Verso, Ben Mabie, who figured out how I could structure an

ALL-AMERICAN NATIVISM

explanation of the entirety of US history through the prism of nativism in roughly 80,000 words, and who advocated for me when that was *way* over the initial word count I had agreed to. Thank you to Andy Hsiao for accepting a rather inchoate book proposal and to Max Thorn, Chris Gelardi, and Will Tavlin who spent dozens of hours ruthlessly fact-checking me. Yet any remaining errors, as they say, remain mine.

Many helped me understand immigration history and politics beyond my personal experience as an activist, through interviews and conversations on *The Dig* and elsewhere, including Juliet Stumpf, Daniel Tichenor, David FitzGerald, Greg Grandin, Mae Ngai, Nick Estes, Paul Frymer, Kelly Lytle-Hernandez, and Charles Kamasaki. Many journalists reported the stories that kept me up to date on Trump's latest barbarities while I buried my brain in history: Dara Lind, Aura Bogado, Monica Campbell, and Jonathan Blitzer. Thanks to the Migration Policy Institute for their voluminous research and responses to my queries. And to Nicholas Kulish for last-minute archival assistance.

An enormous thank you to everyone who read and commented on a portion or the entirety of the book. That includes Nikil Saval (who read a first draft that no one should have ever seen), Peter Andreas, Ana Avendano, Stephanie DeGooyer, César Cuauhtémoc García Hernández, Adam Goodman, Carly Goodman, Hidetaka Hirota, J. Mamana, Thea Riofrancos, Quinn Slobodian, Rick Swartz, Christy Thornton, and Gabriel Winant. Frank Sharry generously read a draft even though it was quite hard on his politics. Aziz Rana not only read multiple drafts but also provided me with a framework for analyzing the history of race, class, and colonialism in the United States. Chris Newman of the National Day Laborer Organizing Network (NDLON) helped form my overarching analysis of immigration reform politics and gave me the idea to write the *Jacobin* article that ultimately became this book. Chris, a frequent draft-reader and constant consultant through every modern communication medium, was indispensable.

My parents Jim and Rangeley encouraged me to read constantly, think critically, and dissent on principle. They no doubt got more than they bargained for and I hope only regretted it all briefly, sometime between my middle school arrest for trespassing and my high school discovery of left-wing politics (and the more noble arrests that followed). And Jamie, Emma, and Jack for surviving being my siblings.

Not one page of this would be possible without Thea Riofrancos, my first and last advisor on everything, perfect companion, constant interlocutor, and radical anchor. I first tried to impress you after Spanish class by talking about the Frankfurt School even though I didn't know a thing about it. You came home sunburnt from the World Social Forum at Porto Alegre, organized against military recruitment in Portland high schools, moved with me to Ecuador because it was a place where we saw something big was happening, and led me to Philly, Rhode Island, and Chile. I have followed you everywhere because I would follow you anywhere. We are constantly striving for the perfect analysis and we are getting there. My takes and life alike would be unimaginably worse without you.

NOTES

Introduction

1 Transcript, "CNN Tonight," transcripts.cnn.com, April 28, 2016.
2 "Executive Order Protecting the Nation from Foreign Terrorist Entry into the United States," whitehouse.gov, January 27, 2017.
3 Adam Liptak and Michael D. Shear, "Trump's Travel Ban Is Upheld by Supreme Court," *New York Times*, June 26, 2018; Melissa Cruz, "Trump's Travel Ban Leaves Thousands of US Citizens Separated from Their Families," immigrationimpact.com, January 29, 2019.
4 Lauren Gambino, "Trump and Syrian Refugees in the US: Separating the Facts from Fiction," *The Guardian*, September 2, 2016.
5 Douglas S. Massey and Karen A. Pren, "Unintended Consequences of US Immigration Policy: Explaining the Post-1965 Surge from Latin America," *Population and Development Review* 38(1), 2012, available at ncbi.nlm.nih.gov.
6 Jynnah Radford, "Key Findings about U.S. Immigrants," pewresearch. org, June 17, 2019.
7 German Lopez, "The War on Drugs, Explained," vox.com, May 8, 2016.
8 "Shifting Public Views on Legal Immigration into the U.S.," people-press.org, June 28, 2018.
9 The Editorial Board, "A Chance to Reset the Republican Race," *New York Times*, January 30, 2016.

Chapter One

1   *Congressional Record*, 104th Congress, 2nd Session, September 25, 1996.

2   W. E. B. Du Bois, *Black Reconstruction in America : Toward a History of the Part Which Black Folk Played in the Attempt to Reconstruct Democracy in America, 1860–1880*, New Brunswick: Routledge, 2012, 10.

3   Daniel J. Tichenor, *Dividing Lines: The Politics of Immigration Control in America*, Princeton: Princeton University Press, 2002, 89; Mark Kanazawa, "Immigration, Exclusion, and Taxation: Anti-Chinese Legislation in Gold Rush California," *The Journal of Economic History* 65(3), 2005, 779–805.

4   Aziz Rana, *The Two Faces of American Freedom*, Cambridge, MA: Harvard University Press, 2010, 183, 186–89.

5   Tichenor, *Dividing Lines*, 24.

6   Laura Grattan, *Populism's Power: Radical Grassroots Democracy in America*, New York: Oxford University Press, 2016, 79–80.

7   Rana, *Two Faces of American Freedom*, 196–200, 215–18.

8   Kerry Abrams, "Polygamy, Prostitution, and the Federalization of Immigration Law," *Columbia Law Review* 641, 2005, 695–96.

9   Tichenor, *Dividing Lines*, 106.

10 Ibid., 115.

11 Janice Fine and Daniel J. Tichenor, "A Movement Wrestling: American Labor's Enduring Struggle with Immigration, 1866–2007," *Studies in American Political Development* 23(2), 2009, 84–95; Justin Akers Chacón, *Radicals in the Barrio: Magonistas, Socialists, Wobblies, and Communists in the Mexican American Working Class*, Chicago: Haymarket Books, 2018; Devra Anne Weber, "Mexican Workers in the IWW and the Partido Liberal Mexicano (PLM)," IWW History Project, depts.washington.edu, 2016.

12 Paul Heideman, "The Rise and Fall of the Socialist Party of America," *Jacobin*, Fall 2016.

13 Douglas Massey et al., *Beyond Smoke and Mirrors: Mexican Immigration in an Era of Economic Integration*, New York: Russell Sage Foundation, 2003, 27–31.

14 Rebecca Onion, "America's Lost History of Border Violence," slate. com, May 5, 2016.

15 The Immigration Commission, *Abstract of the Report on Japanese and*

Other Immigrant Races in the Pacific Coast and Rocky Mountain States, Washington: Government Printing Office, 1911, 76.

16 Abraham Hoffman, *Unwanted Mexican-Americans in the Great Depression: Repatriation Pressures, 1929–1939*, Tucson: University of Arizona Press, 1974, 10.

17 William A. Kandel, "The Trump Administration's 'Zero Tolerance' Immigration Enforcement Policy," Congressional Research Service, crsreports.congress.gov, February 26, 2019.

18 Kelly Lytle Hernández, *City of Inmates: Conquest, Rebellion, and the Rise of Human Caging in Los Angeles, 1771–1965*, Chapel Hill: University of North Carolina Press, 2017, 137–38.

19 Francisco E. Balderrama and Raymond Rodríguez, *Decade of Betrayal: Mexican Repatriation in the 1930s*, Albuquerque: University of New Mexico Press, 2006, 136–51.

20 Tichenor, *Dividing Lines*, 174; Pam Belluck, "Settlement Will Allow Thousands of Mexican Laborers in U.S. to Collect Back Pay," *New York Times*, October 15, 2008.

21 Marc R. Rosenblum et al., "Mexican Migration to the United States: Policy and Trends," Congressional Research Service, crsreports. congress.gov, June 7, 2012, 7.

22 Hiroshi Motomura, *Immigration outside the Law*, New York: Oxford University Press, 2014, 40.

23 Douglas S. Massey et al., *Worlds in Motion: Understanding International Migration at the End of the Millennium*, New York: Oxford University Press, 2002, 73.

24 Mae M. Ngai, *Impossible Subjects: Illegal Aliens and the Making of Modern America*, Princeton: Princeton University Press, 2014, 158–66.

25 Tichenor, *Dividing Lines*, 152.

26 Ibid., 174.

27 Kelly Lytle Hernández, *Migra! A History of the U.S. Border Patrol*, Berkeley: University of California Press, 2010, 171–95.

28 Massey et al., *Beyond Smoke and Mirrors*, 36–37; Mae M. Ngai, *Impossible Subjects: Illegal Aliens and the Making of Modern America*, Princeton: Princeton University Press, 2014, 153; Tichenor, *Dividing Lines*, 225.

29 Arnold R. Weber, "The Role of the US Department of Labor in Immigration," *International Migration Review* 4(3), 1970, 31.

30 Mae M. Ngai, *Impossible Subjects: Illegal Aliens and the Making of*

Modern America, Princeton: Princeton University Press, 2014, 258–64.

31 Jack Jones, "Mexican-American Group Objects to Use of 'Wetbacks,'" *Los Angeles Times*, August 29, 1967; Homer Bigart, "Unions Deplore Influx of Mexican Laborers along the Border," *New York Times*, May 4, 1969; Tichenor, *Dividing Lines*, 226.

32 Joseph Nevins, "The Boycott Legend Sacrifices the Movement: Cesar Chavez and the Renewed Case for Radical Democracy," nacla.org, January 14, 2014.

33 Robert Lindsey, "Criticism of Chavez Takes Root in Farm Labor Struggle," *New York Times*, February 7, 1979.

34 United States Department of Justice, Immigration and Naturalization Service, "Report of the Commissioner of Immigration and Naturalization," hathitrust.org, 1973.

35 Judith Stein, *Pivotal Decade: How the United States Traded Factories for Finance in the Seventies*, New Haven: Yale University Press, 2010, xi–xii.

36 Melinda Cooper, *Family Values: Between Neoliberalism and the New Social Conservatism*, New York: Zone Books, 2017, 27–29.

37 Lane Windham, *Knocking on Labor's Door: Union Organizing in the 1970s and the Roots of a New Economic Divide*, Chapel Hill: University of North Carolina Press, 2017.

38 Matthew D. Lassiter, *The Silent Majority: Suburban Politics in the Sunbelt South*, Princeton: Princeton University Press, 53, 63–64.

39 Garrett Hardin, "The Tragedy of the Commons," *Science*, December 13, 1968.

40 Elinor Ostrom, *Governing the Commons: The Evolution of Institutions for Collective Action*, Cambridge: Cambridge University Press, 1990.

41 Adlai E. Stevenson, last statement before a United Nations body to the Economic and Social Council, Geneva, July 9, 1965, available at archive.org/details/UNFinal.

42 Garrett Hardin, "Lifeboat Ethics: The Case against Helping the Poor," *Psychology Today*, September 1974, available at garretthardinsociety. org.

43 Garrett Hardin, "Lifeboat Ethics," *Bioscience*, October 1974, 561–68.

44 Missing Migrants Project, "Latest Global Figures," missingmigrants. iom.int.

45 Sara Terry, "America's Welcome: Wearing Thin?," *Christian Science Monitor*, June 25, 1981.

46 Leslie Aldridge Westoff, "A Nation of Immigrants: Should We Pull Up the Gangplank?," *New York Times Magazine*, September 16, 1973.

47 Otis L. Graham, *Immigration Reform and America's Unchosen Future*, Bloomington: AuthorHouse, 2008, 45.

48 The Garrett Hardin Society, "Garrett Hardin Oral History Project: Tape 11," accessed September 9, 2019, available at garretthardinsociety.org; Nicholas Kulish and Mike McIntire, "Why an Heiress Spent Her Fortune Trying to Keep Immigrants Out," *New York Times*, August 14, 2019.

49 Robert Scheer, "Law Part of the Problem: Illegal Aliens' Half-Life," *Los Angeles Times*, November 12, 1979; "For the Record," *Los Angeles Times*, November 19, 1979.

50 William Trombley, "Prop. 63 Roots Traced to Small Michigan City," *Los Angeles Times*, October 20, 1986.

51 Kulish and McIntire, "Why an Heiress Spent Her Fortune Trying to Keep Immigrants Out."

52 Brendan O'Connor, "The Eugenicist Doctor and the Vast Fortune behind Trump's Immigration Regime," splinternews.com, July 5, 2018.

53 The Garrett Hardin Society, "Garrett Hardin Oral History Project: Tape 11," accessed September 9, 2019, available at garretthardinsociety.org.

54 Nicholas Kulish, "Dr. John Tanton, Quiet Catalyst in Anti-Immigration Drive, Dies at 85," *New York Times*, July 18, 2019; Southern Poverty Law Center, "John Tanton's Network," available at splcenter.org.

55 Kulish and McIntire, "Why an Heiress Spent Her Fortune Trying to Keep Immigrants Out."

56 William Branigin, "Immigration Policy Dispute Rocks Sierra Club," *Washington Post*, March 7, 1998; Felicity Barringer, "Sierra Club Revisits Issue of Immigration," *New York Times*, April 13, 2005.

57 Otis L. Graham, *Immigration Reform and America's Unchosen Future*, Bloomington: AuthorHouse, 2008, 44.

58 Charles Kamasaki, *Immigration Reform: The Corpse That Will Not Die*, Simsbury, CT: Mandel Vilar Press, 2019, 94.

59 Ibid., 267.

60 Tucker Carlson, "The Intellectual Roots of Nativism," *Wall Street Journal*, October 2, 1997.

61 Tim Weiner, "Pleas for Asylum Inundate System for Immigration," *New York Times*, April 25, 1993.

62 Kamasaki, *Immigration Reform*, 268.

63 Carly Goodman, email to author, August 8, 2019.

64 Kamasaki, *Immigration Reform*, 355.

65 Associated Press, "Wetbacks Flock to Dallas Area," *Austin Statesman*, February 14, 1969.

66 Tichenor, *Dividing Lines*, 224–27.

67 Fine and Tichenor, "A Movement Wrestling," 97–104.

68 Kitty Calavita, "California's 'Employer Sanctions' Law: Now You See It, Now You Don't," *Politics and Society* 12(2), 1983, 205–30.

69 Tichenor, *Dividing Lines*, 208–9.

70 Marjorie Hunter, "James O. Eastland Is Dead," *New York Times*, February 20, 1986.

71 "Eastland Protest Halted '72 Raids on Cotton Gins," *New York Times*, December 31, 1974.

72 David G. Gutiérrez, "'Sin Fronteras?': Chicanos, Mexican Americans, and the Emergence of the Contemporary Mexican Immigration Debate, 1968–1978," *Journal of American Ethnic History* 10(4), 1991, 28–29.

73 Fine and Tichenor, "A Movement Wrestling," 123; Gutiérrez, "'Sin Fronteras?,'" 17–26.

74 M. A. Farber, "Million Illegal Aliens in Metropolitan Area," *New York Times*, December 29, 1974; Roger Sanjek, "Color-Full before Color Blind: The Emergence of Multiracial Neighborhood Politics in Queens, New York City," *American Anthropologist* 102(4), 2000, 762–72; James Nevius, "The Transformation of Jackson Heights: From Planned Community to Neighborhood," curbed.com, April 19, 2017.

75 M. A. Farber, "Unlawful Aliens Use Costly City Services," *New York Times*, December 30, 1974.

76 Ari L. Goldman, "Illegal Aliens Living in Queens Are Assailed at Hearing," *New York Times*, November 24, 1974.

77 Sanjek, "Color-Full before Color Blind," 764.

78 Lee A. Daniels, "Troubled Lefrak City Turning the Corner," *New York Times*, March 11, 1984.

79 Kim Phillips-Fein, *Fear City: New York's Fiscal Crisis and the Rise of Austerity Politics,* New York: Metropolitan Books, 2017, 8.

80 Farber, "Unlawful Aliens Use Costly City Services."

81 Farber, "Million Illegal Aliens in Metropolitan Area."

82 Kelly Lytle Hernández, *Migra! A History of the U.S. Border Patrol,* Berkeley: University of California Press, 2010, 215.

83 John Kendall, "Influx of Illegal Aliens Termed 'Out of Control,'" *Los Angeles Times,* January 9, 1977; Tichenor, *Dividing Lines,* 229.

84 William K. Stevens, "Millions of Mexicans View Illegal Entry to U.S. as Door to Opportunity," *New York Times,* February 12, 1979.

85 Kendall, "Influx of Illegal Aliens Termed 'Out of Control.'"

86 Tichenor, *Dividing Lines,* 230; Muzaffar Chishti et al., "At Its 25th Anniversary, IRCA's Legacy Lives On," migrationpolicy.org, November 6, 2011.

87 Pradnya Joshi and Binyamin Appelbaum, "A History of Fed Leaders and Interest Rates," *New York Times,* December 16, 2015; Samir Sonti, "The World Paul Volcker Made," Jacobinmag.com, December 20, 2018; Cooper, *Family Values,* 25–27.

88 Ronald Reagan, "Republican National Convention Acceptance Speech," reaganlibrary.gov, July 17, 1980.

89 Ronald Reagan, "Ronald Reagan's Announcement for Presidential Candidacy," reaganlibrary.gov, November 13, 1979.

90 Congressional Select Commission on Immigration and Refugee Policy, "U.S. Immigration Policy and the National Interest: The Final Report and Recommendations of the Select Commission on Immigration and Refugee Policy with Supplemental Views by Commissioners," March 1, 1981, 3, 12.

91 Ibid., 11, 62, 74.

92 Mary Thornton, "Raids Nab High-Pay Aliens, Make Jobs, Outrage Clergy," *Washington Post,* May 2, 1982.

93 Frank H. Wu, "Why Vincent Chin Matters," *New York Times,* June 22, 2012.

94 James Reston, "Mondale's Tough Line," *New York Times,* October 13, 1982.

95 Tichenor, *Dividing Lines,* 255–6.

96 Jon Margolis, "Reagan Breaks GOP Tradition, Woos Chicanos," *Chicago Tribune,* September 17, 1980.

97 Kamasaki, *Immigration Reform,* 189, 295.

98 Carla N. Argueta, "Border Security: Immigration Enforcement between Ports of Entry," Congressional Research Service, fas.org, April 19, 2016.

99 Michael E. Miller, "Diversity Visa Lottery, Criticized after New York Terrorist Attack, Was Invented to Help the Irish," *Washington Post*, November 1, 2017; Julia Gelatt, "The Diversity Visa Program Holds Lessons for Future Legal Immigration Reform," Migration Policy Institute, migrationpolicy.org, February 2018.

100 Dolores Acevedo and Thomas J. Espenshade, "Implications of a North American Free Trade Agreement for Mexican Migration into the United States," *Population and Development Review* 18(4), 1992, 729–44; "Report of the Commission for the Study of International Migration and Cooperative Economic Development," hathitrust.org, July 24, 1990.

101 Gil Klein, "Courts Are Next Battleground for Immigration Policy Fight," *Richmond Times-Dispatch*, October 19, 1986; Kamasaki, *Immigration Reform*, 295.

102 Tichenor, *Dividing Lines*, 261–5.

103 George Ramos, "For Some on INS Bus to Tijuana, It's a Round Trip," *Los Angeles Times*, January 1, 1990; Massey et al., *Beyond Smoke and Mirrors*, 138–40.

104 Graham, *Immigration Reform and America's Unchosen Future*, 97–98.

105 Carlos Marichal, "The Vicious Cycles of Mexican Debt," NACLA Report on the Americas, May 31, 2016, 26–28.

106 Tichenor, *Dividing Lines*, 273.

107 Alan K. Simpson, "Will America Control Its Borders?," *Washington Post*, December 5, 1982.

108 Mike Davis, "The Social Origins of the Referendum," *NACLA Report on the Americas* 29(3), 1995; Robert Reinhold, "Welcome for Immigrants Turns to Resentment," *New York Times*, August 25, 1993; James Sterngold, "A Changing California Emerges from Recession," *New York Times*, March 29, 1995.

109 Jeffrey S. Passel et al., "Population Decline of Unauthorized Immigrants Stalls, May Have Reversed," pewhispanic.org, September 23, 2013.

110 Robert Reinhold, "A Welcome for Immigrants Turns to Resentment," *New York Times*, August 25, 1993.

111 Ibid.

112 Leo Chavez, *The Latino Threat: Constructing Immigrants, Citizens, and the Nation*, Stanford: Stanford University Press, 2013; Cooper, *Family Values*, 130–2.

113 Hernández, *City of Inmates: Conquest, Rebellion, and the Rise of Human Caging in Los Angeles, 1771–1965*, 40, 49.

114 Eduardo Obregón Pagán, "Los Angeles Geopolitics and the Zoot Suit Riot, 1943," *Social Science History* 24(1): 223–4.

115 Matthew D. Lassiter, "Pushers, Victims, and the Lost Innocence of White Suburbia: California's War on Narcotics during the 1950s," *Journal of Urban History* 41(5), 2015, 787–9, 795.

116 Scheer, "Illegal Aliens' Half-Life."

117 Ibid.

118 "Voter Information Guide for 1994, General Election," repository, uchastings.edu; Patrick J. McDonnell and Robert J. Lopez, "L.A. March against Prop. 187 Draws 70,000," *Los Angeles Times*, October 17, 1994.

119 "Voter Information Guide for 1994, General Election," repository, uchastings.edu, 91.

120 Daniel Martinez HoSang, *Racial Propositions: Ballot Initiatives and the Making of Postwar California*, Berkeley: University of California Press, 2010, 162–7.

121 Ibid., 166.

122 Ibid., 178.

123 Ibid., 191; Marilyn Kalfus, "Pro-Prop. 187 Group Admits It," *Orange County Register*, October 26, 1994; Paul Feldman, "Group's Funding of Immigration Measure Assailed," *Los Angeles Times*, September 10, 1994.

124 Kenneth Jost, "Cracking Down on Immigration," CQ Researcher, February 3, 1995.

125 "Pete Wilson 1994 Campaign Ad on Illegal Immigration," YouTube video, posted by PeteWilsonCA, February 15, 2010.

126 HoSang, *Racial Propositions*, 172–3; Glenn F. Bunting and Alan C. Miller, "Feinstein Raises Immigration Profile," *Los Angeles Times*, July 18, 1993.

127 George Skelton, "Feinstein Takes Immigration out of Closet," *Los Angeles Times*, July 12, 1992.

128 Bunting and Miller, "Feinstein Raises Immigration Profile."

129 HoSang, *Racial Propositions*, 192.

130 Ngai, *Impossible Subjects*, 258–64.

131 HoSang, *Racial Propositions*, 197.

132 Ibid., 180–1.

133 McDonnell and Lopez, "L.A. March against Prop. 187 Draws 70,000";
     Nicole Hemmer, "Republican Nativism Helped Turn California Blue.
     Trump Could Do the Same for the Whole Country," vox.com, January
     20, 2017.

134 HoSang, *Racial Propositions*, 187.

135 Reuters, "Reno Aims to Control Immigration," *New York Times*,
     September 18, 1994; John Hurst and Sebastian Rotella, "U.S. Weighing
     Controversial Border Crossing Fee, Reno Says," *Los Angeles Times*,
     September 18, 1994.

136 Kitty Calavita, "The New Politics of Immigration: 'Balanced-Budget
     Conservatism' and the Symbolism of Proposition 187," *Social Problems*
     43(3), 1996, 287–9.

137 Ibid., 296.

138 Ibid., 286.

139 Ibid., 284–5.

140 Mike Davis, "The Social Origins of the Referendum"; Mike Davis,
     City of Quartz: Excavating the Future in Los Angeles, London: Verso,
     2018, 164–70.

141 HoSang, *Racial Propositions*, 196.

142 Matthew D. Lassiter, *The Silent Majority: Suburban Politics and the
     Sunbelt South*, Princeton: Princeton University Press, 2006, 8–11.

143 Ibid., 8.

144 Davis, *City of Quartz*, 136.

145 Cooper, *Family Values*, 8.

146 Mark Oppenheimer, "Review: 'We Believe the Children,' on
     Child Abuse Hysteria in the 1980s," *New York Times*, August 6,
     2015.

147 Associated Press, "California Sues U.S. Government over Costs Tied
     to Illegal Aliens," *New York Times*, May 1, 1994; Tony Perry, "State's
     Immigration Suit against U.S. Dismissed," *Los Angeles Times*, February
     14, 1995.

148 Patrick J. McDonnell and Virginia Ellis, "Wilson Acts to Bar Prenatal
     Care for Illegal Immigrants," *Los Angeles Times*, November 2, 1996.

149 Tichenor, *Dividing Lines*, 277.

150 Jost, "Cracking Down on Immigration."

151 David M. Reimers, *Unwelcome Strangers: American Identity and the*

Turn against Immigration, New York: Columbia University Press, 1998, 134.

152 "Text of President Clinton's Announcement on Welfare Legislation," *New York Times*, August 1, 1996; Audrey Singer, "Welfare Reform and Immigrants: A Policy Review," in Philip Kretsedemas and Ana Aparicio, eds., *Immigrants, Welfare Reform, and the Poverty of Policy*, Westport, CT: Praeger Publishers, 2004, 21–34.

153 Motomura, *Immigration outside the Law*, 73.

154 Tichenor, *Dividing Lines*, 276.

155 Rebecca Trounson, "Perot Says Haiti Policy 'Makes No Sense,'" *Los Angeles Times*, September 16, 1994.

156 Roberto Suro, "California's SOS on Immigration," *Washington Post*, September 29, 1994.

157 Michael Lind, "Fatal Attraction," slate.com, October 12, 1999.

158 Dan Balz, "Perot Decries Negative Tactics," *Washington Post*, March 8, 1996.

159 Patrick Joseph Buchanan, "Culture War Speech: Address to the Republican National Convention," voicesofdemocracy.umd.edu, August 17, 1992.

160 Robert Shogan, "Buchanan Attack Upstages Dole at Perot Conference," *Los Angeles Times*, August 13, 1995.

161 Associated Press, "Buchanan, Perot Not Out of Political Picture Yet," *Las Vegas Review-Journal*, March 21, 1996.

162 Robin Toner, "Reform Party Names Perot Its Presidential Candidate," *New York Times*, August 18, 1996; Bob Davis and Hilary Stout, "New Reform Party Finds Enemies Inside and Out," *Wall Street Journal*, August 12, 1996.

163 Patrick J. Buchanan, "America First, NAFTA Never," *Washington Post*, November 7, 1993.

164 Frank Guan, "End of the End of History, Redux," nplusonemag.com.

165 Peter Andreas, *Border Games: Policing the U.S.-Mexico Divide*, Ithaca: Cornell University Press, 2009, 88.

166 Tichenor, *Dividing Lines*, 285–6.

167 Roper Center, "How Groups Voted in 1992," ropercenter.cornell.edu.

Chapter Two

1 Janet Hook, "Clinton Moves to Speed Deportations," *Los Angeles Times*, May 7, 1995.

2 Congressional Select Commission on Immigration and Refugee Policy, "U.S. Immigration Policy and the National Interest: The Final Report and Recommendations of the Select Commission on Immigration and Refugee Policy with Supplemental Views by Commissioners," March 1, 1981, 42.

3 William J. Clinton, "The President's Radio Address," May 6, 1995, presidency.ucsb.edu.

4 Kelly Lytle Hernández, *Migra! A History of the U.S. Border Patrol*, Berkeley: University of California Press, 2010, 36–37.

5 Carla N. Argueta, "Border Security: Immigration Enforcement between Ports of Entry," Congressional Research Service, fas.org, April 19, 2016, 2.

6 Hernández, *Migra!*, 81, 89–91.

7 Ibid., 63, 70.

8 Ibid., 41, 46, 50, 55.

9 Ibid., 104–5.

10 Ibid., 116, 122.

11 L.A. Times Service, "Fences Separating Mexico, U.S. Little Barrier in Some Areas," *Hartford Courant*, November 28, 1980.

12 John M. Crewdson, "In Sister Cities of El Paso and Juarez, 400 Years of History Erase a Border," *New York Times*, July 18, 1981.

13 Charlie Hilinger, "Little Known Agency: The American Border Patrol," *Austin Statesman*, June 24, 1967.

14 Douglas S. Massey and Karen A. Pren, "Unintended Consequences of US Immigration Policy: Explaining the Post-1965 Surge from Latin America," *Population and Development Review*, 38(1), 2012, 1–29.

15 Robert Scheer, "Law Part of the Problem: Illegal Aliens' Half-Life," *Los Angeles Times*, November 12, 1979.

16 Douglas S. Massey and Karen A. Pren, "Unintended Consequences of US Immigration Policy: Explaining the Post-1965 Surge from Latin America," *Population and Development Review*, 38(1), 2012, 1–29.

17 United States Border Patrol, "Southwest Border Sectors: Total Illegal Alien Apprehensions by Fiscal Year (Oct. 1st through Sept. 30th)," cbp.gov.

18 Raúl Delgado-Wise and Luis Eduardo Guarnizo, "Migration and Development: Lessons from the Mexican Experience," migrationpolicy.org, February 1, 2007.

19 Douglas Massey et al., *Beyond Smoke and Mirrors: Mexican Immigration in an Era of Economic Integration*, New York: Russell Sage Foundation, 2003, 15.

20 Raúl Delgado-Wise and Humberto Márquez Covarrubias, "The Reshaping of Mexican Labor Exports under NAFTA: Paradoxes and Challenges," *International Migration Review* 41(3), 2007, 673–5.

21 Joseph A. Reaves, "Battle on the Border," *Chicago Tribune*, April 26, 1983.

22 Ibid.

23 Scheer, "Illegal Aliens' Half-Life."

24 Priscilla Alvarez, "What the Waiting List for Legal Residency Actually Looks Like," *Atlantic*, September 21, 2017.

25 Clara Germani, "Desperate People and a Porous Border," *Christian Science Monitor*, December 17, 1984.

26 Ivor Davis, "Checker Game on the U.S. Border with People as the Pieces," *Globe and Mail*, March 31, 1984.

27 Germani, "Desperate People and a Porous Border."

28 Jay Mathews, "Illegals from Mexico: As Hard to Count as to Stop," *Washington Post*, June 27, 1986.

29 David Harris, "Zone of War: Struggle over Mexican Migrants" *New York Times*, February 17, 1980.

30 Patrick McDonnell, "All-Out Border War to Stem Alien Flow Is High-Tech Affair," *New York Times*, April 13, 1986.

31 Ibid.

32 John M. Crewdson, "Violence, Often Unchecked, Pervades U.S. Border Patrol," *New York Times*, January 14, 1980.

33 Daniel Gonzalez and Rafael Carranza, "Is the Term 'Tronc' an Acronym or a Derogatory Term for Migrants?," azcentral.com, May 19, 2018.

34 Crewdson, "Violence, Often Unchecked, Pervades U.S. Border Patrol."

35 Ibid.; Harris, "Zone of War."

36 John M. Crewdson, "3 Agents of Border Patrol Charged With Beating 8," *New York Times*, July 25, 1980.

37 John M. Crewdson, "2 in Border Patrol Are Found Guilty in First Case on Brutality to Aliens," *New York Times*, January 30, 1980.

38 Hernández, *Migra!*, 207.

39 Stephen Siff, "The Illegalization of Marijuana: A Brief History," *Origins: Current Events in Historical Perspective* 7(8), 2014.

40 Patrick Timmons, "Trump's Wall at Nixon's Border," NACLA Report on the Americas 49(1), 15–24.

41 Matthew D. Lassiter, "Impossible Criminals: The Suburban Imperatives of America's War on Drugs," *Journal of American History* 102(1), 2015, 140.

42 Matthew D. Lassiter, "Pushers, Victims, and the Lost Innocence of White Suburbia: California's War on Narcotics during the 1950s," *Journal of Urban History* 41(5), 2015, 791.

43 Kate Doyle, "Operation Intercept: The Perils of Unilateralism," National Security Archive, April 13, 2003.

44 Michael Agar and Heather Schacht Reisinger, "A Tale of Two Policies: The French Connection, Methadone, and Heroin Epidemics," *Culture, Medicine and Psychiatry* 26(3), 371–96; Nicholas C. Chriss, "Heroin Traffic Takes On Latin Accent: 'Mexican Connection' Hard to Crack, U. S. Agents Find," *Los Angeles Times*, August 1, 1976.

45 Ronald Reagan, "Remarks on Signing Executive Order 12368, Concerning Federal Drug Abuse Policy Functions," June 24, 1982, available at reaganlibrary.gov/research/speeches/62482b.

46 Keith B. Richburg, "Reagan Order Defines Drug Trade as Security Threat, Widens Military Role," *Washington Post*, June 8, 1986.

47 Scott Stewart, "Mexico's Cartels and the Economics of Cocaine," Stratfor, January 3, 2013.

48 Peter Andreas, *Border Games: Policing the U.S.-Mexico Divide*, Ithaca: Cornell University Press, 2012, 43.

49 Ibid., 79; "DEA's Strategies and Operations in the 1990s," United States General Accounting Office, July 1999, 72; Chris Woodyard and Dan Weikel, "5,000 Pounds of Cocaine Seized in 2nd Largest Bust," *Los Angeles Times*, December 19, 1989.

50 Dean Nelson, "The US Border Agents' Challenge," *Boston Globe*, April 28, 1985.

51 "ACLU Releases Crack Cocaine Report: Anti-Drug Abuse Act of 1986 Deepened Racial Inequity in Sentencing," aclu.org, May 26, 2006; Andreas, *Border Games*, 48.

52 William A. Kandel, "Interior Immigration Enforcement: Criminal Alien Programs," Congressional Research Service, fas.org, September 8, 2016, 23.

53 Ibid., Summary; Transactional Records Access Clearinghouse (TRAC), "TRAC Immigration: Aggravated Felonies and Deportation," trac.syr.edu, June 9, 2006.

54 Doug Keller, "Re-thinking Illegal Entry and Re-entry," *Loyola University Chicago Law Journal* 44, 2012, 12.

55 César Cuauhtémoc García Hernández, "Defining Crimmigration Law: Part 1," Crimmigration.com, September 17, 2015.

56 McDonnell, "All-Out Border War."

57 Ibid.; Transactional Records Access Clearinghouse (TRAC), "Graphical Highlights, Immigration: National Trends in Apprehensions and Staffing," trac.syr.edu, 2006.

58 Nelson, "The US Border Agents' Challenge."

59 James Brock, "San Ysidro Border Patrol: A Battle of Technology vs. Superior Numbers," *Baltimore Sun*, February 3, 1985.

60 John Dillin, "Illegal Immigration Surges in '89," *Christian Science Monitor*, December 27, 1989.

61 George Ramos, "For Some on INS Bus to Tijuana, It's a Round Trip," *New York Times*, January 1, 1990.

62 Dillin, "Illegal Immigration Surges in '89."

63 Greg Henderson, "Clinton Administration Defends Bush Haiti Policy," UPI, March 2, 1993; Elaine Sciolino, "Clinton Says U.S. Will Continue Ban on Haitian Exodus," *New York Times*, January 15, 1993.

64 Brandt Goldstein, "Clinton's Guantanamo," Slate.com, December 21, 2005; Mary B.W. Tabor, "Judge Orders the Release of Haitians," *New York Times*, June 9, 1993.

65 "Asylum Seekers Slip through JFK Airport's Strained Security," *Orlando Sentinel*, April 4, 1993.

66 Tim Weiner, "Pleas for Asylum Inundate System for Migration," *New York Times*, April 25, 1993.

67 Maura Ewing, "20 Years Ago, Asylum Seekers Were Not Automatically Put in Immigration Detention," pri.org, December 15, 2016; "Federation for American Immigration Reform," splcenter.org.

68 Weiner, "Pleas for Asylum Inundate System for Migration."

69 Carly Goodman, "Angry That ICE Is Ripping Families Apart? Don't Just Blame Trump. Blame Clinton, Bush and Obama, Too," *Washington Post*, June 11, 2018.

70   Patrick McDonnell, "INS Ponders Border Barricades near San Diego," *Los Angeles Times*, February 12, 1987.

71   Scott Harrison, "Light Up the Border Protests," *Los Angeles Times*, May 25, 1990.

72   Blas Nuñez-Neto and Michael John Garcia, "Border Security: The San Diego Fence," Congressional Research Service, fas.org, May 23, 2007, 2.

73   James Gerstenzang, "Senate Approves NAFTA on 61–38 Vote," *Los Angeles Times*, November 21, 1993; James Gerstenzang and Michael Ross, "House Passes NAFTA, 234–200," *Los Angeles Times*, November 18, 1993.

74   James Bornemeier, "El Paso Plan Deters Illegal Immigrants," *Los Angeles Times*, July 27, 1994; Andreas, *Border Games*, 92.

75   Joel Brinkley, "A Rare Success at the Border Brought Scant Official Praise," *New York Times*, September 14, 1994.

76   Andreas, *Border Games*, 92–93.

77   Kenneth Jost, "Cracking Down on Immigration," CQ Researcher, February 3, 1995.

78   Andreas, *Border Games*, 87–88.

79   Brendan O'Connor, "The Eugenicist Doctor and the Vast Fortune behind Trump's Immigration Regime," splinternews.com, July 5, 2018; Center for Immigration Studies, "Our 2020 Border Tour Will Be Announced This Fall," cis.org; Center for New Community, "Blurring Borders: Collusion between Anti-Immigrant Groups and Immigration Enforcement Agents," newcomm.org, June 30, 2015.

80   Quoted in David M. Reimers, *Unwelcome Strangers: American Identity and the Turn against Immigration*, New York: Columbia University Press, 1998, 80.

81   Ronald Brownstein, "Buchanan Links L.A. Riot to Immigration Problems," *Los Angeles Times*, May 14, 1992.

82   Maria Newman, "After the Riots," *New York Times*, May 11, 1992.

83   Shereen Marisol Meraji, "As Los Angeles Burned, The Border Patrol Swooped In," *All Things Considered*, npr.org, April 27, 2017.

84   Leslie Berger, "Police-INS Actions to Be Probed," *Los Angeles Times*, May 20, 1992; *Civil Disorder: What Do We Know? How Should We Prepare*, Police Foundation National Conference, April 1994, 41.

85   Garrett Hardin to Cordelia Scaife May, June 4 1992, Garrett Hardin papers, Davidson Library, University of California, Santa Barbara.

86 Robert Shogan, "'92 Republican Convention: Platform in Clear Contrast to Rival Democrats' Policies," *Los Angeles Times*, August 17, 1992.

87 *The Vision Shared: The Republican Platform, Uniting Our Family, Our Country, Our World*, American Presidency Project, 1992, available at presidency.ucsb.edu/documents/republican-party-platform-1992.

88 U.S. Border Patrol, "Border Patrol Strategic Plan, 1994 and Beyond," hsdl.org, August 8, 1994, 7.

89 Chad C. Haddal et al., "Border Security: Barriers along the U.S. International Border," Congressional Research Service, March 16, 2009, 3; United States Border Patrol, "Border Patrol Agent Nationwide Staffing by Fiscal Year," cbp.gov, October 1, 2016, 3.

90 Andreas, *Border Games*, 93.

91 Andreas, *Border Games*, 160–1.

92 "Reyes Has Rallied El Pasoans to a New Level of Confidence," *El Paso Times*, October 27, 1996.

93 Robert A. Jones, "It's Quiet—Too Quiet," *Los Angeles Times*, March 22, 1998.

94 Rahm Emanuel, "Memorandum to the President," November 12, 1996.

95 Nathan Gardels, "Salinas' Vision: After NAFTA, the World," *Los Angeles Times*, January 6, 1993.

96 U.S. Border Patrol, "Border Patrol Strategic Plan," 3.

97 Gregory Ross, "NAFTA Can Ease Border Woe," *San Diego Union-Tribune*, October 8, 1993.

98 James McBride and Mohammed Aly Sergie, "NAFTA's Economic Impact," cfr.org, October 1, 2018.

99 Matthew Sanderson and Rebecca Utz, "The Globalization of Economic Production and International Migration," *International Journal of Comparative Sociology* 50(2), 2009, 137–54.

100 Delgado-Wise and Covarrubias, "The Reshaping of Mexican Labor Exports under NAFTA."

101 Carlos Marichal, "The Vicious Cycles of Mexican Debt," NACLA Report on the Americas, 31(3), 1997, 28.

102 R. Jeffrey Smith and Clay Chandler, "Peso Crisis Caught U.S. by Surprise," *Washington Post*, February 13, 1995; Gladys Lopez-Acevedo and Jaime Saavedra, "Mexico: Income Generation and Social Protection for the Poor," documents.worldbank.org, January 1, 2005.

103 Rahm Emanuel, "Memorandum to the President," November 12, 1996.

104   Douglas S. Massey et al., "Border Enforcement and Return Migration by Documented and Undocumented Mexicans," *Journal of Ethnic and Migration Studies* 41(7), 2015, 1015–40.

105   Andreas, *Border Games*, 74–75.

106   June S. Beittel, "Mexico: Organized Crime and Drug Trafficking Organizations," Congressional Research Service, fas.org, April 25, 2017, 8.

107   Andreas, *Border Games*, 59–60; Paul Gootenberg, "Cocaine's Long March North, 1900–2010," *Latin American Politics and Society* 54(1), 2012, 159–80.

108   Beittel, "Mexico: Organized Crime and Drug Trafficking Organizations," 9.

109   Laura Y. Calderón et al., "Organized Crime and Violence in Mexico," Justice in Mexico, April 2019, 38.

110   Andreas, *Border Games*, 78, 80–81.

111   Ibid., 57–60.

112   Ibid., 8.

113   Dylan Riley, "American Brumaire?," *New Left Review*, 103, 2017.

114   Randy Capps et al., "Delegation and Divergence: A Study of 287(g) State and Local Immigration Enforcement," migrationpolicy.org, January 2011, 8; Haddal et al., "Border Security: Barriers along the U.S. International Border," 1, 3.

115   Rahm Emanuel, "Memorandum to the President," November 12, 1996.

116   Alexandra Filindra et al., "20 Years On, Here's How Welfare Reform Held Back Immigrants' Children—in Some States," *Washington Post*, August 22, 2016.

117   Julilly Kohler-Hausmann, *Getting Tough: Welfare and Imprisonment in 1970s America*, Princeton: Princeton University Press, 2017, 2.

118   Daniel Denvir, "How Centrists Failed Immigrants," jacobinmag.com, November 4, 2016.

119   "Remarks by Barbara Jordan, Chair, U.S. Commission on Immigration Reform, to the Immigration and Naturalization Service," Barbara C. Jordan Archives, November 21, 1995, 11.

120   Robert Pear, "Clinton Embraces a Proposal to Cut Immigration by a Third," *New York Times*, June 8, 1995.

121   Dara Lind, "The Disastrous, Forgotten 1996 Law That Created Today's Immigration Problem," *Vox*, April 28, 2016.

122 Charles Kamasaki, *Immigration Reform: The Corpse That Will Not Die*, Simsbury, CT: Mandel Vilar Press, 2019, 364–5; Tichenor, *Dividing Lines*, 365.

123 Office of the Press Secretary, "Remarks by the President, the Vice-President and the Attorney General during Immigration Policy Announcement," clintonwhitehouse6.archives.gov, July 27, 1993.

124 Steven A. Holmes, "The Strange Politics of Immigration," *New York Times*, December 31, 1995; Associated Press, "A Retreat on Denying Welfare to Immigrants," *New York Times*, January 10, 1995.

125 Alison Mitchell, "Clinton Signs Measure on Terrorism and Death Penalty Appeals," *New York Times*, April 26, 1996; Dawn Marie Johnson, "AEDPA and the IIRIRA: Treating Misdemeanors as Felonies for Immigration Purposes," *Journal of Legislation* 27(2), 2001, 481–3; "Analysis of Immigration Detention Policies: Support Fair Detention Policies," aclu.org.

126 Lena Williams, "A Law Aimed at Terrorists Hits Legal Immigrants," *New York Times*, July 17, 1996.

127 Kathleen Belew, *Bring the War Home: The White Power Movement and Paramilitary America*, Cambridge, MA: Harvard University Press, 2018, 7, 236.

128 Douglas S. Massey and Karen A. Pren, "Unintended Consequences of US Immigration Policy: Explaining the Post-1965 Surge from Latin America," *Population and Development Review* 38(1), 2012, 1–29.

129 Robert Pear, "U.S. Strengthening Patrols along the Mexican Border," *New York Times*, January 13, 1996.

130 Andreas, *Border Games*, 89.

131 Dora Schriro, "Immigration Detention Overview and Recommendations," Immigration and Customs Enforcement, October 6, 2009, 2.

132 Sharita Gruberg, "How For-Profit Companies Are Driving Immigration Detention Policies," americanprogress.org, December 18, 2015.

133 Keller, "Re-thinking Illegal Entry and Re-entry," 4, 15, 17.

134 Tracy Wilkinson, "Gangs Find Fresh Turf in Salvador," *Los Angeles Times*, June 16, 1994.

135 Pear, "U.S. Strengthening Patrols along the Mexican Border."

136 Peter Beinart, "The Republican Party's White Strategy," *Atlantic*, July/August, 2016.

137   Cathleen Decker, "Wilson Drops Out of White House Race, Blames Cash Woes," *Los Angeles Times*, September 30, 1995.

138   B. Drummond Ayres Jr., "Wilson, Trailing in Voters' Polls, Drops 1996 Quest," *New York Times*, September 30, 1995.

139   James Bennet, "Candidate's Speech Is Called Code for Controversy," *New York Times*, February 25, 1996.

140   Eric Schmitt, "Milestones and Missteps on Immigration," *New York Times*, October 26, 1996.

141   Adam Nagourney, "Dole Unleashes His Tough Talk on Immigration," *New York Times*, October 18, 1996.

142   The Living Room Candidate: Presidential Campaign Commercials 1952–2016, Museum of the Moving Image, livingroomcandidate.org.

143   Ibid.

144   James Bennet, "Democrats Defend Clinton on Immigration in Striking Manner," *New York Times*, June 27, 1996.

145   Louis Freedberg, "Clinton and Dole's Dueling Immigration Ads," *San Francisco Chronicle*, July 7, 1996.

146   Andreas, *Border Games*, 110.

147   "1996 Democratic Party Platform," August 26, 1996, presidency.ucsb.edu.

148   Robert B. Reich, *Locked in the Cabinet*, New York: Vintage Books, 1998, 339.

149   Pear, "U.S. Strengthening Patrols along the Mexican Border."

150   Denvir, "How Centrists Failed Immigrants."

151   "President Bill Clinton's State Of The Union Address, Part 2," cnn.com, January 27, 1998.

152   Daniel B. Wood, "Controlling Illegal Immigration—but at a Price," *Christian Science Monitor*, October 4, 1999.

153   Andreas, *Border Games*, 85.

154   Mirta Ojito, "Immigrants; Once Divisive, Immigration Now a Muted Issue," *New York Times*, November 1, 1998.

155   Jens Manuel Krogstad et al., "5 Facts about Illegal Immigration in the U.S.," pewresearch.org, June 12, 2019.

156   Steven Greenhouse, "Labor Urges Amnesty for Illegal Immigrants," *New York Times*, February 17, 2000.

157   Don Gonyea, "How the Labor Movement Did a 180 on Immigration," npr.org, February 5, 2013; Ruth Milkman, "Labor and the New Immigrant Rights Movement: Lessons from California," *Items*, items.ssrc.org, July 28, 2006.

158 Nurith C. Aizenman, "INS Raids Follow Union Organizing," *Washington Post*, December 6, 1999.

159 Michael Janofsky, "Candidates Courting Hispanic Vote," *New York Times*, June 25, 2000.

160 Steve Kornacki, "When Trump Ran against Trump-ism: The 1990s and the Birth of Political Tribalism in America," nbcnews.com, October 2, 2018.

161 Haddal et al., "Border Security: Barriers along the U.S. International Border," Summary.

162 Haddal et al., "Border Security: Barriers along the U.S. International Border," 2.

163 "Illegal Immigration: Border-Crossing Deaths Have Doubled since 1995," United States Government Accountability Office, August 2006, 14, 29.

164 "'You Have to Pay with Your Body': The Hidden Nightmare of Sexual Violence on the Border," *New York Times*, March 3, 2019; William Paul Simmons, Cecilia Menjívar, and Michelle Téllez, "Violence and Vulnerability of Female Migrants in Drop Houses in Arizona: The Predictable Outcome of a Chain Reaction of Violence," *Violence against Women* 21(5), 2015.

165 Andreas, *Border Games*, 100–1.

166 Peter Brownell, "The Declining Enforcement of Employer Sanctions," Migration Policy Institute, September 1, 2005.

167 Jeff Greenfield, "Trump Is Pat Buchanan with Better Timing," *Politico*, September, 2016.

168 Eric Schmitt, "Bush Aides Weigh Legalizing Status of Mexicans in U.S.," *New York Times*, July 15, 2001; Kelly Wallace, "Bush in a Tough Place on Immigration Reform," cnn.com, July 27, 2001.

169 Associated Press, "'Guru' Serves as Bush's Lightning Rod," *Billings Gazette*, August 11, 2001.

170 Schmitt, "Bush Aides Weigh Legalizing Status of Mexicans in U.S."

171 Eric Schmitt, "Ambivalence Prevails in Immigration Policy," *New York Times*, May 27, 2001.

172 Terry M. Neal, "Bush's Message Reflects Hispanic Demographics," *Washington Post*, September 15, 1999.

173 Patrick J. McDonnell, "Brash Evangelist," *Los Angeles Times*, July 15, 2001.

174 Patrick J. McDonnell, "Amnesty by Any Name Is Hot Topic," *Los Angeles Times*, July 22, 2001.

175 *How Democracy Works*, episode 2, directed by Catherine Gund (New York: Aubin Pictures, 1997).

176 Peter Andreas, "A Tale of Two Borders: The U.S.-Mexico and U.S.-Canada Lines after 9-11," Center for Comparative Immigration Studies, May 2003, 7.

177 Philip Bump, "How 'Homeland' Became Part of Our American Lexicon," *Washington Post*, September 11, 2014.

178 Argueta, "Border Security: Immigration Enforcement between Ports of Entry," 10.

179 Andreas, *Border Games*, 167–8.

180 9/11 Commission, "The 9/11 Commission Report," 9-11commission. gov, July 22, 2004, 362.

181 Kandel, "Interior Immigration Enforcement," 10.

182 Argueta, "Border Security: Immigration Enforcement between Ports of Entry," 4.

183 Office of Border Patrol, "National Border Patrol Strategy," hsdl.org, 2004.

184 Somini Sengupta and Christopher Drew, "Effort to Discover Terrorists among Illegal Aliens Makes Glacial Progress, Critics Say," *New York Times*, November 12, 2001; "Ashcroft Announces Immigration Crackdown," pbs.org, October 31, 2001.

185 Eric Schmitt, "I.N.S. Chief Stepping Down, Latest to Do So at Justice Dept.," *New York Times*, August 17, 2002.

186 Sengupta and Drew, "Effort to Discover Terrorists among Illegal Aliens Makes Glacial Progress, Critics Say."

187 Eric Lichtblau, "U.S. Report Faults the Roundup of Illegal Immigrants after 9/11," *New York Times*, June 2, 2003; "Department of Justice Inspector General Issues Report on Treatment of Aliens Held on Immigration Charges in Connection with the Investigation of the September 11 Terrorist Attacks," Inspector General of the U.S. Department of Justice, June 2, 2003; "Supplemental Report on September 11 Detainees' Allegations of Abuse at the Metropolitan Detention Center in Brooklyn, New York," Inspector General of the U.S. Department of Justice, December 2003.

188 Maia Jachimowicz and Ramah McKay, "'Special Registration' Program," migrationpolicy.org, April 1, 2003; Rachel L. Swarns, "Special Registration for Arab Immigrants Will Reportedly Stop," *New York Times*, November 22, 2003.

189 Goldstein, "Clinton's Guantanamo"; A. Naomi Paik, "US Turned Away Thousands of Haitian Asylum-Seekers and Detained Hundreds More in the 90s," theconversation.com, June 28, 2018; A. Naomi Paik, "Carceral Quarantine at Guantánamo," *Radical History Review* 115, 2013, 160.

190 Cristina Rodríguez et al., "A Program in Flux: New Priorities and Implementation Challenges for 287(g)," migrationpolicy.org, March 2010, 3.

191 Mike Branom, "35 State Officers to Uphold Federal Immigration," *Miami Herald*, August 16, 2002.

192 Argueta, "Border Security: Immigration Enforcement between Ports of Entry," Summary.

193 *How Democracy Works*, episode 2.

194 Jason DeParle, "The Anti-Immigration Crusader," *New York Times*, April 17, 2011.

195 Rachel L. Swarns, "Senate, in Bipartisan Act, Passes Immigration Bill," *New York Times*, May 26, 2006; "Side-by-Side Comparison of 2013 Senate Immigration Bill with 2006 and 2007 Senate Legislation," migrationpolicy.org, April 2013; Carl Hulse and Jim Rutenberg, "Senate Votes to Extend Fence along Border," *New York Times*, May 17, 2006.

196 Michael A. Fletcher and Jonathan Weisman, "Bush Signs Bill Authorizing 700-Mile Fence for Border," *Washington Post*, October 27, 2006.

197 Haddal et al., "Border Security: Barriers along the U.S. International Border," Summary.

198 Carle Hulse and Rachel L. Swarns, "Senate Passes Bill on Building Border Fence," *New York Times*, September 30, 2006; Calvin Woodward, "AP Fact Check: Trump's Mythical Terrorist Tide from Mexico," apnews.com, January 8, 2019; Salvador Rizzo, "A Guide to Understanding the Administration's Spin on Terrorists at the Border," *Washington Post*, January 14, 2019.

199 Argueta, "Border Security: Immigration Enforcement between Ports of Entry," 6.

200 Julia Preston, "Homeland Security Cancels 'Virtual Fence' after $1 Billion Is Spent," *New York Times*, January 14, 2011; Argueta, "Border Security: Immigration Enforcement between Ports of Entry," 16.

201 Andreas, *Border Games*, 95–96.

202 Pratheepan Gulasekaram, "Why a Wall?," *UC Irvine Law Review* 2, 2012, 157; Ana Campoy and Christopher Groskopf, "The Trump Tax: Human Smugglers at the US-Mexico Border Are Jacking Up Prices," qz.com, March 17, 2017.

203 Office of the Press Secretary, "Statement by Secretary of Homeland Security John Kelly on Southwest Border Security," dhs.gov, March 8, 2017.

204 Sebastian Rotella and Tim Golden, "Despite Trump's Tough Talk about Migrant Smugglers, He's Undercut Efforts to Stop Them," propublica.org, February 21, 2019.

205 Keller, "Re-thinking Illegal Entry and Re-entry," 15.

206 "ENDGAME Office of Detention and Removal Strategic Plan, 2003–2012," U.S. Department of Homeland Security, June 27, 2003.

207 Daniel Gonzalez, "How Many Mexicans Actually Cross the Border Illegally?" azcentral.com, October 9, 2016.

208 Argueta, "Border Security: Immigration Enforcement between Ports of Entry," 24.

209 ACLU Arizona, "Know Your Rights with Border Patrol," acluaz.org; Daniel Denvir, "Curbing the Unchecked Power of the U.S. Border Patrol," citylab.com, October 30, 2015.

210 Nina Bernstein, "Border Sweeps in North Reach Miles into U.S.," *New York Times*, August 29, 2010; Alexia Fernández Campbell, "Why Border Patrol Agents Can Board a Bus or Train and Ask if You're a Citizen," *Vox*, February 9, 2018; Families for Freedom and Immigrant Rights Clinic at New York University School of Law, "Uncovering USBP: Bonus Programs for United States Border Patrol Agents and the Arrest of Lawfully Present Individuals," January 2013.

211 Rebecca Shapiro, "Customs Officers Demand ID from Passengers Leaving Domestic Flight at JFK," huffpost.com, February 24, 2017.

212 ACLU, "The Constitution in the 100-Mile Border Zone," aclu.org.

213 Noelle K. Brigden, "A Visible Geography of Invisible Journeys: Central American Migration and the Politics of Survival," *International Journal of Migration and Border Studies* 4(1–2), 2018, 72; Christopher Wilson and Pedro Valenzuela, "Mexico's Southern Border Strategy: Programa Frontera Sur," Mexico Institute, July 11, 2014.

214 Brigden, "A Visible Geography of Invisible Journeys," 72.

215 Robert M. Morgenthau, "The US Keeps 34,000 Immigrants in Detention Each Day Simply to Meet a Quota," *The Nation*, August 13, 2014.

216 United States Department of Homeland Security, *Yearbook of Immigration Statistics: 2017*, Washington, D.C.: U.S. Department of Homeland Security, Office of Immigration Statistics, 2017: 103.

217 E. Ann Carson, "Prisoners in 2016," Bureau of Justice Statistics, January 2018, 13.

218 Transactional Records Access Clearinghouse (TRAC), "TRAC Immigration: Immigration Now 52 Percent of All Federal Criminal Prosecutions," trac.syr.edu, November 28, 2016.

219 Jennifer Chan, "Immigration Detention Bed Quota Timeline," immigrantjustice.org, January 13, 2017.

220 César Cuauhtémoc García Hernández, "Immigration Detention Population Drops in FY '13, While Removals Increase to All-Time High," crimmigration.com, October 8, 2014.

221 Gruberg, "How For-Profit Companies Are Driving Immigration Detention Policies."

222 Jeff Sommer, "Trump Immigration Crackdown Is Great for Private Prison Stocks," *New York Times*, March 10, 2017.

223 Ellen Powell, "Sessions Memo: Reversal on Private Prisons Could Portend Shift on Justice, Observers Say," *Christian Science Monitor*, February 24, 2017.

224 Christopher Dean Hopkins, "Private Prisons Back in Mix for Federal Inmates as Sessions Rescinds Order," npr.org, February 23, 2017.

225 The Geo Group, Inc., Form 8-K, February 22, 2017.

226 United States Border Patrol, "Border Patrol Agent Nationwide Staffing by Fiscal Year."

227 Sarah Hauer, "Is Donald Trump Right That Hillary Clinton Once 'Wanted a Wall' on the Mexican Border?," politifact.com, August 15, 2016.

Chapter Three

1 Nicholas Kulish, "Dr. John Tanton, Quiet Catalyst in Anti-Immigration Drive, Dies at 85," *New York Times*, July 18, 2019.

2 Michael Kagan, "Is the Chinese Exclusion Case Still Good Law? (The President Is Trying to Find Out)," *Nevada Law Journal Forum* 1, 2017, 80–91.

3 Barbara Jeanne Fields, "Slavery, Race and Ideology in the United States of America," *New Left Review*, May/June 1990.

4 Aziz Rana, *The Two Faces of American Freedom*, Cambridge, MA: Harvard University Press, 2010, 58–60; Aaron S. Fogleman, "From Slaves, Convicts, and Servants to Free Passengers: The Transformation of Immigration in the Era of the American Revolution," *Journal of American History*, 85(1), 1998, 44–71.

5 Rana, *Two Faces of American Freedom*, 89–90.

6 Ibid., 95.

7 Donald Ratcliffe, "The Right to Vote and the Rise of Democracy, 1787–1828," *Journal of the Early Republic* 33(2), 2013, 220.

8 Tichenor, *Dividing Line*, 53–5.

9 Paul Frymer, *Building an American Empire: The Era of Territorial and Political Expansion*, Princeton: Princeton University Press, 2017, 9, 18, 132.

10 Hidetaka Hirota, *Expelling the Poor: Atlantic Seaboard States and the Nineteenth-Century Origins of American Immigration Policy*, New York: Oxford University Press, 2017, 42; Anna O. Law, "Lunatics, Idiots, Paupers, and Negro Seamen—Immigration, Federalism and the Early American State," *Studies in American Political Development* 28(2), 2014, 107–17.

11 Hiroshi Motomura, *Americans in Waiting: The Lost Story of Immigration and Citizenship in the United States*, New York: Oxford University Press, 2007, 70–71.

12 Ian Haney López, *White by Law: The Legal Construction of Race*, New York: New York University Press, 2006, 1–3, 70.

13 Ariela J. Gross, "The Caucasian Cloak: Mexican-Americans and the Politics of Whiteness in the Twentieth-Century Southwest," *Georgetown Law Journal* 95, 2007, 347–8.

14 Erika Lee, "The Chinese Exclusion Example: Race, Immigration, and American Gatekeeping, 1882–1924," *Journal of American Ethnic History* 21(3), 2002, 46.

15 Frymer, *Building an American Empire*, 203–4.

16 Law, "Lunatics, Idiots, Paupers, and Negro Seamen," 115.

17 Tichenor, *Dividing Lines*, 61–63.

18 Hirota, *Expelling the Poor*, 3–8.

19 Eric Foner, *The Fiery Trial: Abraham Lincoln and American Slavery*, New York: W.W. Norton, 127–31, 236–60.

20 DeNeen L. Brown, "When Portland Banned Blacks: Oregon's Shameful History as an 'All-White' State," *Washington Post*, June 7, 2017.

21 Rana, *The Two Faces of American Freedom*, 89–90.

22 Tichenor, *Dividing Lines*, 100.

23 Walter M. Merrill and Louis Ruchames, eds., *The Letters of William Lloyd Garrison*, vol. 6, 1868–1879, Cambridge, MA: Belknap Press of Harvard University, 1981, 558.

24 Frymer, *Building an American Empire*, 152.

25 Ibid., 132.

26 William H. Seward, [Untitled letter to the diplomatic and consular officers of the United States], "Papers Relating to Foreign Affairs, Accompanying the Annual Message of the President to the First Session Thirty-Eighth Congress," Part II, history.state.gov.

27 Michael C. Dawson and Megan Ming Francis, "Black Politics and the Neoliberal Racial Order," *Public Culture* 28(1), 2016, 34–36, 38.

28 Donna R. Gabaccia, "Nations of Immigrants. Do Words Matter?," *The Pluralist* 5(3), 2010, 13.

29 Rana, *Two Faces of American Freedom*, 189.

30 Theodore Roosevelt, "National Life and Character," *Sewanee Review* 2(3), 1894, 366.

31 Beth Lew-Williams, *The Chinese Must Go: Violence, Exclusion, and the Making of the Alien in America*, Cambridge, MA: Harvard University Press, 2018, 32.

32 Matthew Frye Jacobson, *Barbarian Virtues: The United States Encounters Foreign Peoples at Home and Abroad, 1876–1917*, New York: Hill and Wang, 2001, 231–4.

33 Paul A. Kramer, introduction to *The Blood of Government: Race, Empire, the United States, and the Philippines*, Chapel Hill: University of North Carolina Press, 2006.

34 Jacobson, *Barbarian Virtues*, 4–5, 97.

35 Kramer, "Empire and Exclusion: Ending the Philippine Invasion of the United States," chap. 6 in *The Blood of Government*.

36 Ibid.

37 Tichenor, *Dividing Lines*, 127, 145.

38 Mae M. Ngai, *Impossible Subjects: Illegal Aliens and the Making of Modern America*, Princeton: Princeton University Press, 2014, 39–40.

39 Rana, *Two Faces of American Freedom*, 188.

40 W.E.B. Du Bois, *Darkwater: Voices from within the Veil*, Mineola, NY: Dover Thrift Editions, 1999, 123.

41 Tichenor, *Dividing Lines*, 115.

42 Ibid., 70–75.

43 Hirota, *Expelling the Poor*, 5–10.

44 Lee, "The Chinese Exclusion Example," 37, 47–48.

45 Hirota, *Expelling the Poor*, 5.

46 Ibid., 180–4, 191.

47 Ibid., 201–4.

48 Tichenor, *Dividing Lines*, 138; Jack Citrin et al., "The 'Official English' Movement and the Symbolic Politics of Language in the United States," *Western Political Quarterly* 43(3), 1990, 536–7.

49 Tichenor, *Dividing Lines*, 142.

50 Katherine Benton-Cohen, *Invention the Immigration Problem: The Dillingham Commission and Its Legacy*, Cambridge, MA: Harvard University Press, 2018, 2–7.

51 Ibid., 15.

52 Cold Spring Harbor Laboratory's Image Archive on the American Eugenics Movement, "Fitter Family Contests," eugenicsarchive.org.

53 Tichenor, *Dividing Lines*, 116–17.

54 Ibid., 76–77.

55 Lee, "The Chinese Exclusion Example," 49.

56 Gray Brechin, "Conserving the Race: Natural Aristocracies, Eugenics, and the U.S. Conservation Movement," *Antipode* 28(3), 1996, 233.

57 Tichenor, *Dividing Lines*, 143.

58 Brechin, "Conserving the Race," 236–7.

59 Tichenor, *Dividing Lines*, 118–9.

60 Ibid., 71.

61 Joshua Rothman, "When Bigotry Paraded through the Streets," *The Atlantic*, December 4, 2016.

62 Tichenor, *Dividing Lines*, 119–120; Benton-Cohen, *Inventing the Immigration Problem: The Dillingham Commission and Its Legacy*, 203–5.

63 Tichenor, *Dividing Lines*, 142.

64 Ibid., 145.

65 Lee, "The Chinese Exclusion Example," 51.

66 Ibid., 145; Ngai, *Impossible Subjects*, 25–37.

67 Philip Eric Wolgin, "Beyond National Origins: The Development of Modern Immigration Policymaking, 1948–1968," PhD diss., University of California, Berkeley, 2011.

68 Tichenor, *Dividing Lines*, 164.

69 David Scott FitzGerald and David Cook-Martin, *Culling the Masses: The Democratic Origins of Racist Immigration Policy in the Americas*, Cambridge, MA: Harvard University Press, 2014, 7.

70 Brechin, "Conserving the Race," 231.

71 Tichenor, *Dividing Lines*, 191.

72 Ibid., 188–196.

73 Leti Volpp, "Obnoxious to Their Very Nature: Asian Americans and Constitutional Citizenship," *Citizenship Studies* 5(1), 2001, 74

74 Kelli Y. Nakamura, "Alien Enemies Act of 1798," *Densho Encyclopedia*, encyclopedia.densho.org; Kelly Lytle Hernández, *Migra!: A History of the U.S. Border Patrol*, Berkeley: University of California Press, 2010, 103.

75 Kramer, "Empire and Exclusion," chap. 6 in *The Blood of Government*.

76 "President Lyndon B. Johnson's Remarks at the Signing of the Immigration Bill, Liberty Island, New York," October 3, 1965, lbjlibrary.org.

77 FitzGerald and Cook-Martin, *Culling the Masses*, 118–20; Ngai, *Impossible Subjects*, 243–5.

78 Ngai, *Impossible Subjects*, 263.

79 "President Lyndon B. Johnson's Remarks at the Signing of the Immigration Bill."

80 Bill Ong Hing, *Defining America through Immigration Policy*, Philadelphia: Temple University Press, 2004, 95.

81 Muzaffar Chishti et al., "Fifty Years On, the 1965 Immigration and Nationality Act Continues to Reshape the United States," migrationpolicy.org, October 15, 2015.

82 Ngai, *Impossible Subjects*, 258–64.

83 Matthew Frye Jacobson, *Roots Too: White Ethnic Revival in Post–Civil Rights America*, Cambridge, MA: Harvard University Press, 7–13, 41.

84 Ibid., 21.

85 Ibid., 350; Ngai, *Impossible Subjects*, 246, 263; Jacobson, *Roots Too*, 201–2, 390.

86 Leo Chavez, *The Latino Threat: Constructing Immigrants, Citizens, and the Nation*, Stanford: Stanford University Press, 2013, 30–32.

87 Evan Maxwell, "Immigrant Tide Brings Public Health Concern," *Los Angeles Times*, July 23, 1979.

88 Kathleen Belew, *Bring the War Home: The White Power Movement and Paramilitary America*, Cambridge, MA: Harvard University Press, 2018, 159.

89 Associated Press, "Klan Border Watch to Continue," *Prescott Courier*, October 26, 1977.

90 Belew, *Bring the War Home*, 41–50.

91 Tichenor, *Dividing Lines*, 248.

92 Tribune Wire Services, "Carter Won't Bargain over Cuban Refugees," *Chicago Tribune*, May 9, 1980.

93 Carl Lindskoog, "How the Haitian Refugee Crisis Led to the Indefinite Detention of Immigrants," *Washington Post*, April 9, 2018.

94 Tichenor, *Dividing Lines*, 247.

95 Joanne Omang, "Contra Aid Rejected by Two Panels," *Washington Post*, March 6, 1986.

96 Belew, *Bring the War Home*, 97.

97 Susan Gzesh, "Central Americans and Asylum Policy in the Reagan Era," migrationpolicy.org, April 1, 2006.

98 Belew, *Bring the War Home*, 85.

99 Ibid., 350, 97–9.

100 Ibid., 350, 193–4.

101 George H. W. Bush, "Address before a Joint Session of the Congress on the State of the Union," January 29, 1991, presidency.ucsb.edu.

102 Maureen Dowd, "War Introduces a Tougher Bush to Nation," *New York Times*, March 2, 1991.

103 Ira. R. Allen, "Hayakawa Proposes English as Official Language," UPI, April 27, 1981.

104 "About Language Minority Voting Rights," justice.gov, March 27, 2019.

105 Sandra Stencel, "The New Immigration," CQ Researcher, December 13, 1974.

106 Sara Terry, "America's Welcome: Wearing Thin?," *Christian Science Monitor*, June 25, 1981.

107 Sarah Henry, "Fighting Words: California's Official-Language Law Promises to Preserve and Protect English," *Los Angeles Times*, June 10, 1990; Richard L. Berke, "Buchanan Co-leader Quits under Fire," *New York Times*, February 16, 1996; Belew, *Bring the War Home*, 201.

108 Geoffrey K. Pullum, "Here Come the Linguistic Fascists," *Natural Language and Linguistic Theory* 5, 1987, 603; "English-Only Plea Called," *Houston Chronicle*, December 3, 1986.

109 HoSang, *Racial Propositions: Ballot Initiatives and the Making of Postwar California*, Berkeley: University of California Press, 2010, 146, 157.

110 Henry, "Fighting Words."

111 HoSang, *Racial Propositions*, 131–40.

112 Carly Goodman, email to author, August 8, 2019.

113 "English Spoken Here, but Unofficially," *New York Times*, October 29, 1988; HoSang, *Racial Propositions*, 158; "'Witan MEMO' III," *Intelligence Report*, splcenter.org; Associated Press, "Cronkite Quits English-Only Campaign Body," *Los Angeles Times*, October 14, 1988.

114 Jason DeParle, "The Anti-Immigration Crusader," *New York Times*, April 17, 2011; Carly Goodman, "John Tanton Has Died," *Washington Post*, July 18, 2019; Southern Poverty Law Center, "Federation for American Immigration Reform," available at splcenter.org.

115 John Fairhall, "Buchanan Courts Voters Who Feel Jilted by Bush," *Baltimore Sun*, January 20, 1992; Patrick J. Buchanan, "What Will America Be in 2050?," *Los Angeles Times*, October 24, 1994; David M. Kennedy, "Can We Still Afford to Be a Nation of Immigrants?," *The Atlantic*, November 1996.

116 "In Buchanan's Words," *Washington Post*, February 29, 1992.

117 Patrick J. Buchanan, "Who Voted for Clinton's Revolution?," buchanan.org, July 1, 1997.

118 Elaine Woo, "Barbara Coe Dies at 79," *Los Angeles Times*, September 4, 2013.

119 Ben Ehrenreich, "Eyes Wide Shut," *LA Weekly*, September 1, 2005; Mike Davis, *City of Quartz: Excavating the Future in Los Angeles*, London: Verso, 2018, 167.

120 David M. Reimers, *Unwelcome Strangers: American Identity and the Turn against Immigration*, New York: Columbia University Press, 1998, 113; "American Border Patrol/American Patrol," splcenter.org.

121 Chavez, *The Latino Threat*, ix–x.

122 Robert Pear, "Citizenship Proposal Faces Obstacle in the Constitution," *New York Times*, August 7, 1996.

123 John Tierney, "A San Francisco Talk Show Takes Right-Wing Radio to a New Dimension," *New York Times*, February 14, 1995.

124 David Gilson, "Michael Savage's Long, Strange Trip," salon.com, March 6, 2003.

125 Associated Press, "Multicultural History Standards Rejected by Senate in 99–1 Vote," *Los Angeles Times*, January 19, 1995.

126 Roy Beck, "The Ordeal of Immigration in Wausau," *The Atlantic*, April 1994.

127 Osita Nwanevu, "How *National Review* Helped Build the Alt-Right," slate.com, March 23, 2017.

128 Ernest Van Den Haag, "More Immigration?," *National Review*, September 21, 1965, 821–2; "Camp of the Saints," *National Review*, September 30, 1977, 1096–7; Daniel Pipes, "The Muslims Are Coming! The Muslims Are Coming!," *National Review*, November 19, 1990, 28–31.

129 Peter Brimelow, "Time to Rethink Immigration?," *National Review* 44(12), June 22, 1992.

130 Peter Brimelow, *Alien Nation: Common Sense about America's Immigration Disaster*, New York: Random House, 1995.

131 Heidi Beirich, "Courting Conservatives," *Intelligence Report*, splcenter. org, November 30, 2008.

132 Jack Miles, "The Coming Immigration Debate," *The Atlantic*, April 1995.

133 Richard Bernstein, "The Immigration Wave: A Plea to Hold It Back," *New York Times*, April 19, 1995.

134 Richard Bernstein, "The Rising Hegemony of the Politically Correct," October 28, 1990; Moira Weigel, "Political Correctness: How the Right Invented a Phantom Enemy," *The Guardian*, November 30, 2016.

135 Beirich, "Courting Conservatives."

136 "The Nativists Are Restless," *New York Times*, January 31, 2009.

137 Jean Raspail, "Full Text of 'Camp of the Saints by Jean Raspail,'" archive.org.

138 William F. Buckley Jr., "No Irish Need Apply," *National Review*, July 23, 2004.

139 "The Social Contract Press," splcenter.org.

140 Sarah Jones, "The Notorious Book That Ties the Right to the Far Right," *New Republic*, February 2, 2018; Paul Blumenthal and JM Rieger, "This Stunningly Racist French Novel Is How Steve Bannon Explains the World," huffpost.com, March 6, 2017; Chris Massie, "Steve King: Blacks and Hispanics 'Will Be Fighting Each Other' before Overtaking Whites in Population," cnn.com, March 14, 2017.

141 Allan Bloom, *The Closing of the American Mind*, New York: Simon and Schuster, 1987, 29, 31, 38.

142 Dinesh D'Souza, "Illiberal Education," *The Atlantic* 267(3), March 1991, 51–79; *Illiberal Education: The Politics of Race and Sex on Campus*," New York: Free Press, 1991.

143 Weigel, "Political Correctness: How the Right Invented a Phantom Enemy."

144 Quinn Slobodian, "Anti-'68ers and the Racist-Libertarian Alliance: How a Schism among Austrian School Neoliberals Helped Spawn the Alt Right," forthcoming in *Cultural Politics*, academia.edu.

145 Ibid., 339.

146 Patrick J. McDonnell, "Brash Evangelist," *Los Angeles Times*, July 15, 2001.

147 Alicia A. Caldwell et al., "With Eight Mexican Deaths, El Paso Shooting Prompts New Cross-Border Anxiety," *Wall Street Journal*, August 6, 2019.

148 Tim Arango et al., "Minutes before El Paso Killing, Hate-Filled Manifesto Appears Online," *New York Times*, August 3, 2019; Vincent Schilling, "U.S. Cities El Paso, Dayton and Gilroy Racked by Three Deadly Mass Shootings in One Week," *Indian Country Today*, August 4, 2019.

149 Tendayi Achiume, "Migration as Decolonization," *Stanford Law Review* 71, 2019, 1509.

150 CBS/Associated Press, "Donald Trump Doubles Down on Mexican Immigrant Remarks," cbsnews.com, July 6, 2015.

151 NBC News, "Here's the Full Text of Donald Trump's Speech in Poland," nbcnews.com, July 6, 2017.

152 K. Larry Storrs, "CRS Report for Congress: Mexico-United States Dialogue on Migration and Border Issues, 2001–2005," Congressional Research Service, fas.org, June 2, 2005; "Bush Calls for Changes on Illegal Workers," cnn.com, January 8, 2004.

153 "Bush Calls for Changes on Illegal Workers."

154 John M. Broder, "Immigration, from a Simmer to a Scream," *New York Times*, May 21, 2006.

155 Ralph Blumenthal, "Citing Violence, 2 Border States Declare a Crisis," *New York Times*, August 17, 2005.

156 Raymond Hernandez, "The Evolution of Hillary Clinton," *New York Times*, July 13, 2005.

157 "Hillary Goes Conservative on Immigration," *Washington Times*, December 13, 2004.

158 Commission on Presidential Debates, "October 13, 2004 Debate Transcript," debates.org.

159 Elisabeth Bumiller, "Bush Would Give Illegal Workers Broad New Rights," *New York Times*, January 7, 2004.

160 Katharine Q. Seelye, "Moral Values Cited as a Defining Issue of the Election," *New York Times*, November 4, 2004.

161 David Paul Kuhn and David Hancock, "Buchanan Reluctantly Backs Bush," cbsnews.com, October 18, 2004.

162 Jeffrey S. Passel, "Size and Characteristics of the Unauthorized Migrant Population in the U.S.," pewhispanic.org, March 7, 2006.

163 Connie Bruck, "Supermoderate!," *New Yorker*, June 28, 2004.

164 Peter Nicholas and Robert Salladay, "Gov. Praises 'Minuteman' Campaign," *Los Angeles Times*, April 29, 2005.

165 Paul A. Gigot, "Mainstream Left Is Silent about Nativist Right," *Wall Street Journal*, March 31, 2000.

166 Lawrence Downes, "The Terrible, Horrible, Urgent National Disaster That Immigration Isn't," *New York Times*, June 20, 2006.

167 David Leonhardt, "Truth, Fiction and Lou Dobbs," *New York Times*, May 30, 2007.

168 *Lou Dobbs Tonight*, transcripts.cnn.com, May 22, 2007.

169 Leonhardt, "Truth, Fiction and Lou Dobbs."

170 Ken Auletta, "Mad as Hell," *New Yorker*, December 4, 2006.

171 Beau Hodai, "Selling the Anti-immigration Story," fair.org, June 1, 2011; *Lou Dobbs Tonight*, transcripts.cnn.com, December 9, 2005.

172 Mark Engler and Paul Engler, "Op-Ed: The Massive Immigrant-Rights Protests of 2006 Are Still Changing Politics," *Los Angeles Times*, March 4, 2016.

173 "The 287(g) Program: Ensuring the Integrity of America's Border Security System through Federal State Partnerships, Hearing before the Subcommittee on Management, Integration, and Oversight of the Committee on Homeland Security, House of Representatives," govinfo.gov, July 27, 2005.

174 Aarti Shahani and Judith Greene, "Local Democracy on ICE: Why State and Local Government Have No Business in Federal Immigration Law Enforcement," Justice Strategies, justicestrategies.org, February 2009.

175　Adam Liptak, "Justices Block Law Requiring Voters to Prove Citizenship," *New York Times*, June 17, 2003.

176　Hiroshi Motomura, *Immigration outside the Law*, New York: Oxford University Press, 2014, 73–75

177　Muzaffar Chishti and Claire Bergeron, "Hazleton Immigration Ordinance That Began with a Bang Goes Out with a Whimper," migrationpolicy.org, March 28, 2014.

178　Associated Press, "Philly Officials Warn Eatery for English-Only Sign," nbcnews.com, June 12, 2006; James Coomarasamy, "Mind Your Language at Geno's," news.bbc.co.uk, June 30, 2007.

179　News Report, "Mass. Governor, ICE Sign Immigration Enforcement Pact," govtech.com, December 13, 2006.

180　Alexander Mooney, "Romney, McCain Ad Wars Continue in New Hampshire," politicalticker.blogs.cnn.com, December 29, 2007.

181　Joseph Berger, "Danbury Mayor Cuts the Noise on Immigration," *New York Times*, June 9, 2006.

182　David Kelly, "Illegal Immigration Fears Have Spread," *Los Angeles Times*, April 25, 2005.

183　Douglas Massey et al., *Beyond Smoke and Mirrors: Mexican Immigration in an Era of Economic Integration*, New York: Russell Sage Foundation, 2003, 126–8.

184　Office of the Press Secretary, "'Islam Is Peace,' Says President," georgewbush-whitehouse.archives.gov, September 17, 2001.

185　"Bush on State of War," *Washington Post*, October 11, 2001.

186　Nikhil Pal Singh, *Race and America's Long War*, Oakland: University of California Press, 2017, 13.

187　Pew Research Center, "Post September 11 Attitudes," people-press.org, December 6, 2001.

188　Pew Research Center, "7. How the U.S. General Public Views Muslims and Islam," in "U.S. Muslims Concerned about Their Place in Society, but Continue to Believe in the American Dream," pewforum.org, July 26, 2017.

189　Pew Research Center, "Growing Number of Americans Say Obama Is a Muslim," pewforum.org, August 18, 2010.

190　Andrea Elliott, "White House Quietly Courts Muslims in U.S.," *New York Times*, April 18, 2010; Andrea Elliott, "Muslim Voters Detect a Snub from Obama," *New York Times*, June 24, 2008.

191　Associated Press, "Muslim Demands Apology from Obama over Seat Snub," *Boston Globe*, June 19, 2008.

192 Elliott, "Muslim Voters Detect a Snub from Obama."

193 Emily Stewart, "Watch John McCain Defend Barack Obama against a Racist Voter in 2008," vox.com, September 1, 2018.

194 Drew DeSilver and David Masci, "World's Muslim Population More Widespread than You Might Think," pewresearch.org, January 31, 2017.

195 Pew Research Center, "Growing Number of Americans Say Obama Is a Muslim."

196 Jane Mayer, "The Making of the Fox News White House," *New Yorker*, March 4, 2019.

197 Ashley Parker and Steve Eder, "Inside the Six Weeks Donald Trump Was a Nonstop 'Birther,'" *New York Times*, July 2, 2016.

198 "Rep. Tom Tancredo: Bomb Mecca," democracynow.org, July 19, 2005.

199 Ken Maguire, "Sikhs Lament Obama Plan to Bypass India Temple," *New York Times*, October 21, 2010.

200 Pew Research Center, "7. How the U.S. General Public Views Muslims and Islam."

201 "FBI: Bias Crimes against Muslims Remain at High Levels," *Intelligence Report*, splcenter.org, February 27, 2013.

202 Sheryl Gay Stolberg and Laurie Goodstein, "Domestic Terrorism Hearing Opens with Contrasting Views on Dangers," *New York Times*, March 10, 2011.

203 Chris Hawley, "NYPD Monitored Muslim Students All over Northeast," ap.org, February 18, 2012.

204 Chris Lisee/Religion News Service, "Rep. Michele Bachmann's Muslim Brotherhood Claims Draw Fierce Fire," *Washington Post*, July 19, 2012; Russell Goldman, "Bachmann Opposed to Sharia Law, Says It 'Usurps' Constitution," abcnews.go.com, November 2, 2011.

205 Pew Research Center, "After Boston, Little Change in Views of Islam and Violence," people-press.org, May 7, 2013; Pew Research Center, "7. How the U.S. General Public Views Muslims and Islam."

206 Nir Rosen, "The Flight from Iraq," *New York Times*, May 13, 2007.

207 Rubén G. Rumbaut, "A Legacy of War: Refugees from Vietnam, Laos and Cambodia," in *Origins and Destinies: Immigration, Race, and Ethnicity in America*, ed. Silvia Pedraza and Rubén G. Rumbaut, Belmont, CA: Wadsworth, 1996.

208 "Iraq: Gallup Historical Trends," gallup.com.

209 Mohammad-Mahmoud Ould Mohamedou, *A Theory of ISIS: Political Violence and the Transformation of the Global Order*, London: Pluto Press, 2018, 205–6.

210 Mohamedou, *A Theory of ISIS*.

211 International Physicians for the Prevention of Nuclear War (German Affiliate) et al., "Body Count: Casualty Figures after 10 Years of the 'War on Terror,'" calculators.io, March 2015, 15.

212 Neta C. Crawford, "United States Budgetary Costs of the Post-9/11 Wars through FY2019: $5.9 Trillion Spent and Obligated," watson. brown.edu, November 14, 2018.

213 Fred Kaplan, "A Debt of Gratitude," slate.com, March 13, 2007.

214 Daniel Schorn, "Transcript: Bush Interview," *60 Minutes*, cbsnews. com, January 14, 2007.

215 James Traub, "The Mess Obama Left behind in Iraq," *Foreign Policy*, October 7, 2016.

216 Tal Kopan, "Donald Trump: I Meant That Obama Founded ISIS, Literally," cnn.com, August 12, 2016.

217 John Greenberg, "War of Words: The Fight over 'Radical Islamic Terrorism,'" politifact.com, December 11, 2015; Andrew Prokop, "Why Republicans Want Obama to Denounce 'Radical Islam'—and Why He Won't Do It," *Vox*, July 18, 2016.

218 "Declaration of Jihad against the Americans Occupying the Land of the Two Holiest Sites," ctc.usma.edu; "Full Text: Bin Laden's 'Letter to America,'" theguardian.com, November 24, 2002; Daniel Immerwahr, *How to Hide an Empire: A History of the Greater United States*, New York: Farrar, Straus and Giroux, 2019, 381–2.

219 Christopher Mathias, "Americans Think There Are 54 Million Muslims in America. There Are Only 3 Million," huffpost.com, December 16, 2016.

220 Theodore Schleifer, "Donald Trump: 'I Think Islam Hates Us,'" cnn. com, March 10, 2016.

221 Khaled A. Beydoun, "Islamophobia: Toward a Legal Definition and Framework," *Columbia Law Review Online*, 116, 2016, columbialawreview.org.

222 Ryan Teague Beckwith, "Read Hillary Clinton and Donald Trump's Remarks at a Military Forum," time.com, September 7, 2016.

223 Liz Robbins, "On Long Island, Sessions Vows to Eradicate MS-13 Gang," *New York Times*, April 28, 2017.

224   "Attorney General Jeff Sessions Delivers Remarks on Violent Crime to Federal, State and Local Law Enforcement: Central Islip, NY, Friday, April 28, 2017," justice.gov.

225   Eugene Kiely, "Fact Check: Trump's Gross Exaggeration on MS-13 Gang," *USA Today*, June 29, 2017.

226   Aiden Quigley, "Trump Blames Obama for Allowing MS-13 Gang to Form in America," politico.com, April 18, 2017.

227   "Remarks by the President in Address to the Nation on Immigration," obamawhitehouse.archives.gov, November 24, 2010; "Remarks by the President on Comprehensive Immigration Reform in El Paso, Texas," obamawhitehouse.archives.gov, May 10, 2011.

228   Laura Figueroa, "Donald Trump Cites Newsday Article on Gangs," *Newsday*, December 7, 2016.

229   Michael Scherer, "2016 Person of the Year: Donald Trump," *Time*, December 19, 2016.

230   Gabriel Stargardter, "U.S. Coaxes Mexico into Trump Plan to Overhaul Central America," Reuters, May 4, 2017.

Chapter Four

1   Barack Obama, "Remarks by the President in Address to the Nation on Immigration," November 20, 2014, available at obamawhitehouse.archives.gov.

2   Lynn Waltz, "The Price of Cheap Meat? Raided Slaughterhouses and Upended Communities," *Washington Post*, April 11, 2018.

3   Nancy Lofholm, "Fear from Swift Plant Raid Resonates in Greeley Six Years Later," *Denver Post*, January 4, 2013, updated April 30, 2016.

4   Miriam Valverde, "Did Senate Pass Immigration Bills in 2006, 2013 and House Failed to Vote on Them?," *PunditFact*, politifact.com, January 26, 2018.

5   Chuck Plunkett and Anne Mulkern, "Raids Point to Call for Reform," *Denver Post*, January 28, 2007, updated May 8, 2016.

6   Carl Hulse and David Herszenhorn, "Defiant House Rejects Huge Bailout; Next Step Is Uncertain," *New York Times*, September 29, 2008.

7   George W. Bush, "President Bush Addresses the Nation on Immigration Reform," May 15, 2006, available at georgewbush-whitehouse.archives.gov.

8   Ricardo Alonso-Zaldivar, "U.S. to Bolster Arizona Border Security," *Los Angeles Times*, March 30, 2005.

9   Leo Chavez, *The Latino Threat: Constructing Immigrants, Citizens, and the Nation*, Stanford: Stanford University Press, 2013, 140.

10 Fernanda Santos, "Day Laborers' Lawsuit Casts Spotlight on a Nationwide Conflict," *New York Times*, September 17, 2006.

11 Karin Brulliard, "Herndon Group to Keep Eye on Day Labor Sites," *Washington Post*, October 22, 2005.

12 Ibid., 140.

13 Jennifer Delson, "One Man's Convictions Launched a Border Crusade," *Los Angeles Times*, April 11, 2005.

14 Tyche Hendricks, "Civilian Border Patrols across the Country Have Helped Polarize Political Debate over Immigration Reform," sfgate. com, December 5, 2005.

15 Jerry Seper, "Border Vigil Ends on Wary Note," *Washington Times*, May 1, 2005.

16 Carla N. Argueta, "Border Security: Immigration Enforcement between Ports of Entry," Congressional Research Service, fas.org, April 19, 2016, 7.

17 Andorra Bruno, "Immigration-Related Worksite Enforcement: Performance Measures," Congressional Research Service, fas.org, June 23, 2015, 5–6.

18 "Briefing Materials Submitted to the United Nations Special Rapporteur on the Human Rights of Migrants," Detention and Deportation Working Group, Lutheran Immigration and Refugee Services and the Detention Watch Network, April 2007, 24.

19 George Lakoff and Sam Ferguson, "The Framing of Immigration," Rockridge Institute, May 19, 2006.

20 Benton-Cohen, *Inventing the Immigration Problem*, 2–3.

21 Matthew Continetti, "Immigration Nation," *New York Times*, November 8, 2006.

22 Ryan Grim, "Maureen Dowd Asked Rahm Emanuel to Weigh In on an Immigration Debate. His Record Is Abysmal," theintercept.com, July 17, 2019.

23 Rachel L. Swarns, "Some Democrats Send a More Conservative Immigration Message," *New York Times*, October 17, 2006.

24 Eunice Moscoso, "Both Parties' Candidates Talk Tough on Immigration," *Austin American-Statesman*, October 29, 2006.

25 Ibid.

26 "Split in Organized Labor over Immigration," Associated Press, June 21, 2007.

27 Robert Pear and Carl Hulse, "Immigration Bill Fails to Survive Senate Vote," *New York Times*, June 28, 2007.

28 Ibid.

29 "Media Coverage of Campaign Rises, War Coverage Falls, during the Second Quarter of 2007," Pew Research Center, Project for Excellence in Journalism, August 20, 2007, 21.

30 Chris McGreal, "Shock Jocks: Voice of America or Voice of Hate?," *The Guardian*, May 8, 2009.

31 Nicole Gaouette, "Talk Radio Fans Unite on Immigration," *Los Angeles Times*, April 28, 2007.

32 "Media Coverage of Campaign Rises," 21.

33 Trevor Zimmer, "Savage: 'Bring in 10 Million More from Africa . . . They Can't Reason, but Bring Them in with a Machete in Their Head,'" mediamatters.org, January 31, 2008.

34 Julia Preston, "Immigrants' Speedy Trials after Raid Become Issue," *New York Times*, August 8, 2008.

35 Courtney Crowder and MacKenzie Elmer, "Postville Raid Anniversary: A Timeline of Events in One of America's Largest Illegal Immigration Campaigns," *Des Moines Register*, May 10, 2018.

36 Randy Capps, Marc Rosenblum, Cristian Rodríguez, and Muzaffar Chishti, "Delegation and Divergence: A Study of 287(g) State and Local Immigration Enforcement," Migration Policy Institute, January 2011, 10.

37 Michael Kiefer, "Sheriff Joe Arpaio Has Always Done It His Way," *Arizona Republic*, September 11, 2015, updated September 22, 2015.

38 Nicholas Riccardi, "Migrants Survive Arizona Desert," *Los Angeles Times*, July 20, 2006.

39 Jim Hill, "Arizona Criminals Find Jail Too In-'Tents,'" cnn.com, July 27, 1999.

40 Tom Zoellner, "Partners in Pink Underwear," slate.com, November 24, 2008.

41 "Sheriff Helping Inquiry, U.S. Says," *Dallas Morning News*, September 12, 1995.

42 Richard Ruelas, "Arpaio Repaying Favor to Napolitano," *Arizona Republic*, October 14, 2002.

43 Richard Ruelas, "No Governor Bid for Arpaio," *Arizona Republic,* April 3, 2002.

44 Simon van Zuylen-Wood, "The Chaos Candidate Returns to His Favorite Tinderbox," *Politico Magazine*, August 23, 2017.

45 Stephen Lemons, "Neo-Nazis and Extreme Right-Wingers Love Joe Arpaio, and There's Evidence that the MCSO Keeps Them Close," *Phoenix New Times*, May 14, 2009.

46 Robert Anglen and Susan Carroll, "Case Sounds Vigilante Alarm," *Arizona Republic*, April 13, 2005.

47 Paul Rubin, "Dangerous Mind," *Phoenix New Times*, August 26, 2004.

48 Fernanda Santos, "Sheriff Joe Arpaio Loses Bid for 7th Term in Arizona," *New York Times*, November 9, 2016.

49 Daniel Gonzalez, "Arpaio Keeps the Heat on Migrants," *Arizona Republic*, October 17, 2007.

50 John Grooms, "Pendergraph Ties to Prison Industry Raise Questions," clclt.com, October 26, 2010.

51 Capps, Rosenblum, Rodríguez and Chishti, "Delegation and Divergence," 22.

52 Janet Napolitano, letter to Michael Chertoff, July 1, 2005.

53 Mike Sunnucks, "Napolitano, Arpaio Say Immigration Cooperation Lacking," *Phoenix Business Journal*, August 15, 2006.

54 Elvia Diaz, "Step against 'Coyotes,'" *Arizona Republic*, March 15, 2005.

55 Randal Archibold, "Arizona County Uses New Law to Look for Illegal Immigrants," *New York Times*, May 10, 2006.

56 Robert Robb, "Governor Is Focused on Immigration," *Arizona Republic*, September 4, 2005.

57 Rene Gutel, "Gov. Napolitano's Move Leaves Some Arizonans Angry," *Day to Day*, npr.org, November 25, 2008.

58 Dan Nowicki, "McCain, Kyl Pressing Napolitano on Arpaio," *Arizona Republic*, December 13, 2009.

59 Randal Archibold, "Immigration Hard-Liner Has His Wings Clipped," *New York Times*, October 6, 2009.

60 Janet Napolitano, Speech at the Center for American Progress, Washington, DC, November 13, 2009.

61 John Podesta, Remarks at the Center for American Progress, Washington, DC, November 13, 2009.

62 "STATEMENT: CAP Applauds Secretary Napolitano's Stance on

Immigration Reform," Center for American Progress, November 13, 2009.

63 Carrie Budoff Brown, "Dems' Tough New Immigration Pitch," politico.com, June 10, 2010; Alfonso Gonzales, *Reform without Justice: Latino Migrant Politics and the Homeland Security State*, New York: Oxford University Press, 2014, 128–9.

64 "Secure Communities," ICE.gov (archived May 5, 2009).

65 Ana Gonzalez-Brown, "More Mexicans Leaving than Coming to the U.S.," Pew Research Center, November 19, 2015, 5.

66 Transactional Records Access Clearinghouse (TRAC), "TRAC Immigration: Removals under the Secure Communities Program; ICE Data through October 2018," trac.syr.edu (accessed August 9, 2019).

67 Daniel Denvir, "How Centrists Failed Immigrants," *Jacobin*, November 4, 2016.

68 Julia Preston, "Firm Stance on Illegal Immigrants Remains Policy," *New York Times*, August 3, 2009.

69 Bonnie Honig, *Democracy and the Foreigner*, Princeton: Princeton University Press, 2001, 76.

70 "Southwest Border Sectors: Total Illegal Apprehensions by Fiscal Year," published by the United States Border Patrol; "Tucson Sector Arizona," cbp.gov, modified June 10, 2019.

71 "Arizona Sheriff Joe Arpaio, Who Grew Up in Springfield, Being Probed for Treatment of Illegal Immigrants," *The Republican*, March 29, 2009.

72 Marc Perry, "State-to-State Migration Flows: 1995 to 2000," United States Census, August 2003.

73 Wan He and Jason P. Schachter, "Internal Migration of the Older Population: 1995 to 2000," United States Census Bureau, August 2003.

74 "John Tanton's Network," splcenter.org (accessed August 4, 2019).

75 "American Border Patrol/American Patrol," splcenter.org (accessed August 4, 2019).

76 Phillip Reese, "California Exports Its Poor to Texas, Other States, While Wealthier People Move In," *Sacramento Bee*, March 5, 2017; James Allen and Eugene Turner, "Migrants between California and Other States," *California Geographer* 47, 2007, 1–26.

77 Patrick McDonnell, "Brash Evangelist," *Los Angeles Times*, July 15, 2001.

78 "American Border Patrol/American Patrol."

79 Jazmine Ulloa, "Bilingual Education Has Been Absent from California Public Schools for Almost 20 Years. But That May Soon Change," *Los Angeles Times*, October 12, 2016.

80 Richard Marosi, "Decade Later, Prop. 187 Has an Echo in Arizona," *Los Angeles Times*, October 23, 2004.

81 Tyche Hendricks, "Issue of Illegals Roiling Arizona / New Law Denies Public Services to Such Immigrants," sfgate.com, February 28, 2005.

82 Michael Kiefer, "Another Ariz. Immigration Law Shot Down by 9th Circuit," *Arizona Republic*, October 15, 2014.

83 Alia Beard Rau, "Limit on Illegal-Immigrant Lawsuits Faces Test of Constitutionality," *Arizona Republic*, May 30, 2011.

84 Mike Madden and Yvonne Wingett, "Initiatives Curbing Migrant Rights Win Majorities," *Arizona Republic*, November 9, 2006.

85 Jesse McKinley, "Arizona Law Takes a Toll on Nonresident Students," *New York Times*, January 27, 2008.

86 Scott Jordan, "A State on the Borderline," National Institute on Money in Politics, followthemoney.org, January 4, 2008.

87 Randal Archibold and Jennifer Steinhauer, "Welcome to Arizona, Outpost of Contradictions," *New York Times*, April 28, 2010.

88 Nigel Duara, "Arizona's Once-Feared Immigration Law, SB 1070, Loses Most of Its Power in Settlement," *Los Angeles Times*, September 15, 2016.

89 Cindy Carcamo, "Arizona Loses Appeal over Part of Law Aimed at Day Laborers," *Los Angeles Times*, March 4, 2013.

90 Alia Beard Rau, "Arizona Immigration Law Was Crafted by Rising Star Activist," *Arizona Republic*, May 31, 2010.

91 Michele Waslin, "Discrediting 'Self Deportation' as Immigration Policy," Immigration Policy Center, American Immigration Council, February 2012.

92 Laura Sullivan, "Prison Economics Help Ariz. Immigration Law," *Morning Edition*, npr.org, October 28, 2010.

93 Nicole Santa Cruz, "Arizona Bill Targeting Ethnic Studies Signed into Law," *Los Angeles Times*, May 12, 2010.

94 Tim Gaynor, "Arizona Lawman Joe Arpaio's Re-election Bid Divides County," *Chicago Tribune*, November 1, 2012.

95 Morley Safer, "'60 Minutes Footage Shows Arpaio When He Was Ruthless 'Joe the Jailer,'" cbsnews.com, August 26, 2017; Marc Lacey,

"U.S. Finds Pervasive Bias against Latinos by Arizona Sheriff," *New York Times*, December 14, 2011.

96 Jennifer LaFleur, "Tale of Three Cities: Foreclosures Don't Always Follow the Script," propublica.com, December 17, 2010.

97 "Arizona: Population and Labor Force Characteristics, 2000–2006," Pew Research Center, Pew Hispanic Center, January 23, 2008, 9.

98 "RealtyTrac Year-End Report Shows Record 2.8 Million U.S. Properties with Foreclosure Filings in 2009," RealtyTrac, January 14, 2010.

99 Arizona Unemployment Statistics, Bureau of Labor Statistics, data.bls.gov (accessed August 5, 2019).

100 Mark Muro and Kenan Fikri, "Mountain Monitor–Second Quarter 2011," Brookings Mountain West, September 2011, 5.

101 Conor Dougherty, "Sun Belt Loses Its Shine," *Wall Street Journal*, March 24, 2010.

102 Theda Skocpol and Vanessa Williamson, *The Tea Party and the Remaking of Republican Conservatism*, New York: Oxford University Press, 2013, 30.

103 Priscila Diaz, Delia Saenz, and Virginia Kwan, "Economic Dynamics and Changes in Attitudes toward Undocumented Mexican Immigrants in Arizona," *Analyses of Social Issues and Public Policy* 11(1), 2011, 300–313.

104 Paul Frymer, *Building an American Empire: The Era of Territorial and Political Expansion*, Princeton: Princeton University Press, 2017, 204.

105 Elizabeth Tandy Shermer, *Sunbelt Capitalism: Phoenix and the Transformation of American Politics*, Philadelphia: University of Pennsylvania Press, 2013, 7–8.

106 Shermer, *Sunbelt Capitalism*, 7–8, 239.

107 Ibid., 303–8.

108 Shermer, *Sunbelt Capitalism*, 336.

109 Nathan Thornburgh, "The Politics of Arizona's Great Divide," *Time*, February 7, 2011.

110 Skocpol and Williams, *The Tea Party and the Remaking of Republican Conservatism*, 24.

111 "SB 1070 Foes Blast Pearce E-mails," *Arizona Republic*, July 20, 2012.

112 Dustin Gardiner, "Birthright Citizenship Past Target in Arizona," *Arizona Republic*, November 1, 2016.

113   Robert Farley, "Gov. Jan Brewer Talks of Beheadings in the Arizona Desert," politifact.com, September 8, 2010.

114   Deborah Weissman, "The Politics of Narrative: Law and the Representation of Mexican Criminality," *Fordham International Law Journal* 38(141), 2015, 183.

115   Randal Archibold, "Ranchers Alarmed by Killing near Border," *New York Times*, April 4, 2010.

116   Nigel Duara, "Death on the Border: Arizona Used Rancher's Killing to Justify Harsh Immigration Laws, but the Truth of the Case Is Unclear," *Los Angeles Times*, June 23, 2017.

117   Nigel Duara, "Arizona's Once-Feared Immigration Law, SB 1070, Loses Most of Its Power in Settlement," *Los Angeles Times*, September 15, 2016.

118   "Arizona v. United States," scotusblog.com, June 25, 2012.

119   Donald Verrilli Jr. et al., Brief for the United States, *State of Arizona et al v. United States of America*, Supreme Court of the United States, March 11, 2012.

120   Linda Greenhouse, "The Lower Floor," *New York Times*, May 2, 2012.

121   Transactional Records Access Clearinghouse (TRAC), "TRAC Immigration: Deportations under ICE's Secure Communities Program," trac.syr.edu, April 25, 2018.

122   Stephen Lemons, "SB 1070 Rage: Salvador Reza, Alfredo Gutierrez, Scores of Others Arrested in Phoenix," *Phoenix New Times*, July 29, 2010.

123   "Secretary Napolitano and ICE Assistant Secretary Morton Announce That the Secure Communities Initiative Identified More than 111,000 Criminal Aliens in Its First Year," Immigration and Customs Enforcement, November 12, 2009.

124   "Groups Condemn Arizona Bill, Warn of Dangers of ICE-Police Collaboration in Suit Challenging Government Secrecy in ICE Program," Center for Constitutional Rights, ccrjustice.org, April 26, 2010.

125   Tim Craig, "D.C. Council: Boycott Arizona, Don't Share Arrest Data with Feds," *Washington Post*, May 4, 2010.

126   Gretchen Gavett, "Why Three Governors Challenged Secure Communities," *Frontline*, pbs.org, October 18, 2011.

127   "Arizona Governor Signs Immigration Bill," cnn.com, April 24, 2010.

128   Michael Shear and Spencer Hsu, "President Obama to Send More

National Guard Troops to U.S.-Mexico Border," *Washington Post*, May 26, 2010.

129 Kirk Semple and Julia Preston, "Deal to Share Fingerprints Is Dropped, Not Program," *New York Times*, August 6, 2011.

130 Paloma Esquivel, "Secure Communities' Documents Show Immigration Officials Misled Public, Judge Says," *Los Angeles Times*, August 18, 2011.

131 Marc Lacey, "Justice Dept. Sues Sheriff over Bias Investigation," *New York Times*, September 2, 2010.

132 Ana Avendaño, personal communication to author, July 26, 2019.

133 Gonzales, *Reform without Justice*, 122.

134 "Rick Santelli and the 'Rant of the Year,'" YouTube video, aired on *CNBC* on February 19, 2009, posted by "Todd Sullivan," February 19, 2009.

135 Vanessa Williamson, Theda Skocpol, and John Coggin, "The Tea Party and the Remaking of American Conservatism," *Perspectives on Politics* 9(1), 2011, 33.

136 Ibid., 33.

137 Marc Lacey, "Activists Take Fight on Immigration to Border," *New York Times*, August 15, 2010.

138 Jocelyn Fong, "Did J.D. Hayworth Inspire Fox News' New 'Third War' Series about the Border?" mediamatters.org, November 16, 2010.

139 "McCain TV Ad: 'Complete the Danged Fence,'" YouTube video, posted by "John McCain," May 7, 2010.

140 Juliet Eilperin, "Palin's 'Pro-America Areas' Remark: Extended Version," *Washington Post*, October 17, 2008, available voices.washingtonpost.com.

141 Jessica Tores and Cristina López G., "The Most Absurd Anti-Immigrant Myths of 2014," mediamatters.org, December 17, 2014.

142 "Mexican Empire Will Rise to Challenge the USA Economy," YouTube video, uploaded by "DellaRobbiaMX," posted August 1, 2011.

143 Philip Bump, "Even in Death, Barack Obama's Aunt Zeituni Is a Talking Point," *The Atlantic*, April 23, 2014.

144 "Glenn Beck on Illegal Immigration," aired on *Fox News* on April 26, 2010, uploaded by "odom2008dotcom," April 26, 2010.

145 Manuel Roig-Franzia, "Mark Krikorian: The Provocateur Standing in the Way of Immigration Reform," *Washington Post*, June 17, 2013.

146 Alfonso Aguilar, "Immigration and the Party Of Reagan," *Wall Street Journal*, December 2, 2011.

147 Manuel Roig-Franzia, "Mark Krikorian: The Provocateur Standing in the Way of Immigration Reform," *Washington Post*, June 17, 2013.

148 Bradley Jones, "Majority of Americans Continue to Say Immigrants Strengthen the U.S.," Pew Research Center, January 31, 2019.

149 Ana Gonzalez-Barrera and Jens Manuel Krogstad, "U.S. Deportations of Immigrants Reach Record High in 2013," Pew Research Center, October 2, 2014.

150 Peter Slevin, "Deportation of Illegal Immigrants Increases under Obama Administration," *Washington Post*, July 25, 2010.

151 Barack Obama, Speech in El Paso, Texas, May 10, 2011.

152 Julia Preston, "At Rally, Call for Urgency on Immigration Reform," *New York Times*, March 21, 2010.

153 Gonzales, *Reform without Justice*, 135.

154 Lisa Mascaro and Michael Muskal, "Dream Act Fails to Advance in Senate," *Los Angeles Times*, December 18, 2010.

155 Julia Preston, "Deportations under New U.S. Policy Are Inconsistent," *New York Times*, November 12, 2011; John Morton, "Exercising Prosecutorial Discretion Consistent with the Civil Immigration Enforcement Priorities of the Agency for the Apprehension, Detention, and Removal of Aliens," Memo for Immigration and Customs Enforcement, June 17, 2011.

156 Gonzalez-Barrera and Krogstad, "U.S. Deportations of Immigrants Reach Record High in 2013."

157 "President Barack Obama Keynote Address at 2011 NCLR Annual Conference," YouTube video, uploaded by "UnidosUS," July 29, 2011.

158 Julia Preston and John H. Cushman, "Obama to Permit Young Migrants to Remain in U.S.," *New York Times*, June 15, 2012.

159 Fernanda Santos and Charlie Savage, "Lawsuit Says Sheriff Discriminated against Latinos," *New York Times*, May 10, 2012.

160 Barack Obama, Speech in Washington, DC, June 15, 2012, nytimes.com/2012/06/16/us/transcript-of-obamas-speech-on-immigration-policy.html.

161 Daniel Denvir, "How Centrists Failed Immigrants," *Jacobin*, November 4, 2016.

162 Dan Balz, "Mitt Romney's Immigration Problem," *Washington Post*, June 26, 2012; Alexander Burns, "Immigration, Social Security Dominate," politico.com, September 22, 2011.

163 Julia Preston, Benyamin Appelbaum, and Trip Gabriel, "Romney's Lawn Care History and the Fight over Immigration," *New York Times*, October 18, 2011.

164 Edward Wyatt, "Cain Proposes Electrified Border Fence," *New York Times*, October 15, 2011.

165 Commission on Presidential Debates, "October 16, 2012 Debate Transcript," debates.org.

166 Mark Hugo Lopez and Paul Taylor, "Latino Voters in the 2012 Election," Pew Research Center, Pew Hispanic Center, November 7, 2012, 4.

167 Garance Franke-Ruta, "What You Need to Read in the RNC Election-Autopsy Report," *The Atlantic*, March 18, 2013.

168 Ted Hesson, "As One Immigration Enforcement Program Fades Away, Another Rises," abcnews.com, December 27, 2012.

169 Ashley Parker and Jonathan Martin, "Senate, 68 to 32, Passes Overhaul for Immigration," *New York Times*, June 27, 2013.

170 Ted Hesson, "Where Do Unions Stand on Immigration Reform?," abcnews.com, January 23, 2013.

171 "Comprehensive Immigration Reform in the 113th Congress: Major Provisions in Senate-Passed S. 744," Congressional Research Service, July 9, 2013.

172 Andrew Stiles, "Building a Human Wall on the Border," *National Review*, July 2, 2013.

173 "A Guide to S. 744: Understanding the 2013 Senate Immigration Bill," Immigration Policy Center, American Immigration Council, July 10, 2013, 9.

174 Fredreka Schouten and Alan Gomez, "Tech Companies Driving the Lobbying on Immigration," *USA Today*, April 29, 2013.

175 "Senate Passes Bipartisan Immigration Bill While House Continues to Stall," unidosus.org, June 28, 2013.

176 Ed O'Keefe, "Senators Reach Deal on Border Security Proposals," *Washington Post*, June 20, 2013.

177 Ana Avendaño, personal communication to author, July 26, 2019.

178 Benjy Sarlin, "Democrats Let GOP Name Their Price on Immigration," msnbc.com, June 20, 2013, updated on September 13, 2013.

179 "CMSC Newsletter Vol. 2, No. 2–July 26, 2013," California-

MexicoCenter.org, July 27, 2013 (accessed August 8, 2019).

180 Andrew Stiles, "Building a Human Wall on the Border," *National Review*, July 2, 2013.

181 Burgess Everett, "No Tea Party Recess on Immigration," politico. com, June 30, 2013.

182 Tim McCarthy, "The Evolution of Immigration Reform under Obama—a Timeline," *The Guardian*, November 20, 2014; Ashley Parker and Michael S. Schmidt, "Boehner Rules Out Negotiations on Immigration," *New York Times*, November 13, 2013.

183 Gonzalez-Barrera and Krogstad, "U.S. Deportations of Immigrants Reach Record High in 2013."

184 Brian Bennett, "High Deportation Figures Are Misleading," *Los Angeles Times*, April 1, 2014.

185 Argueta, "Border Security," 7–10.

186 Rory Carroll and Ed Pilkington, "Dream Nine Immigration Activists Freed," *The Guardian*, August 7, 2013.

187 Roque Planas, "Undocumented Youths Stopped Crossing Border Back to U.S. in Immigration Protest," huffpost.com, July 22, 2013.

188 Lizbeth Mateo, "The Fight to Keep Families Together Does Not End at Deportation," huffpost.com, July 22, 2013, updated September 21, 2013.

189 Mary Schmich, "Undocumented and Unafraid," *Chicago Tribune*, March 10, 2010.

190 "One Year Later, Obama's Immigration Heckler Feels Vindicated," nbcnews.com, December 2, 2014.

191 Jennifer Epstein, "Obama Challenges Immigration Heckler," politico. com, November 25, 2013.

192 Reid Epstein, "W.H. Faces Rising Grass-Roots Heat," politico.com, February 20, 2014.

193 Elise Foley, "Cecilia Munoz Named to Top White House Post," huffpost.com, January 10, 2012.

194 Maegan Ortiz, "How Do You Solve a Problem Like Cecilia?," *American Prospect*, November 9, 2011.

195 Julia Preston, "The Big Money behind the Push for an Immigration Overhaul," *New York Times*, November 14, 2014.

196 Daniel Tichenor, *Dividing Lines*, 231–2.

197 Walter Nicholls, Justus Uitermark, and Sander van Haperen, "The

Networked Grassroots. How Radicals Outflanked Reformists in the United States' Immigrant Rights Movement," *Journal of Ethnic and Migration Studies* 42(6), 2016, 1036–54.

198 Epstein, "W.H. Faces Rising Grass-Roots Heat."

199 Reid Epstein, "NCLR Head: Obama 'Deporter-in-Chief,'" politico. com, March 4, 2014; Nicholls, Uitermark, and van Haperen, "The Networked Grassroots," 1049–50.

200 Denvir, "How Centrists Failed Immigrants."

201 "Immigration Advocates Rally to Curb Deportations," nbcnews.com, April 5, 2014.

202 "National Groups Weigh In on Immigration Reform Timetable," sojo. net, May 27, 2014.

203 Josh Lederman, "Obama Delays Deportation Review," Associated Press, May 28, 2014.

204 Seung Min Kim, "Immigration Groups Push Action," politico.com, September 19, 2019.

205 Seung Min Kim, "Cantor Loss Kills Immigration Reform," politico. com, June 10, 2014.

206 "Eric Cantor a Casualty of Immigration Reform," nbcnews.com, June 10, 2014.

207 Transactional Records Access Clearinghouse (TRAC), "TRAC Immigration: Has Cooperation by State and Local Law Enforcement Agencies Improved ICE's Apprehension Numbers?," trac.syr.edu, August 12, 2016.

208 Seung Min Kim and Jennifer Epstein, "Obama, Interrupted," politico. com, November 3, 2014.

209 Patrick McGreevy, "Signing Trust Act Is Another Illegal-Immigration Milestone for Brown," *Los Angeles Times*, October 5, 2013.

210 "RE: Draft Letter," email, sent from redacted to John Morton, September 28, 2012.

211 "Third Circuit Appeals Court Rules That Immigration Detainers Are Non-Binding Requests in Ground-Breaking Case," American Civil Liberties Union, March 4, 2014.

212 Janice Stewart, Opinion and Order, *Maria Miranda-Olivares v. Clackamas County*, United States District Court, District of Oregon, April 11, 2014.

213 Andrea Castillo, "Immigration Detainer Changes Spreading across Oregon; National Implications Possible," oregonlive.com, April 17, 2014.

214 Ted Hesson, "Is Fear of Immigrant Criminals Overblown?," abcnews. com, July 15, 2013.

215 Tony Lee, "Media Ignore Americans Killed by Illegal Alien 'DREAMers,'" breitbart.com, August 26, 2013.

216 Jonathan Blitzer, "The Hard-Liners Standing behind Trump against Sanctuary Cities," *New Yorker*, January 30, 2017.

217 "The Remembrance Project," splcenter.org (accessed August 8, 2019).

218 Kitty Calavita, "The New Politics of Immigration: 'Balanced-Budget Conservatism' and the Symbols of Proposition 187," *Social Problems* 43(3), 1996, 284–9.

219 Marc Rosenblum and Isabel Ball, "Trends in Unaccompanied Child and Family Migration from Central America," Migration Policy Institute, January 2016.

220 Wil S. Hylton, "The Shame of America's Family Detention Camps," *New York Times Magazine*, February 4, 2015.

221 Julia Preston, "Detention Center Presented as Deterrent to Border Crossings," *New York Times*, December 15, 2014.

222 Molly Hennessy-Fiske and Richard Simon, "Republicans Blame Obama Policies for Immigration Crisis on Border," *Los Angeles Times*, June 19, 2014; Jeff Sessions, Remarks in Washington, DC, September 5, 2017.

223 Julia Preston, "G.O.P.'s Inroads with Latinos Hint at a Path for 2016," *New York Times*, November 5, 2014.

224 McCarthy, "The Evolution of Immigration Reform under Obama."

225 Michael Shear, "Obama, Daring Congress, Acts to Overhaul Immigration," *New York Times*, November 20, 2014.

226 "FACT SHEET: Immigration Accountability Executive Action," White House, Office of the Press Secretary, November 20, 2014.

227 "Secure Communities" Memorandum from Jeh Johnson, for Thomas Winkowski, Megan Mack, and Philip McNamara, November 20, 2014.

228 TRAC, "Has Cooperation by State and Local Law Enforcement Agencies Improved ICE's Apprehension Numbers?"

229 Denvir, "How Centrists Failed Immigrants."

230 Jeremy Peters, "After Obama's Immigration Action, a Blast of Energy for the Tea Party," *New York Times*, November 25, 2014.

231 Randy Capps et al., "Revving Up the Deportation Machinery:

Enforcement under Trump and the Pushback," Migration Policy Institute, May 2018.

232 Time Staff, "Here's Donald Trump's Presidential Announcement Speech," *Time*, June 16, 2015.

233 Peter Beinart, "The Republican Party's White Strategy," *The Atlantic*, July/August 2016.

234 Jason DeParle, "The Anti-Immigration Crusader," *New York Times*, April 17, 2011.

235 Mitchell Sunderland, "How Ann Coulter Created Donald Trump," *Vice*, September 8, 2016.

236 Jessica Torres, "Ann Coulter Credits White Nationalist as 'Intellectual Influence' on Her Anti-Immigrant Book," mediamatters.org, August 10, 2015.

237 Thomas Peele, "Kate Steinle Killing: Bullet Apparently Ricocheted before Hitting Steinle, Expert Says," *Mercury News*, August 26, 2015.

238 Kevin Fagan, "Defendant's Lawyer in Kate Steinle Murder Trial: It Was an Accident," *San Francisco Chronicle*, July 8, 2017.

239 "Immigrant Acquitted in Kate Steinle's Shooting Death Wants Gun Conviction Overturned," Associated Press, January 16, 2019; Brittny Mejia and Alene Tchekmedyian, "Immigrant Deported Multiple Times Found Not Guilty in Slaying of Kathryn Steinle; Trump Calls Verdict 'Disgraceful,'" *Los Angeles Times*, November 20, 2017.

240 Alex Emslie, "Not Guilty: S.F. Jury Delivers Verdict in Kathryn Steinle Slaying," KQED, November 30, 2017.

241 Cassandra Vinograd, "Donald Trump: Kathryn Steinle Death on Pier 14 Shows Need for Border Wall," nbcnews.com, July 4, 2015.

242 Max Ehrenfreund, "Understanding Trump's Plan to End Citizenship for Undocumented Immigrants' Kids," *Washington Post*, August 17, 2015.

243 Deena Zaru, "Coulter: After Immigration Plan, I Don't Care If Trump 'Performs Abortions,'" cnn.com, August 17, 2015.

244 Joshua Green, "Attack, Attack, Attack," *New York Magazine*, July 10, 2017.

245 Blitzer, "The Hard-Liners Standing behind Trump against Sanctuary Cities."

246 Mark Krikorian, "Knowing What We Know Now, Mrs. Clinton, Would You Still Support Sanctuary Cities?," *National Review*, July 6, 2015.

247 John Hayward, "With Blood on Their Hands, Democrats Suddenly Act Concerned about Illegal Immigration," breitbart.com, July 8, 2015.

248 "Clinton: San Francisco Erred in Case of Deported Man Now Charged with Murder," Reuters, July 7, 2015.

249 "Feinstein Calls on San Francisco to Join DHS Immigration Program," feinstein.senate.gov, July 7, 2015.

250 Dara Lind, "Obama Just Picked a Fight with Border Agents," vox.com, January 29, 2015.

251 Daniel Denvir, "The Scapegoating of Sanctuary Cities," citylab.com, July 8, 2015.

252 Miriam Valverde, "Trump Says Secure Communities, 287(g) Immigration Programs Worked," politifact.com, September 6, 2016.

253 "Trump in Phoenix: 10-Point Plan to End Illegal Immigration," *Arizona Republic*, August 21, 2016; Tara Golshan, "Donald Trump Introduced Us to "Angel Moms." Here's Why They Matter," vox.com, September 1, 2016.

254 Blitzer, "The Hard-Liners Standing behind Trump against Sanctuary Cities."

255 Ian Hanchett, "Trump: 'Nobody Wants to Talk About' Crimes Committed by Illegal Immigrants," breitbart.com, July 4, 2015.

256 Betsy Woodruff, "Donald Trump Pledges to Deport 'Bad Hombres' and Praises . . . Obama?," thedailybeast.com, April 13, 2017.

257 Michael John Garcia, "Barriers along the U.S. Borders: Key Authorities and Requirements," Congressional Research Service, fas.org, November 18, 2016.

258 Allison Graves, "Fact-Check: Did Top Democrats Vote for a Border Wall in 2006?," politifact.com, April 23, 2017.

259 Donald Trump, Speech at the Republican National Convention, July 21, 2016.

260 Rory Carroll, "'No Amnesty': Trump Vows to Deport Millions during 'First Hour in Office,'" *The Guardian*, September 1, 2016.

261 D'Angelo Gore and Eugene Kiely, "Trump's Border Boast," factcheck.org, July 31, 2017.

262 Michael Shear and Julie Hirschfeld Davis, "Trump Moves to End DACA and Calls on Congress to Act," *New York Times*, September 5, 2017.

263 Josh Dawsey and Nick Miroff, "The Hostile Border between Trump and the Head of DHS," *Washington Post*, May 25, 2018.

264 Lydia O'Connor, "Trump Still Enabling George Soros Conspiracy Theory after Bomb Threats, Synagogue Shooting," huffpost.com, October 31, 2018.

265 Makini Brice and Roberta Rampton, "Trump Backtracks on Suggestion U.S. Troops Could Fire on Migrants," *Reuters*, November 2, 2018.

266 Masha Gessen, "Why the Tree of Life Shooter Was Fixated on the Hebrew Immigrant Aid Society," *New Yorker*, October 27, 2018.

Conclusion

1 Julie Hirschfeld Davis and Peter Baker, "How the Border Wall Is Boxing Trump In," *New York Times*, January 5, 2019.

2 Julie Hirschfeld Davis, "President Wants to Use Executive Order to End Birthright Citizenship," *New York Times*, October 30, 2018.

3 Miriam Valverde, "Donald Trump's Border Wall: How Much Has Been Built?," August 30, 2019, politifact.com.

4 "30 of Donald Trump's Wildest Quotes," cbsnews.com.

5 "Transcript of Donald Trump's Immigration Speech," *New York Times*, September 1, 2016.

6 David Lauter and Brian Bennett, "No More Nation of Immigrants: Trump Plan Calls for a Major, Long-lasting Cut in Legal Entries," *Los Angeles Times*, September 2, 2016.

7 Richard Spencer, Twitter Post, August 31, 2016, 10:26 PM.

8 Brendan O'Connor, "The Eugenicist Doctor and the Vast Fortune behind Trump's Immigration Regime," splinternews.com, July 5, 2018; Pema Levy, "Long before Trump, Kellyanne Conway Worked for Anti-Muslim and Anti-Immigrant Extremists," *Mother Jones*, December 9, 2016.

9 Jonathan Blitzer, "How Stephen Miller Single-Handedly Got the U.S. to Accept Fewer Refugees," *New Yorker*, October 13, 2017; Jonathan Blitzer, "Jeff Sessions Is Out, but His Dark Vision for Immigration Lives On," *New Yorker*, November 8, 2018.

10 "President Donald J. Trump Backs RAISE Act," whitehouse.gov, August 2, 2017.

11 Dylan Scott, "The Senate Put 4 Immigration Bills Up for a Vote. They

All Failed," vox.com, February 15, 2018.

12 Michael D. Shear, "Trump Has Right to End DACA, Justice Dept. Tells Supreme Court," *New York Times*, August 19, 2019; Leigh Ann Caldwell, nbcnews.com, "SCOTUS decision gives Congress reprieve on DACA legislation," February 26, 2018.

13 Justin Sink and Erik Wasson, "Trump Stages Shutdown Face-Off with Democrats over Wall Funding," bloomberg.com, December 11, 2018.

14 Erica Werner et al., "Congress Approves Border Deal to Avert Shutdown; Trump to Sign It and Seek Wall Money Elsewhere," *Washington Post*, February 14, 2019; Sarah D. Wire and Jennifer Haberkorn, "Congress Passes Bill to Avert Shutdown as Trump Vows to Declare National Emergency to Build Wall," *Los Angeles Times*, February 14, 2019.

15 Jess Bravin and Louise Radnofsky, "Trump Scores Two Victories on Border," *Wall Street Journal*, July 26, 2019.

16 Michael Brice-Saddler, "'This Is Tyranny of Talk Radio Hosts, Right?': Limbaugh and Coulter Blamed for Trump's Shutdown," *Washington Post*, December 22, 2018.

17 Kristina Peterson, "Senate Approves Stopgap Spending Bill to Avert Shutdown," *Wall Street Journal*, December 19, 2018; Chad Groening, "Freedom Caucus Begging Trump to Veto Bill, Fight for Wall," onenewsnow.com, December 20, 2018.

18 Franco Ordoñez, "Why Some on the Right Are Grateful to Democrats for Opposing Trump's Border Wall," mcclatchydc.com, December 20, 2018.

19 Mark Krikorian, "Mass Legal Immigration Will Finish Conservatism," *National Review*, August 31, 2015.

20 Erik Ruark, "A Wall Is a Wall Is a Wall . . . ," numbersusa.com, January 5, 2019.

21 Julie Hirschfeld Davis and Peter Baker, "How the Border Wall Is Boxing Trump In," *New York Times*, January 5, 2019.

22 Sahil Kapur, "Trump Calls for More Legal Immigration after Pushing to Cut It," bloomberg.com, February 6, 2019.

23 Otis L. Graham Jr., "A Skirmish in a Wider War: An Oral History of John H. Tanton, Founder of FAIR, the Federation for American Immigration Reform," splcenter.org, April 20–21, 1989, 65; Jason DeParle, "The Anti-immigration Crusader," *New York Times*, April

17, 2011; Richard Bernstein, "In U.S. Schools, a War of Words," *New York Times Magazine*, October 14, 1990.

24   Red Robbins, "'America's Toughest Sheriff' Takes on Immigration," *Morning Edition*, npr.org, March 10, 2008.

25   Greg Grandin, "The Myth of the Border Wall," *New York Times*, February 20, 2019.

26   Julie Hirschfeld Davis and Peter Baker, "How the Border Wall Is Boxing Trump In," *New York Times*, January 5, 2019.

27   "Shifting Public Views on Legal Immigration into the U.S.," Pew Research Center, people-press.org, June 28, 2018.

28   "Public Charge," Immigrant Legal Resource Center.

29   Jeanne Batalova, Michael Fix, and Mark Greenberg, "Millions Will Feel Chilling Effects of U.S. Public-Charge Rule That Is Also Likely to Reshape Legal Immigration," *Migration Policy Institute*, August 2019.

30   Ted Hesson, "Exclusive: Visa Denials to Poor Mexicans Skyrocket under Trump's State Department," *Politico*, August 6, 2019.

31   Theda Skocpol and Alexander Hertel-Fernandez, "The Koch Network and Republican Party Extremism," *Perspectives on Politics* 11(3), 2016, 681–99.

32   Nicholas Kulish and Mike McIntire, "Why an Heiress Spent Her Fortune Trying to Keep Immigrants Out," *New York Times*, August 14, 2019.

33   Margaret E. Peters, *Trading Barriers: Immigration and the Remaking of Globalization*, Princeton: Princeton University Press, 2017, 3–4.

34   Nicholas P. De Genova, "Migrant 'Illegality' and Deportability in Everyday Life," *Annual Review of Anthropology* 31(1), 2002, 438.

35   Claire Brockway and Carroll Doherty, "Growing Share of Republicans Say U.S. Risks Losing Its Identity If It Is Too Open to Foreigners," pewresearch.org, July 17, 2019.

36   "2018 Midterm Voters: Issues and Political Values," Pew Research Center, people-press.org, October 4, 2018.

37   Bradley Jones, "Americans' Views of Immigrants Marked by Widening Partisan, Generational Divides," pewresearch.org, April 15, 2016.

38   Aziz Rana, *Two Faces of American Freedom*, Cambridge, MA: Harvard University Press, 2010.